Interest Projects

for Cadette and Senior Girl Scouts

Girl Scouts of the U.S.A.

420 Fifth Avenue

New York, N.Y. 10018-2798

http://www.gsusa.org

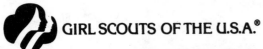

GIRL SCOUTS OF THE U.S.A.®

Elinor Johnstone Ferdon, *National President*

Mary Rose Main, *National Executive Director*

Inquiries related to *Interest Projects for Cadette and Senior Girl Scouts* should be directed to Membership and Program, Girl Scouts of the U.S.A., 420 Fifth Avenue, New York, N.Y. 10018-2798.

Authors

Sandy Ayala
Chris Bergerson
LaVerne Bolling
Trina Brooks
María L. Cabán
Odette Cabrera
Rosemarie Cryan
Jan Cummings
Wendy DeGiglio
Martha Jo Dennison, Ed.D.
Toni Eubanks
Nancy Garfield
Sharon Woods Hussey
Carolyn Kennedy
Sheila K. Lewis
Chris Francis Lightbourne
Lauraine Merlini
Harriet S. Mosatche, Ph.D.
Rita Niemeyer
Donna Nye
Patricia J. Paddock
Nancy H. Richardson
Dottie Ruvel
Judy Seigler
Verna Simpkins
Karen White

Contributors

Patricia Blake
Leslie Collins
Susan S. Davis
Melissa Harris
Susan Hutchinson
Frances A. Karnes, Ph.D.
Theresa Lechton
Bobbi Olson
Rebecca Pagan
Janet Robison
Sara Schwebel
Denise Scribner
Hillary Strilko

Project Coordinators

Harriet S. Mosatche, Ph.D.
Sharon Woods Hussey
Sheila K. Lewis
Rosemarie Cryan

Design Studio/Designer

Designworks, Stephen Vann

Table of Contents

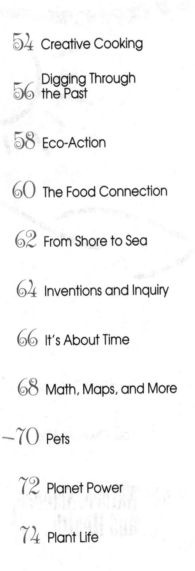

Table of Contents

84 Communications

112 The Arts and History

Introduction

SKILL BUILDERS

When you daydream, what do you envision? Do you think of yourself as an astronaut exploring far-off galaxies? Do you see yourself drawing, painting, or photographing the world around you? Perhaps you have visions of being a star athlete or concert pianist.

Dreams are unique to each person and generally reflect an individual's interests and aspirations. As a Girl Scout you have many opportunities to fulfill your dreams or simply to start hobbies that will enrich your daily life. Completing interest projects can be the first step along the way.

How Do You Begin?

Choosing an interest project that is relevant to you is particularly important. Some of your friends might choose Backpacking or The Performing Arts, but unless these topics interest you, you will probably be bored completing all the required activities. In order to make the experience of earning the patch far more enjoyable, pick an interest project that stimulates your imagination and curiosity, or that is on a topic you want to explore. Take time to read through the table of contents. Then skim some of the actual interest projects, and try one that seems like fun.

TECHNOLOGY

In some cases, it might be advantageous for a troop or group of girls to work together on the same interest project. In this situation, you can learn from one another and share a common set of resources in completing the requirements. For each girl to benefit from her experience, equal participation from everyone involved should be expected.

Anatomy of an Interest Project

SERVICE PROJECTS

Each interest project contains numerous activities, which are organized into four different categories: **Skill Builders**, **Technology**, **Service Projects**, and **Career Exploration**. By doing these activities, you will gain insights about yourself—your strengths and weaknesses, your likes and dislikes. You will have a range of new experiences, and you will develop valuable skills and expertise in specific areas. To earn an interest project patch, you must complete at least seven activities as follows:

- Two Skill Builders activities.

- One Technology activity.

- One Service Project activity.

- One Career Exploration activity.

- Two activities from any category that you choose.

CAREER EXPLORATION

Skill Builders: These activities will help you to develop the technical skills associated with your area of interest. For example, if you choose **On the Playing Field**, the Skill Builders activities will help you learn how to dribble a basketball or throw a softball. To earn an interest project patch, at least **two** Skill Builders activities are required.

Technology: The activities in this category provide exposure to the ever-expanding world of technology. You should, however, view the term "Technology" as including not just computers, disks, and the Internet, but also advances and applications in areas such as media, sports, and medical equipment. At least **one** Technology activity is required.

Service Projects: As Girl Scouts you are familiar with lending a helping hand and contributing to your community. The activities in this category will help you organize your endeavors in your community. At least one activity in this category is required.

Career Exploration: The Career Exploration activities will help you begin to associate professions with your interests and hobbies. By talking to and observing people in various fields, reading about the education and expertise required, and trying out career exploration exercises, you will gain insights into the preparation needed for the career you might like to pursue.

Common Elements Among the Interest Projects

Many of the interest projects that you will find in this book rely on a common set of skills and instructions. For example, you will frequently be asked to interview an individual who works in a particular career or to create an exhibit that you can display in a public area in an effort to educate others about a topic or idea. Some of the basic skills and guidelines that comprise many interest projects are discussed below.

Working with Consultants

People who are willing to share their expertise can make doing an interest project a unique and rewarding experience. Before you ask a person to help you, anticipate questions she or he may have. For example, you should be able to explain your reasons for doing this interest project; estimate the amount of time you are requesting; and describe the resources you will need (materials, equipment, facilities). In all your discussions with consultants, your enthusiasm for Girl Scouting and this project should be contagious. Let the consultants know that their contributions will be personally satisfying while they are helping you to fulfill a worthwhile goal. Also, while the text, for ease of reading, uses female pronouns to describe consultants, expertise rather than gender should determine who will assist you with your project.

Interviewing

Set up the interview in advance: Establish a convenient time and place for the interview. People may choose to talk at home, on the job, or at places like the library or a coffee shop. Keep in mind that their schedules come first. Exchange phone numbers in case you have to reschedule the interview. Always ask about the best times to call.

Be prepared: Prepare a list of questions ahead of time or at least have an idea of the kinds of things you want to know. Have a notebook and at least two pens or pencils handy. You may want to bring a tape recorder (ask first if it's okay to tape the interview).

Take accurate notes: Take good notes. If a person talks too fast for you, ask her to repeat the information. She won't mind and will be impressed with your desire for accuracy. If you plan to quote someone, it's especially important that you write down *verbatim* (word for word) what that person says. Even omitting one little word by mistake can change the entire meaning of a sentence.

Display good manners: Be on time, dress well, and be enthusiastic. Not everyone you interview may reveal astonishing facts, but the person has gone through the trouble of giving you her time, so be patient and appreciative.

Relax and have fun: If you are shy about calling a "stranger," relax! Most people feel this way. You can practice with a friend, or pretend you are your favorite TV personality conducting the interview. What would *she* say?

Most interviews are fun. People generally appreciate your interest and are willing to give you the information you request. If someone declines to answer a question, don't take it personally. Just ask another one. Sometimes it is best just to let the person talk. In telling a story she may reveal an interesting bit of information or give you insight you never expected into a topic. Before you leave, be sure to ask the person if you can contact her again in case you think of something else to ask.

Role-Playing

In general, role-playing is an effective teaching technique. Some people, however, do not like to share their thoughts and feelings in a public forum. The following guidelines will help to ensure that the role-playing experience is successful and beneficial for all participants:

Be a good listener and never make fun of another person's performance.

Establish a supportive and nonthreatening environment in which to conduct the role-plays. Remind all participants that role-playing is simply acting out hypothetical situations. It is not real life.

Solicit volunteers to act out the scenes. Never cajole or force anyone into participating.

Ensure that participants have time to prepare for the role-play before they begin to act. Allow participants to choose the role that they wish to portray.

Nurture one another's self-esteem and self-confidence by praising participation and performance.

Suggest that the audience observe the role-play carefully, noticing both verbal and nonverbal communication clues.

Initiate a dialogue upon completion of the role-play that allows all participants to process their thoughts, feelings, and emotions about what they have seen or heard.

Talk about your feelings only if you are comfortable doing so. Don't pressure anyone to react or to share their thoughts unless they do so willingly.

Investigate those areas or topics that participants would like to have more information about or those that make participants feel uncomfortable.

Voice controversial opinions tactfully, and support arguments with facts.

Entertain new ideas and viewpoints and ensure that all participants have an equal opportunity to express their ideas and opinions.

As you can see, the overall rule for role-playing is to *be sensitive*. Role-playing is a great, nonthreatening way to address sensitive issues and to anticipate the type of dialogue and feelings that might occur in a given situation. It is important, however, to respect people's privacy and to allow for the strong emotional reactions that the role-play might evoke.

Working with Younger Girls

■ Be realistic in terms of your expectations. It is important for activities or discussions to be tailored to the ages and attention spans of participants. Generally, children can sustain a directed activity for 20–30 minutes, but they prefer to be involved. This is why many of the activities are "hands-on."

■ Be equally attentive to all children. Do not pick favorites.

■ If a girl is not acting appropriately, determine why she is misbehaving and try to redirect her attention to the activity at hand.

■ When you are giving directions to younger girls, try to do so visually as well as verbally. In other words, demonstrate tasks before you ask girls to do them.

■ Be flexible in your directions and requirements for projects. Every girl has her own way of approaching a task. There are probably a variety of ways to accomplish most activities.

"Find Out About"/"Investigate"

You may be asked to "find out about" or to "investigate" a particular topic and, in many cases, a specific time period is not assigned to these activities. It is expected that you will work on your investigation until you feel satisfied that you have gained a greater understanding of the topic or that you have more knowledge of the subject than when you started the interest project. Overall, "finding out" or "investigating" a particular topic should not take less than one hour, although it may certainly take more.

Safety Issues

As with all Girl Scout activities, you must adhere to the guidelines for safety that are outlined in *Safety-Wise*. This publication is sure to be available at your council and/or from your Girl Scout leader.

Making It All Fit In

A juggling act, that's what your life may seem like. Between school projects, extracurricular activities, religious education, and part-time jobs, there hardly seems to be enough time in the day. It is important, therefore, to make connections between your various activities and responsibilities, and Girl Scouting. For example, if you have just completed an essay for your history class that applies to the requirements for an interest project you are working on, that is a valid link. Or maybe your religious education has components that address interpersonal skills or helping others. Using these ideas or projects toward completing the **Understanding Yourself and Others** or **A World of Understanding** patches is acceptable.

Similarly, use your creativity in finding ways to fund your interest projects. In general, you should try to complete the requirements without investing too much money. For example, use common resources or recycled products. If you need materials that are costly, perhaps an individual or a business owner would be willing to donate them to you.

Tap into your ingenuity and knowledge of finance and business to sell your own products at crafts fairs or at neighborhood bazaars. For instance, if you design a terrific T-shirt for your patch requirements, you might want to have a number of them printed and then you can sell them.

Interest Projects and the Girl Scout Silver and Gold Awards: How Do They Relate?

The requirements for earning Girl Scout Gold and Silver Awards state that the interest project patches must relate to the topic of the award. This, however, does not mean that if you choose to devise an interpretive nature walk in a local park, each of your interest projects must have an out-of-doors theme. In fact, you might choose to complete the **Graphic Communications** interest project and create an original design in stencil or silk-screen. Having this skill will certainly facilitate your Gold or Silver Award project because it will enable you to make aesthetically pleasing signs for the trail that you are developing. Similarly, another girl might decide to host a health fair for her Girl Scout Gold Award project, and she will be able to publicize her event by employing what she has learned from doing the **Public Relations** interest project. It is important, therefore, for you to work with your Gold Award advisers, Girl Scout leaders, and parents or guardians to draw parallels between the skills you have learned in one context and the manner in which they can be used in another.

Writing Your Own Interest Project

Have you read through the whole table of contents searching for a particular topic only to come up empty-handed? If this is the case, don't despair, because you can write your own interest project. To create your own recognition, you must follow these steps:

1 Follow the format established for all the other interest projects included in this book. In other words, you must develop two activities in the Skill Building category, and at least one activity in each of the other three categories. You must also create two additional activities in any categories that you choose. When you are done writing, you will have created a series of seven activities.

2 Decide if you will work on your interest project alone or in a group.

3 Make sure you include your leader or adviser and perhaps an interest project consultant, too. They can help you plan and should be aware of safety standards.

As you create your interest project, try to vary the types of things that you will be doing. For example, seven activities requiring trips or interviews would probably not be practical or interesting. Make sure your activities are appropriate for your knowledge and skill levels. If they are too easy, you'll get bored; if they are too hard, you'll give up in the middle.

Know the resources available in your community, and those you can realistically attain elsewhere. Do some research to ensure that a resource or a consultant will be available.

When you have written your interest project, share it with the following people:

1 Your Girl Scout council. The council needs to know what you are doing and can help you by suggesting consultants, council events, or projects that can be helpful as you do the activities in your interest projects.

2 Your Girl Scout troop or group, and friends and schoolmates who may not be Girl Scout members. See if they would like to join your interest project group as new or continuing members of Girl Scouting.

3 Consultants — for suggestions on improving it.

4 Your family. Let family members know what you are interested in. Perhaps they can help you.

Now you are ready to begin. Flip the pages and find the interest projects that will start you on the way to new hobbies, new adventures, new skills, and lots of fun! Use the charts located on pages 180–184 to track your progress.

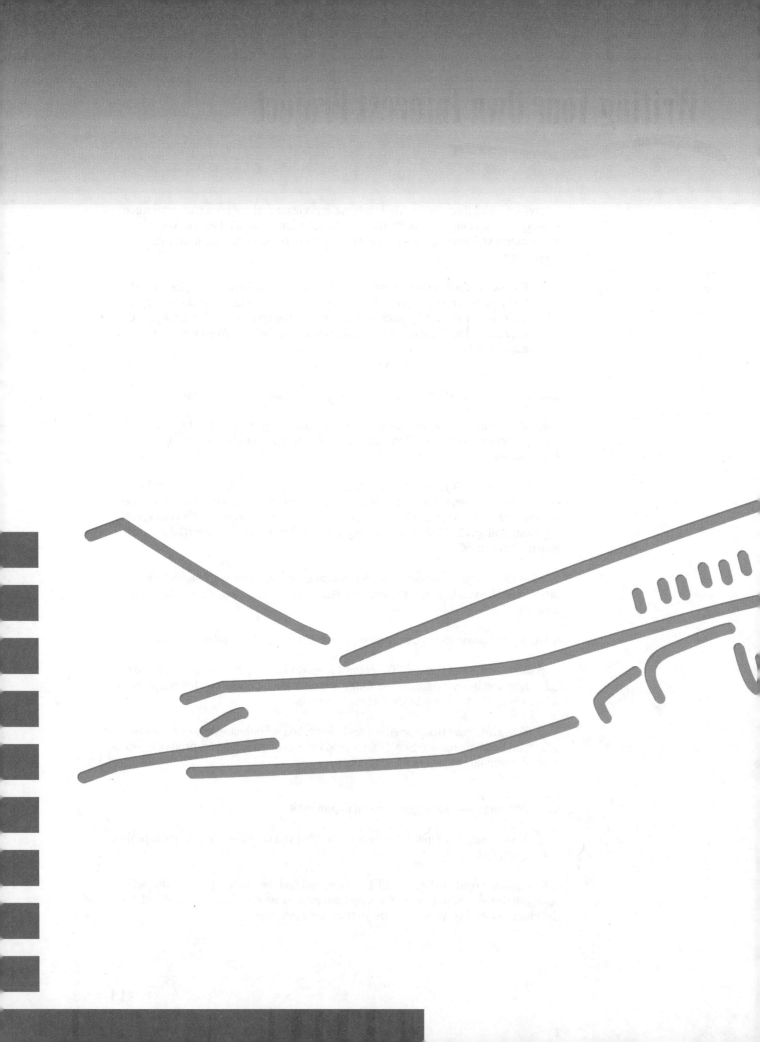

Life Skills

Car Sense ▪ Child Care ▪ Conflict Resolution ▪ Cookies and Dough ▪ Dollars and Sense ▪ Family Living ▪ From Fitness to Fashion ▪ From Stress to Success ▪ Generations Hand in Hand ▪ Home Improvement ▪ Law and Order ▪ Leadership ▪ Travel ▪ Understanding Yourself and Others ▪ Your Best Defense ▪ Your Own Business

Car Sense

Learning to drive a car is something that you have probably looked forward to for a long time. Once you have your driver's license, you are responsible for the safe use and maintenance of the vehicle you are driving, as well as for the safety of your passengers. This interest project will give you an opportunity to recognize and meet the challenges you'll face as the driver and caretaker of a car. Common sense or "car sense" can mean the difference between safety and danger on the road.

Skill Builders

1 Check the engine oil, automatic transmission fluid, brake fluid, and power steering fluid in several vehicles. Find out how often the following procedures should be done on a vehicle and obtain some cost estimates for each:

- Change oil and automatic transmission fluid.
- Reline brakes.
- Realign wheels and balance tires.
- Replace belts, steering lines, and hoses.
- Replace damaged or loose parts in exhaust system.
- Replace shock absorbers.

2 With an adult, change the oil and oil filter on a vehicle. Dispose of or recycle the old oil using an ecologically sound method.

3 Check tire pressure with a gauge. Observe a tire being changed by an experienced adult. Make a list of the steps taken. With adult supervision, follow the steps you have outlined and change a tire on a car.

4 Find out what the procedures are in your state for obtaining a learner's permit and a driver's license. What driver's education courses are available? Also find out what's involved in registering a vehicle. Visit the motor vehicle department and get copies of forms, information, and regulations.

5 Visit a car dealership with an adult and evaluate the costs, options, and availability of two different types of cars, both new and used. Find out about financing: where you can borrow money and at what rates, and the costs of leasing a car.

6 Read pages 122–123 in *A Resource Book for Senior Girl Scouts*. Using the information provided, assemble a vehicle emergency tool kit for the car you will be driving.

7 Contact different insurance companies and find out what types of coverage are required by your state. Find out how your driving and choice of car affect your insurance rates. Investigate the legal liabilities of a driver who is uninsured or underinsured.

Technology

1 Find out how an anti-lock braking system (ABS) works and how it differs from traditional braking systems. Find out how ABS affects your driving in emergency situations and inclement weather.

2 How does the rising number of automobiles on the road affect the environment? Survey an automobile for its energy use. Does it use gas economically or not? Has the engine been tuned recently? Do the tires have the proper inflation? Are the air and oil filters clean? Find out about driving habits that save gas. Talk to a car owner, mechanic, or car dealer about energy conservation in the use and maintenance of cars. What has the auto industry been doing to curtail air pollution and make cars more efficient in their use of gas?

3 Air bags have recently become a standard safety feature. Locate the air bags in a car. Read the owner's manual and discover the strengths and limitations of air bags, as well as any dangers. Identify five safety rules to follow when operating a vehicle that has air bags. Share that information with two other drivers.

4 From car ignitions to theft detection, cars are becoming more and more computerized. Describe in what ways cars are computerized. What does that mean for mechanics and servicers? What are the implications for drivers and car owners? Talk with someone who serviced cars before and after computers were installed. Discover the advantages and disadvantages of these changes.

5 Find information about purchasing a car by browsing through the Internet. Explore purchasing and/or leasing two vehicles of your choice, used or new. Use the Internet to compare the cost, safety, resale value, size, storage space, and options such as air conditioning, automatic transmission, and anti-lock brakes.

6 Compute the cost of running a car for a year. Include the cost of gasoline, insurance, registration, parking, taxes, and maintenance. Compare this with the cost of using public transportation. Is the convenience of a car worth the expense?

Service Projects

1 Volunteer at a vehicle safety event or workshop emphasizing safety through preventive maintenance. Activities might include inspecting tires, changing wiper blades, and checking car fluids.

2 Create a car safety campaign focusing on one or more of the following topics: use of safety belts; use of air bags; obscured vision; behavior during and following an accident or breakdown; drunk driving. Display the information in two prominent areas of your town, or ask the local newspaper or schools to print the information.

3 Using the poem "Young and Dumb" on page 123 and the information on pages 47–48 in *A Resource Book for Senior Girl Scouts*, run a discussion group with other teens about driving under the influence. Discuss the severity of the issue and steps you can take to avoid riding with a drunk driver. Role-play what to do if you think your friend is under the influence and is about to drive.

4 Volunteer with a car-based community service: for example, one that delivers groceries or meals to the homebound or takes library books to isolated communities or schools.

Career Exploration

1 Interview a mechanic, car service manager, or car assembler. Find out what factors led to choosing that career, what school training, courses, or on-the-job experiences prepared her for this work.

2 Prepare a cartoon with the theme "Teaching novices to drive." What skills are most critical to becoming a good driving instructor?

3 Interview a highway patrol officer or traffic enforcement officer. Ask about traffic laws and the most common violations for the area. What steps does one take to become a highway patrol or a traffic enforcement officer? How do they handle motorists who have been stopped for driving while intoxicated or for speed violations? How often do teenagers commit these types of violations? How often are they involved as victims?

4 Tour an auto design or assembly plant. Discover what goes into the designing and/or assembling of an automobile. Ask about future occupations and trends in the auto industry.

And Beyond

IF YOU LIKED "SPINNING YOUR WHEELS" with Car Sense, learn more about car safety, design, and travel with these related interest projects:

- Emergency Preparedness
- Inventions and Inquiry
- Travel
- Law and Order

Child Care

*D*o you take care of your younger brothers and sisters? Earn money as a baby sitter? Want to prepare for a career working with children? Think that being a parent may be part of your future? In this interest project, you will find suggestions for taking care of children.

Skill Builders

1 Pick a particular developmental level, such as infancy, childhood, or adolescence, and learn about either the physical, emotional, intellectual, or social growth that takes place during that stage.

2 Learn how to care for children in an emergency situation. Take a course such as fire safety, lifesaving, or baby sitting at your local Girl Scout council, the American Red Cross, or your local fire department. Share your information with at least three friends.

3 Become familiar with local, state, and federal laws that protect children. Review and clip related articles from newspapers and magazines. Hold a discussion, debate, or lecture on a topic of interest such as children's television, discipline, sibling rivalry, or fostering creativity. Invite people interested in child care to attend.

4 What were you like when you were a baby? When you were two, three, or four years old? When you started school? What do you remember about yourself? Talk to people who knew you at different ages. Do they have pictures of you, stories about you, information about your health, where you lived, or who took care of you? Ask yourself, "What are those things in my life that make me the special person I am today?" Record what you find in a story about yourself, a poem, a song, a tape recording, a diary, a play, or a picture.

5 Keep a file of games, songs, finger plays, and stories that children like. Include such things as recipes for play dough and finger paints. Talk to parents, teachers, day-care workers, or librarians for suggestions. Keep adding to your file and use these ideas when you take care of your own younger brothers or sisters, baby-sit, or do volunteer work with children.

Technology

1 Visit a computer store and find out about software and video games for children. Focus on resources for a specific age group. Evaluate the software. Some key questions to consider:

■ Are the graphics exciting for the child?
■ Are the activities fun? Are the activities designed to teach or merely entertain?
■ If the video or software is designed to be educational, is there a better way to learn the subject?
■ Do the images send negative messages?

2 Visit a store where educational toys, and games are sold. What is the educational value of some of the items? Write down the names of two or three items you would recommend for a child of a certain age. Then, observe a child at play in one of the following age groups: birth to two years, three to five years, six to ten years. Do you still agree with the choices you made in the store? If not, adjust your choices to accommodate what you have learned. Based on your findings, make recommendations about age-appropriate toys to a child's family.

3 Compare two types of toys that a child might typically use today with similar toys available 20 or more years ago. Have the toys changed because of technological advances?

4 Familiarize yourself with some toys and games available for children. With that in mind, design your own game or toy for a specific age group. Or modify one already on the market. Present your toy (actual or model) to an adult who spends time with children of that age group. Ask the adult to critique your design.

5 Create television viewing guidelines for your family or a family with young children. Create a time sheet to monitor the number of viewing hours, a tip sheet suggesting appropriate programs for children of particular ages, and a list of programs to avoid viewing.

teer to read stories to the children. Determine your goals, and work on a plan for reaching them. Recruit others to help you with the plan.

3 Become involved in tutoring a student after school. For example, you can devise a "homework help" program to use at home with a younger sibling. Keep a notebook or log of the skills you are emphasizing and of your student's progress. Share it with the parents or guardians.

4 Create a "baby-sitter's club" with girls in your troop or with friends. Advertise your group's services in a brochure. Or create a newsletter for the club. The baby-sitters' newsletter can include such features as do's and don'ts while baby sitting and first-aid tips. Meet regularly with other baby sitters to exchange ideas and tips.

5 Where can children in your community play and have fun? Locate the playgrounds and other recreational facilities in your area. Find out what ages can use them. Are they safe? What equipment do they provide? Create a recreation guidebook to share in your community.

child with a disability. Read the poem "Building Your Character Up with Down's" on page 67 of the *Cadette Girl Scout Handbook*. Describe the poet's relationship with her brother. How has her brother influenced her personal goals?

3 Invite four professionals who work with children, such as a pediatric dentist, nurse, teacher, psychologist, or pediatrician, to speak at a troop or group meeting about their work. How does each professional help and work with parents and with children? Ask questions about their training and experience.

4 Interview a mother who works for pay outside the home full-time, one who works for pay outside the home part-time, and one who does not work outside the home. Find out their child-care arrangements. What are the roles played in child-rearing by fathers, grandparents, other family members, and professional child-care workers? What did the mothers tell you about the advantages and disadvantages of each arrangement?

Service Projects

1 Work with a local school, religious center, library, or other site where parents and children gather. Volunteer to organize a child-care event or program. Determine what your responsibilities will be: for example, leading activities or registration.

2 Determine a service you can provide for a local day-care or after-school facility. Arrange a meeting with the director to find out which service or resource is needed. You might organize a toy drive to provide new or slightly used toys and games for the facility, or volun-

Career Exploration

1 Discover how many colleges or agencies in your area offer courses for day-care providers. Contact a local child-care referral agency or college and learn what you need to do to become a professional day-care provider. Find out what courses you need to take, if any, for certification. Visit a college that offers day care and talk with the students/child-care providers about their work experiences.

2 Learn from a child-care provider, teacher, or parent the special needs of caring for a

And Beyond

SELECT AN ACTIVITY FROM THE GIRL Scout book *Fun and Easy Nature and Science Investigations* to use with a group of Brownie Girl Scouts.

From child care to child's play, enjoy these related interest projects:

- Family Living
- Understanding Yourself and Others
- Games for Life
- Pets
- Museum Discovery
- Heritage Hunt
- It's About Time
- From Stress to Success

Conflict Resolution

The reasons for conflicts vary, but they all have one thing in common— the potential to escalate, even to the point of violence, if mishandled. But violence isn't the only troublesome product of conflict. When attempts to compromise fail in personal relationships, or don't take place at all, friendships break, feelings are hurt, and neither party wins. In this interest project, learn effective ways to help resolve conflict—personal, social, or even global.

Skill Builders

1 Read and do the activities on pages 76–81 in the *Cadette Girl Scout Handbook*, or read pages 79–85 in *A Resource Book for Senior Girl Scouts* and identify five techniques for resolving conflict. Give examples of how three of these techniques are used in the "real world."

2 Keep a journal for two weeks and record all of your conflicts with other people. Note how you handled each conflict and whether or not it was resolved. Do you see a pattern? For example, did you use confrontation, avoidance, or compromise? What other techniques might you try in the future?

3 With a group of four to six people, carry out the following active listening exercises. Have participants take turns as group facilitators, recorders, and observers.

■ Have two people simultaneously talk about a topic for three minutes, without regard to what the other person is saying.
Question for participants: What does it feel like to talk to someone who isn't listening?

■ Have one participant spend three minutes talking about something important to her while another participant disagrees or responds negatively.
Question for participants: If someone is negative or disagrees with you, what do you do? What are three other ways to change the direction of the conversation?

■ For three minutes, have one participant try to convince another of a particular point of view. While one is talking, have the other participant close her eyes or turn her back to demonstrate her lack of interest.
Question for participants: What role does body language play in active listening?

4 Respecting the values of other people improves relationships and communication. Read "Your Values" on pages 56–57 of the *Cadette Girl Scout Handbook* or "Values and Conflict" on page 81 of *A Resource Book for Senior Girl Scouts*. Rate the values on the chart on page 21 according to their importance in your life. Compare your outcomes with those of a friend:

5 In the world of competitive sports, fair play is the ideal. Yet cursing at, shoving, and bullying opponents often occur. With friends, attend or watch on television several different sports events. Note the athletes' behavior. After the events, address the following questions:

■ Did you witness fair or unfair conduct? What kind?
■ Were certain sports more likely than others to have athletes engage in foul play?
■ What methods of conflict resolution did the referees, umpires, and other sports officials use?

Technology

1 In sports, players and referees frequently disagree

THIS IS...	VERY IMPORTANT	SOMEWHAT IMPORTANT	NOT IMPORTANT AT ALL
Being popular at school		PKM S	
Getting good grades	mKPS		
Spending time with my family	m	KPS	
Taking part in my religion	SM	KP	
Making my own decisions	SmKP		
Exercising and eating nutritiously	pmS	K	
Wearing the latest styles	P	mKS	
Spending time with my friends	mPKS	S	m
Caring for the environment	Sm	P	K
Improving my community		SM	PK

about calls. How does the use of instant replays facilitate the resolution of these disputes? What techniques were used before instant replay was available?

2 Watch or play several video or computer games. Which ones seem too violent? Think of ways to make them less violent and still interesting. Write to the manufacturer with your suggestions.

3 What messages do television shows, music videos, and print and broadcast ads give about resolving conflict? View two or three of your favorite television shows. Are these shows realistic in portraying conflict and its resolution? Rewrite the ending of a show, portraying a better way to resolve conflict.

4 Watch the evening news or read a daily newspaper for three days in a row, paying particular attention to opinions about global, social, and political conflicts. How do the opinions of influential people alter our perceptions of conflict? How do inflammatory headlines and round-the-clock broadcast coverage of conflicts affect our viewpoints?

Service Projects

1 Use a mock court to mediate or resolve a dispute. You could use a real situation or create one that concerns issues of interest for you and your friends. Arrive at a resolution that meets the interests of both parties.

2 Learn to officiate your favorite sport. You can visit the library or a bookstore for a book on the sport and also ask a coach at your school for help. Plan ahead of time how you will deal with conflicts over questionable calls, fighting between players, etc. Then serve as an official in a sports event in your community.

3 Introduce a group of younger children to the concept of conflict resolution. Show them how to express hurt or angry feelings in a nonthreatening way, how to listen to another person without judging or criticizing, or other resolution skills.

4 Learn about peer mediation strategies and then set up a

Career Exploration

1 Make a list of professionals whose jobs require skills in conflict resolution. Pick one profession or occupation to learn more about by arranging to speak with someone in that field.

2 Professional mediators help settle disputes between different parties. Interview a professional mediator in your community. Find out what skills they use to help opposing parties find mutually satisfying solutions.

3 Obtain information about the role that United Nations delegates, ambassadors, and diplomats play in solving international conflicts.

4 Interview people in three different jobs to find out how they resolve conflicts in the workplace.

And Beyond

WORK AT USING YOUR SKILLS SENSIBLY IN a "hot" situation. Take the plunge from conflict to peace by exploring these related interest projects:

- A World of Understanding
- Law and Order
- Family Living
- Do You Get the Message?

Cookies and Dough

Girl Scouts have been selling cookies since the 1920s when Juliette Low began the practice as a way for Girl Scouts to become self-reliant. In the beginning, girls baked their own cookies. In 1934, the first documented councilwide sale of commercially baked cookies took place in Philadelphia.

Today's Girl Scouts develop their entrepreneurial and public speaking skills while earning money for special events, projects, supplies, equipment, and facilities.

Skill Builders

1 To hone your marketing skills, write a 30- or 60-second television or radio commercial for this year's Girl Scout cookie varieties. Or create a public service announcement (PSA) on the benefits of cookie sales for Girl Scout activities, projects, and trips.

2 Choose an activity that your group or troop would like to do, research the expenses involved (including things like admission fees, transportation, food) and then figure out how many boxes of cookies you would need to sell to finance the project. Read page 44 in the *Cadette Girl Scout Handbook* or pages 120–121 in *A Resource Book for Senior Girl Scouts* to find out how to create a budget.

3 Design a poster or flier for your cookie campaign that you could post at local stores, businesses, religious institutions, etc.

4 Brainstorm 10 new locations in your community for selling cookies—for example, at train stations, parades, tag sales, malls. Then, narrow down your choices by conducting an informal "test." Keep tabs on the numbers of sales made in each of these locations over the course of one week.

5 Research the history of Girl Scout cookie production and sales. Then, with your troop, recreate some of the old ad campaigns for fun. Could they still generate sales today? Take a poll.

6 One of the ways to ensure successful product sales is to develop a marketing plan. Do a market survey of your community to determine the ages and occupations of those who buy certain kinds of cookies and use the results to help in your sales efforts.

7 Selling cookies requires skills in areas such as customer service, public speaking, and perseverance. Role-play different scenarios that might occur during the sale. You might want to include the customer who is cranky, obnoxious, or very inquisitive.

8 Create a press kit to send to media outlets and places where cookies are sold. Include information on Girl Scouting, the purpose of the cookie campaign, a current council newsletter or list of projects and activities for girls, and a glossy flier of the cookie order form.

Technology

1 Surf the Internet for marketing ideas for food products. Download the information for your troop or group's cookie campaign.

2 Survey at least 10 people for their favorite cookies and their reasons. On your computer or by hand, make a bar graph or chart showing the results, and interpret them.

3 Study the design of a Girl Scout cookie box. How does it protect the product? How is it appealing? Look at the colors, print styles, artwork, or photography. Can you list five things the design says about Girl Scouting?

4 Prepare a spreadsheet that will help you keep track of your troop, group, or council's cookie sales and the profits. Use graph paper or a computer program.

5 Start a "cookies coast to coast" newsletter on the Internet.

Service Projects

1 Develop a cookie board game for Brownie Girl Scouts that will teach them skills like counting, matching, and following rules. Hold an informal contest to come up with a great name for the game.

2 Hold a cookie-tasting party at a senior citizens' facility, child-care center, or homeless shelter.

3 Swap sales techniques with another troop or group.

4 Recycle cookie boxes into an art project you have designed, constructed, and decorated. Or create something functional like a small toolbox or tissue holder.

5 Send thank-you notes to major supporters or helpers of your cookie campaign and share with them one project that came about as a result of the cookie sales.

6 Create a poster for a younger troop promoting the benefits of a healthy beverage (such as milk or juice) to go with their cookie snack.

Career Exploration

1 Examine different careers in the food industry. Don't forget jobs like those in marketing, sales, photography, and advertising, including the graphic arts and copy writing. Interview a professional in at least two of these fields. Ask about the job's responsibilities, education requirements or training, and benefits.

2 Be an entrepreneur and start your own business selling a product or service that you think will appeal to a specific group: for example, weekend baby-sitting services or a lemonade and cookie stand. Read about one Girl Scout's experiences with setting up her own business on pages 97 and 98 of the *Cadette Girl Scout Handbook.* Learn how to create a budget.

3 Get some writing tips from a local reporter, freelance writer, or teacher, and then write a feature story about your cookie campaign for the council newsletter.

4 Arrange a factory tour for a food product and see what is involved in the making and packaging of that item. Share what you have learned with your Girl Scout troop or group, or others.

And Beyond

FIND OUT HOW MANY GIRL SCOUT COOKies are sold each year in your council and nationally. Keep a visual tally at your council office or meeting place.

Write to Girl Scouts in other states to see what activities their cookie sales support. Display clippings, letters, or photos.

Try these related interest projects to improve your sales skills and marketing strategies:

- Your Own Business
- Leadership
- Dollars and Sense
- Graphic Communications
- The Food Connection
- Games for Life
- Collecting
- Creative Cooking
- Writing for Real

Dollars and Sense

Do you know how to manage your money wisely? Can you make a little go a long way? Do you have short- or long-term goals that involve significant amounts of money? Completing the following activities will help you to accomplish these goals with common sense and dollar savings.

Skill Builders

1 Read pages 97–98, "Life Success Skill #5: Earning and Managing Money," in the *Cadette Girl Scout Handbook* or "Money Management" on pages 120–121 in *A Resource Book for Senior Girl Scouts*. Prepare a troop or group budget, with a balance sheet that shows both income and expenses. Include troop money-earning projects as well as the Girl Scout cookie sale and other product sales. Plan activities for the year that keep your troop or group within its budget.

2 Work with a group to make a long-term financial plan for a goal that will require considerable financial reserves: for example, a trip to the Juliette Low Girl Scout National Center in Savannah, Georgia, or to Our Cabaña in Cuernavaca, Mexico.

3 Many shoppers try to find bargains or to get the best value for their money. Read "Life Success Skill #6: Becoming a Responsible Consumer" in the *Cadette Girl Scout Handbook*, or "Money Management" in *A Resource Book for Senior Girl Scouts*. Select a product and, over the course of two months, chart how the price changes in the same store. Or comparison shop for an item in three or four different stores. You can use the phone, visit the stores directly, or check prices through advertising circulars and catalogs. Make sure that you compare the quality of similar items as well as their cost.

4 Select a country you'd like to visit. Investigate the following:

■ The rate of exchange on United States currency and how, when, and where to exchange money into foreign currency.

■ The customs concerning bartering and bargaining practices. For instance, it's customary to "bargain down" prices when shopping at outdoor bazaars in some countries.

■ The cost of an item in the country's currency and its equivalent in U.S. dollars.

5 Play a stock market game in your troop or group or with other friends. Use an allotted amount of money to "buy" stocks or mutual funds. Over a designated period of time, "sell" your stocks and buy new ones as you or your group sees fit. Compare your group's performance with that of a professional money manager.

6 Talk with your family about its budget. Keep track of the cost of your family's meals, transportation, clothing, and other costs for two weeks. Designate three ways you could help your family cut costs and increase its savings. Share that information with your family.

Technology

1 Find out about two different software packages that create and analyze budgets. Prepare a letter to a hypothetical employer, a friend, or your family, explaining the advantages and disadvantages of these programs and recommending the one you think should be purchased.

2 Automatic teller machines (ATMs) have revolutionized the banking industry. Find out from an employee at your local bank how an ATM is operated and maintained. Brainstorm in your troop or group sensible and safe ways to use ATMs.

3 When people travel, they need to plan for all their expenses plus emergency funds. "Wiring" for money should only be used in real emergencies. Brainstorm with other traveling Girl Scouts the best ways to access funds while traveling. Compare the advantages and disadvantages of letters of credit, debit cards, travelers' checks, cash, and other methods of accessing money while away from home.

4 Find out the finances behind credit cards. Compare the "purchase" interest rate with the "cash advance" interest rate on a variety of cards. Figure out how much interest will add to the total cost of a cash advance. Compare "billing cycles" of different bank cards. Find out if they offer different grace periods before interest gets added to the cost of the purchase or advance. Find out about credit cards that offer check writing and the costs of using them. Compare the advantages and disadvantages of credit and debit cards.

5 Find out how computers have altered trading on the stock exchanges. If possible, visit a brokerage house, talk with an experienced trader, or read up on the "crash" of 1987.

Service Projects

1 Volunteer to be treasurer for an event or activity that is being planned by your troop or another group to which you belong.

2 Conduct a money management presentation for another Girl Scout troop or group. Enlist the advice and aid of adults with careers in finance or business. Choose topics that will interest your group, such as budgeting, savings, ways to earn money, checking accounts, how credit works, and income taxes.

3 From food to clothes and shelter, each aspect of daily living incurs an expense. For people with limited income, this is especially difficult. Arrange a drive for goods for disadvantaged individuals. Work with adults and philanthropic organizations in your community to distribute the items that you collect.

4 Reading and completing tax forms can be quite daunting for the average citizen. With your troop or group, set up a tax fair, in which volunteer accountants or other experts explain how to complete these forms.

5 Help a troop or group of younger girls to develop and implement a money-earning plan.

Career Exploration

1 Go to your local library or school guidance office and ask to see the *Encyclopedia of Associations*. Look under titles such as Finance, Accounting, or Computer Systems. Choose an organization that sounds interesting, and contact it with any questions about careers in that field.

2 Ask to review the résumé of an individual who works in a finance-related career. Talk to that person about her education and work history. Discuss what steps you might take now to prepare yourself for a similar career.

3 List a variety of part-time or summer jobs available to you. Compare the actual take-home pay from at least three different types of jobs. Also compare career growth from each job for increased earnings in the future. For example, a part-time job as a sales clerk in a department store now will help you later to be a manager, a buyer, or a display artist.

4 Learn about the responsibilities of operating your own business. Visit at least two businesses run by women. Ask them what's difficult and what's exciting about being self-employed.

5 Talk to three people who have very different jobs and find out how they use money management skills at work.

And Beyond

READ A WEEKLY NEWSPAPER OR JOURNAL with a financial or business section.

Obtain a part-time or summer job that involves some aspect of money management.

Improve your "money sense" and skills by trying these related interest projects:

- Your Own Business
- Cookies and Dough
- Leadership
- Math, Maps, and More
- Travel

Family Living

Your family influences you in many ways. Learn more about different family roles, how families communicate, how family life has changed over time, and the pleasures, problems, and pastimes that are a part of family living.

Skill Builders

1 Read magazines, newspapers, books, and other material on family life topics for one month. Keep a journal, noting current trends. Select one issue to discuss in your troop or group, or in a personal essay.

2 What does it cost your family to operate the household for one month? Work with your parents or guardian to create a family budget. Include costs for food, housing, clothing, transportation, child care, children's allowances, entertainment, insurance, and debt repayment. Compare your family's monthly expenses with their monthly income. Discuss with your family the types of financial problems you can avoid when using a budget.

3 Invite a financial planner or consultant to a troop or group meeting to discuss the services financial planners or agencies provide to families.

4 Arrange a family meeting to discuss two or three important issues that your family has experienced some conflict over: too much TV, curfews, household responsibilities, and sibling arguments are some possibilities. Each person should have an opportunity to express her or his feelings as well as listen respectfully to others.

Aim at reaching an agreement on at least one of the issues.

5 Prepare your family chronology (time line). The chronology can be displayed on a collage, a chart, or through a tape recording. Include the important events (births, moves, marriages, deaths, etc.) that have taken place since you were born. Highlight the events that caused significant changes in your family. Briefly discuss how these changes were handled. Do this activity with your family and share your chronology with your group.

6 Create a "family time" activity. Family members have busy schedules. Quality time together is often limited. Think of activities that will preserve and reinforce your family relationships, like reading to a younger sibling, helping a parent or grandparent learn computer skills, or playing board games.

7 Plan a family reunion. Form a committee of relatives to work with you in planning the event. Decide where and when you will hold it, and how you can involve relatives who live far away. In addition, create a display of old photos to share at the reunion.

Technology

1 Find out how technology has changed family life through the years. Talk to individuals of four different ages about what family life was like when they were children. Talk to both women and men. Ask someone who is in her or his twenties or thirties, forties or fifties, sixties, seventies, or older. How do their descriptions compare with what you know of family life today? Document and share your findings with others.

2 Take a trip to a computer store. Gather information about computer software that could be used in your household for task management and for fun. Which software programs are most worthwhile?

3 Develop a family media and technology center and storage area for labeled videocassettes, tapes, and compact discs. Regularly recycle or share your tapes with others.

4 Use a computer search to find information about family life in two cultures other than your own. Compare the similarities and differences.

5 Design a family T-shirt for a family reunion or gathering. This may be an original design in stencil or silk-screen or some other technique. Or design and print your family's greeting cards.

Service Projects

1 Compile a community directory of medical, legal, educational, financial, and recreational services for families. Make it available to troop or group family members or other community members.

2 With your family, prepare and deliver a holiday basket for a homebound, elderly, or ill person in your community.

3 Through your school or religious institution, find out how to help families in need in your community. Consider providing clothing, food, or information on child care. Share with your troop or group, or others, how they may also be of help.

4 Set up two or three meetings with other families with whom you share a common interest. Meet to plan an event, such as a parks beautification project. Come up with realistic goals and time lines.

5 Plan a special family meal. Choose people to do the following: shop for the food, cook the meal, set the table, and do the cleanup. Be certain to assign tasks to all family members.

Career Exploration

1 Identify at least five careers that involve family living. Find resources or books about three of these careers, and answer the following questions:

■ How much and what type of schooling is required?

■ What are the daily job responsibilities?

■ Where would a person in this field work (schools, hospitals, etc.)?

2 There are many different ways that parents today juggle having a career and raising a family. Some do it alone, and some with the support of spouses or other family members. Interview at least three parents in diverse situations and with children of varying ages. Ask them questions about the challenges and rewards of managing a career and family life, such as:

■ Are there different responsibilities for mother or father?

■ If you could do it differently, what would you change?

■ What supports do you rely on?

■ What are creative solutions you have worked out in your family to help get household jobs done?

3 Take on an area at home that you will personally be responsible for, like laundry, food shopping, or menu planning. Come up with timely and creative ways to tackle tedious chores.

4 Invite representatives from agencies that provide services for families to a troop or group meeting. Have them discuss the types of services provided, the costs involved, and the major family issues challenging their agencies. You might also invite parents or guardians to the meeting.

And Beyond

FOR HELP ON FAMILY MATTERS, TRY THESE related interest projects:

■ A World of Understanding
■ Generations Hand in Hand
■ Child Care
■ Understanding Yourself and Others
■ From Stress to Success

From Fitness to Fashion

*L*ooking your best has a lot to do with taking care of your body. The fashions you wear only complement your healthy habits of good nutrition, physical activity, and rest. This interest project takes you from personal fitness to the exciting world of fashion, and will help you develop a style of your own.

Skill Builders

1 With your parent's permission, do aerobic exercises—for example, cycling, swimming, skating, jumping rope, or walking—at least three times a week for at least six weeks. These exercises tone your body *and* burn fat. Gradually increase either the time of your workouts, or your repetitions, whichever applies. Keep a personal fitness log. Make sure to increase your fluid intake.

2 Learn how to take care of your skin. Start by eating right! (See the food pyramid in the *Cadette Girl Scout Handbook*.) Determine your skin type (oily, dry, normal, or combination), and develop a skin-care routine to fit your needs. Follow it for at least two weeks. Learn the meaning of the following skin-care terms: hypoallergenic, toner, astringent, exfoliate, mask, moisturizer, sun protection factor (SPF), antiperspirant, deodorant. Learn what natural, organic, and botanical cosmetics are.

3 Change your hairstyle. You don't need a radical cut to acquire a new look. Start with clean, conditioned hair. Try a zigzag part down the middle or side, French braids or cornrows using ribbons, beads, or other ornaments. If you usually wear your hair loose, try a topknot or French twist. If you wear it up, try it loose. Add a headband or barrettes. Look through magazines for an appealing style. Keep in mind the shape of your face, whether or not you wear glasses, and how difficult the style is to maintain.

4 Learn how to build a wardrobe. Begin with five basic pieces in your current wardrobe—jacket, skirt, pants, dress or jumper, blouse. This is your wardrobe's foundation. Create 10 or 12 outfits by interchanging these pieces. Try adding an additional blouse or sweater. Build onto these pieces with shoes, belts, scarves, jewelry, and other accessories. Some people build a wardrobe around their favorite colors.

5 Develop a project on fashions in history. Select a period in history, such as eighteenth-century America, the Victorian period, or the 1920s. Learn what styles were popular during that time. Or trace one item, such as hats, shoes, or bathing suits, and show how styles have changed over the years. Or develop your project on the fashions and cosmetics of another culture. Plan a presentation on your topic.

6 With today's emphasis on natural products, you might try making your own cosmetics. Look through beauty guides, magazines, and books for recipes on how to make facial cleansers, masks, skin moisturizers, skin conditioners, shampoos, and hair conditioners. Some of the ingredients will come from your own kitchen; others you may have to buy. Compile a "cosmetic resources" scrapbook for common beauty problems, and list your resources and recipes. With the permission of a parent or guardian, try some of the recipes.

Technology

1 Discover how cosmetics are made. Learn about the ingredients, testing procedures, manufacturing techniques, and packaging involved in producing a product.

2 Learn about natural and synthetic fabrics. Select five fabrics such as silk, linen, and polyester. Learn how each fabric is created, and what types of clothes it is used for. Are clothes made from these fabrics suitable to wear in only certain seasons? Make a collage with illustrations of fashions in a variety of fabrics for different occasions.

3 Fashion design has entered the computer age. Find out what software is used by the fashion industries. Check with your local computer store or a fashion school for information.

4 Design a fashion or accessory item. Or invent an article of clothing or accessory that has a special function.

5 Collect several different fashion magazines or different issues of the same magazine to review. Collect enough to draw some conclusions about them. What kinds of stories are highlighted? Describe the model(s) on the covers. Is there much diversity with regard to age, race, and physical features? Would the average girl relate to these models? Formulate your conclusions and present them to your group.

Service Projects

1 There are alternatives to shopping in the more expensive department stores. Choices include thrift shops, consignment shops, discount stores, garage sales, and outlets. Make a directory that includes the names and addresses of several of these stores, and the bargains available. Distribute it in your community, particularly to the local library.

2 Direct a "toiletries" drive in your council to help women in need. Collect soaps, shampoos, combs, lotions, and deodorants. Place sets in individual decorated bags for distribution.

3 Host a fashion show for teens as a troop money-earning project. Include "models" with special needs, if possible. Consider extending the fashion show concept to include skin-care, hair, and wardrobe tips.

4 Hold a From Fitness to Fashion Fair at a senior citizens' center or for younger Girl Scouts in your community.

5 Find out about unfair labor practices that exploit garment workers in this and other countries. Plan and implement actions you can take to raise public awareness of this issue in your community.

Career Exploration

1 To get ideas about careers in the fashion magazine industry, study the masthead in your favorite fashion magazine. List the careers represented there. Select a career that interests you, and learn more about it.

2 Discover which schools are noted for their fashion programs. Where are they located? What are the requirements for entrance? Speak to a guidance counselor about careers in the fashion industry. Send away for brochures and program descriptions of occupations and careers in fashion, make-up, fitness, and related fields.

3 Interview two of the following:

■ Buyer in a department store.

■ Fashion consultant in the merchandising division.

■ Tailor.

■ Cosmetics representative.

■ Hairstylist.

4 Achieving a personal style is a matter of choosing what's right for you—for your age, your build, your complexion. It means adding your own touch: an antique pin you found at a flea market, an old sweater that just happens to match the stripe in your new skirt, a belt your sister gave you. If you have a flare for personalizing your wardrobe, explore a career or avocation as a fashion consultant. Offer to help two of your friends personalize their wardrobes with accessories.

And Beyond

IF YOU ENJOY THE CREATIVE END OF FASHION, try your hand at these related interest projects:

■ Fashion Design
■ Visual Arts
■ Textile Arts
■ Just Jewelry

For tips on ways to beautify the world around you, look at Home Improvement. And for fitness's sake, try:

■ Women's Health
■ Sports for Life
■ The Food Connection
■ From Stress to Success
■ Your Best Defense

From Stress to Success

*D*o you have stress in your life? Chances are that you do. In this interest project, you will learn about sources of stress, how to manage it, and even how to turn it into a positive asset!

Skill Builders

1 Find out how the human body responds to stress. How are the following affected by stress: metabolism, blood pressure, heart rate, breathing? What happens to the body if it is continually under stress?

2 Feelings of stress can be reduced by using relaxation techniques. Sit in a quiet, comfortable place. Close your eyes. Relax all your muscles, breathe slowly, and repeat the word "one" each time you exhale. Using a word helps to erase other thoughts. Continue this exercise of focusing on each exhalation for 10–15 minutes. Slowly open your eyes. How do you feel? Find time to do this exercise once a day for a week.

3 Effective time management is the ability to plan your time well. Such planning often eliminates stressful situations. Plan your time by creating a reasonable schedule for yourself for one week. Fit in each activity you hope to accomplish from the time you get up to the time you go to bed. Be sure to designate some time to practice relaxation techniques. Try it out. What were your results? What did you learn?

4 Massage can relieve stress in muscles. Learn several massage strokes that help in relaxation. Try working on your feet, hands, or someone's shoulders. For example, a hand can be massaged by making firm circular patterns with your thumb between the tendons on the back of the hand. Then grasp each finger one at a time with your hand, and with a slight twisting motion slide your hand slowly from the base of the finger to the tip. Similar patterns can be used on the feet. A little hand lotion or oil will help to make the motion more soothing.

5 Some stresses are caused by problems for which you cannot readily see a solution. Choose one of these problems and brainstorm at least five ways you could cope with it. Read chapter 5 in the *Cadette Girl Scout Handbook* for some ideas. Or ask parents or guardians, friends, and teachers for possible solutions. Practice one of the "solutions" regularly.

6 Some of the symptoms of stress can be relieved by physical activity. Make room in your schedule to participate in one of the following activities at least three times a week. Do this for at least one month. Compare how you feel before and after the one-month period.

■ Play an active sport.

■ Participate in a movement or dance activity that makes you feel more flexible.

■ Go for a 20-minute walk or ride a bicycle for several miles.

■ Participate in a vigorous physical activity that lasts at least 25 minutes.

Make a list of the different methods people use to reduce stress, such as listening to music, soaking in a hot tub, or pursuing a hobby. Star those that would work for you and use one the next time you feel stressed.

Technology

1 Find out how biofeedback works. What ailments respond well to biofeedback techniques? Which are less responsive? Why? How does the biofeedback machinery help to treat the ailment? How can you use this information to reduce stress in your own life?

2 Hold a discussion at your troop or group meeting about the advantages and disadvantages of technology in today's society. Questions to consider: Does the computer enslave us or does it reduce our workload? Is the increasing reliance on computers having negative as well as positive effects on our lives? Support your viewpoints with personal experiences.

3 Take time to listen to the sounds in your environment. Listen to a variety of types of music and find pieces that evoke different emotions in you—happiness, sorrow, anger, playfulness, etc. Use tension-reducing music or sounds when you are feeling stressed, perhaps by making a tape recording of your favorite music or taking a walk outdoors.

4 Muscles tense under stress, sometimes without our realizing it. Hunched shoulders from hours of studying, for example, can bring on shoulder and neck pains. Learn to monitor your body and relax tight muscles. Find a cassette tape with a recorded relaxation exercise on it that you can use, or record your own with instructions from a resource on relaxation exercises.

Service Projects

1 Help to plan a workshop on stress among teenagers for your troop or group, school, or religious organization. Invite teens, their parents or guardians, and experts in your community to attend. Include discussion time and hands-on activities. You may want to include a role-play in which teen and parent participants reverse roles and enact a familiar scene of conflict (staying out late, consequences of not doing schoolwork).

2 School is a cause of stress for many teens. Volunteer as a peer counselor or tutor for a semester at your school or community center. Be sure that you receive training in counseling or teaching techniques!

3 Contact local organizations, such as youth centers, gyms, health clubs, and hospitals, to identify stress management programs and resources for youth. Make a list available through your council or school.

4 Set up a time with your family members in which you can practice a relaxation or stress management technique together: for example, exercise, breathing techniques, prayer, listening to music, singing. Keep a record of everyone's progress over a two- to three-month period. What changes do you notice in family interactions?

Career Exploration

1 Read about or interview two professionals from among the following: biofeedback consultant, sports trainer, relaxation therapist, massage therapist, recreation therapist, nutritionist/dietitian, yoga instructor, or physical therapist. Ask them about their field, how they were trained, and how they see their field expanding or changing in the next 10 years.

2 In the last 10 years, how has the medical field incorporated stress management in the prevention and treatment of illness and disease? Read about these changes in magazines or books, or learn about them elsewhere. Discuss your findings in a meeting of your troop or group or club.

3 Educators are exploring the connection between stress and success. Speak to at least three teachers about how they think stress affects student performance, and tips they have for dealing with it.

4 Counseling is a field that helps people handle or reduce stress in their lives. Find out how psychologists, psychiatrists, and clinical social workers are educated and trained. What is each trained and/or licensed to do?

And Beyond

REGULARLY PRACTICE RELAXATION TECHniques that you enjoy. Do you notice improved grades or health?

If you'd like to further de-stress, try any of the interest projects that offer you positive recreation and fun as well as:

- The Food Connection
- Women's Health
- It's About Time
- Understanding Yourself and Others
- From Fitness to Fashion

Generations Hand in Hand

Years ago grandparents often shared the same household with their children and grandchildren. Aunts and uncles may not have been far away. Today, because of economics and easy mobility, many young people do not have the opportunity to live with or even interact on a regular basis with older people. This interest project provides a series of activities that will help you to bridge the "generation gap" as you get to know older people.

Skill Builders

1 Investigate your heritage. Talk with family members and friends to get information about your family's history. Go back as many generations as you can. Ask about special family traditions, names, and foods. Make a heritage book for your family.

2 Interview at least five people who lived in your community over the past 25 to 50 years. Complete an oral history and/or pictorial record focusing on their experiences when they were your age. How is your life the same as or different from a girl of 50 years ago?

3 Complete a project with members or residents of a senior center or home. The project could be a musical performance or a dance workshop, low-impact aerobics class or another fun physical activity.

4 Team up with a group of senior citizens to complete a civic project such as a voter registration drive or a community celebration.

5 Invite retirees from a variety of professional fields to lend their expertise to a project you or your group are planning. Suggested projects are a health fair or career workshop.

6 Contact your local high school and get the names of graduates from the 1930s, 1940s, or 1950s and help them organize a class reunion.

7 Invite a senior citizen or older relative to accompany you to an outing she or he would enjoy—a baseball game, movie, play, or zoo. Plan a second outing based on your evaluation of your first.

8 Find out about the elderly in different societies and cultures. What are their roles? How are they treated? Create an artwork that reflects what you have learned.

Technology

1 The average life span of Americans today is longer than ever before. Find out about the factors that have contributed to this increase in longevity and the ability to stay active. Find out what the expected life span of someone your age is. Compare it with the life span of girls your age in other countries.

2 Interview a few older people to find out about the technological advances they've observed over the years. What effect did these changes have on themselves or their families?

3 Select a medical service or procedure available today that was not in existence 50 years ago, like open-heart surgery, laser treatments, hepatitis vaccines, etc. Talk with someone who has benefited from these services or procedures. Discuss their impact.

4 Teach an introductory lesson on the use of computers, including CD-ROMs, fax machines, and voice mail, to an older person who would like to keep up with the latest technology.

Service Projects

1 Develop a service project that will help an elderly person. Here are some ideas:

■ After getting permission, work with an animal shelter and your Girl Scout troop or group to bring pets to a local nursing home on a regular basis.

■ Set up a program for girls to read to or write letters for the visually impaired.

■ Set up a telephone network with a religious group or organization to have the homebound contacted once a day.

2 Recruit volunteers to participate in a food-shopping program for the elderly in your community. Find out if there is an agency or group that has established such a program and volunteer your time. Design a project that will provide shopping or food-delivery services.

3 Work with a senior citizen to provide assistance to children in need. For example, visit children in a hospital or emergency day-care center.

4 Compile a list of community organizations and services for the elderly. Distribute the list to senior centers, nursing homes, or individuals. Post the list for young people to view, so they can volunteer their time, too.

Career Exploration

1 Hold a career-day workshop with retired professionals. Topics could include résumé writing, interviewing, interpersonal skills in the workplace, and business etiquette. Find out who might be available for consultation and develop a list of consultants.

2 Talk to a retired person about her volunteer work. Find out whether her volunteer work relates to a previous career or whether it represents a recently acquired interest.

3 Learn about the field of geriatrics. How have advances in gerontology careers enhanced the quality of life of the elderly?

4 Find out about career opportunities in fields offering goods and services to retired people. Write to an organization that represents people over age 50—for example, the American Association of Retired People (AARP)—or refer to a magazine or newsletter written to this audience. Make a list of the advertisers and announcements and identify career opportunities suggested to them.

And Beyond

HAVE FUN WITH FAMILY AND FRIENDS OF all ages with these related interest projects:

■ Child Care
■ Family Living
■ Women's Health
■ Heritage Hunt
■ It's About Time
■ Writing for Real
■ Once Upon a Story
■ Artistic Crafts
■ Folk Arts
■ Paper Works
■ Just Jewelry
■ On a High Note
■ Invitation to the Dance
■ Sports for Life

Home Improvement

Would you like to learn how to restore old furniture? Connect your family's VCR or your friend's new stereo system? Decorate a room or wall in your home? If so, this interest project is "custom made" for you.

Skill Builders

1 Accessories such as pillows, curtains, or collectibles can really enhance the look of a room. Create your own room accessory such as a needlepoint or hand-stitched pillow, a decorative window treatment, wall hanging, or a display of your collectibles.

2 With the permission of an adult in your family, brighten up a room, a wall, or the trim (molding) around the doors, floors, and ceiling with paint! You may want to sponge paint or use stencils to add an interesting touch.

3 Create a family gallery! With a friend or family member, collect family photos and memorabilia. Then arrange them into an attractive display for all to enjoy.

4 Sometimes all a drab-looking piece of furniture or woodwork really needs is a face-lift! Check the condition of a piece of furniture. If the item is sturdy, it might be worth investing a little elbow grease. With the assistance of an experienced adult, try one or more of the following refurbishing methods on a piece of furniture:

- Stripping and refinishing.

- Faux finishes such as marbling or crackling.

- Cleaning and painting.

5 Find out how to connect a VCR to a television, a television to a stereo system, or your house lights to a timing system. Then teach someone else in your family how to do these things, too.

6 Learn to unclog a toilet using a plunger and a snake. Investigate how the basic mechanism inside the tank operates. When needed, use your newly acquired knowledge and skills at home.

Technology

1 From wall and window treatments to upholstery and carpeting, there's a wide choice in fibers today. Find out about two natural fibers and two chemically created fibers. Then, learn about the process each undergoes to become fabric. If possible, obtain samples of the fibers and fabric. What are the strengths and weaknesses of each fiber? How are natural fibers chemically treated to make them stain-resistant and flame-retardant? You could consult a teacher, a carpet or fabric store owner, or a textile manufacturer's Web site to get this information. Share what you learn with others.

2 Educate yourself about home hazards. For example, read about carbon monoxide poisoning, lead poisoning, and fire hazards. Then check the safety of the water in your home by contacting the health department for a water-testing kit. Or install a carbon monoxide or smoke detector.

3 Technology enables people with disabilities to live more independently in their own homes. A flashing light lets someone who is hearing-impaired know when the doorbell or phone rings. Doorknobs, doorways, sinks, and counter heights can be adjusted to allow those who use wheelchairs more independence. Find out about other technologies used in homes to increase the independence of people with disabilities. Then assess the accessibility of your home for people with disabilities.

4 Put together a tool kit for basic home repair. Include a claw hammer, flathead screwdriver, Phillips screwdriver, pliers, monkey wrench, wrenches, level, and staple gun. Demonstrate the correct use of five of these tools. When using tools, be sure to wear protective eye guards and follow safety guidelines.

5 Learn about three safety features found in houses or apartments today. Share information with others about how these features work and how to maintain them.

6 Investigate home water filter systems—those installed under the sink as well as container-based systems. How often do filters have to be changed? Do these systems remove all contaminants? What are the costs? Make a poster displaying the benefits of each system.

Service Projects

1 With your Girl Scout troop or group, plan a "spruce-up" party for a nursing home, children's center, or another place of your choosing. Paint walls and install shelving, as needed. Use some of your skills to paint furniture or decorate windows.

2 Volunteer for a weekend construction program. Make sure you follow all safety guidelines as you work with an adult.

3 Make and donate a "design box" for younger girls in your council. Include in each box such items as a color wheel, graph paper, pencils, T-squares, paint sample cards, and fabric swatches.

4 Organize a home safety workshop for parents or guardians of infants and young children. Ask a child psychologist and pediatrician, or another child safety expert, to address the group and answer questions.

Career Exploration

1 Find out what training is required in your state to be a licensed carpenter, plumber, or electrician. Explore different ways of obtaining that training. Talk with a member of that trade and find out what she would suggest for girls interested in that field.

2 The best way to find out if a job is right for you is to try it! Volunteer as an apprentice painter, carpenter, or decorator.

3 Shadow an interior decorator. Find out about her training, how she solicits clients, and how she reconciles their budgets with their decorating preferences. What other type of professionals work inside the home to improve it? Look at related books and magazines at a bookstore.

4 Design a "dream" room or house to scale. Use your creativity as you paint, wallpaper, and furnish this space.

5 Get a part-time job at a local hardware, fabric, or home-decorating store.

And Beyond

IF THE SKILLS YOU'VE LEARNED SPARKED your interest, keep improving them with these related interest projects:

- Build a Better Future
- Visual Arts
- Fashion Design
- Math, Maps, and More
- Inventions and Inquiry

Law and Order

Laws guide and protect civilized societies. They regulate the behavior of individuals, small groups, and big businesses. The laws a society has established reflect what it considers important. If you would like to know more about law and order, this interest project is for you.

Skill Builders

1 See the law in action. Observe at least two of these proceedings: a town/city council meeting, a live or televised trial, or a special court session (such as juvenile justice, landlord/tenant, small claims). Record and present your observations.

2 Arrange to interview a law enforcement official. What are the penalties a violator might face if convicted of particular categories of crime? What are the rights of a person who is arrested? Use this and other information in creating a poster or other visual aid.

3 Find out about defamation law (slander and libel) as it relates to the media. For example, what is a journalist's best defense against a defamation lawsuit? Why are newspapers able to print embarrassing pictures without permission? Why do people get on network news programs without their knowledge? Why can the personal problems of public figures be discussed on the news?

4 Read the local newspaper for several weeks to track crime in your community. What patterns do you observe? Is one type of crime more prevalent than others? Ask your neighbors if they have been victims of a crime.

5 Investigate laws and lawsuits that affect students. Consider locker or backpack searches for weapons or drugs, and uniform and clothing codes. Hold a debate on an issue that affects or interests you and your friends.

6 Should parents be held responsible for crimes committed by their children? Who should face the penalties and why? Organize a debate on this topic.

7 Learn the common terms used in parliamentary procedure by reading the section "Parliamentary Procedure" in *A Resource Book for Senior Girl Scouts*. Hold a meeting following parliamentary procedures.

Technology

1 Host a video slumber party with friends with the theme of "crime and justice." View one or two movies or TV shows in which a youth is involved in a crime. Discuss the issues of justice or injustice that were presented in these movies or TV shows.

2 Find out what role computers play in law enforcement. How do they make it easier to track criminals?

3 What are polygraph tests? When and why are they used? How do they work? Create a police drama, in which you and a partner take turns "polygraphing" each other about a made-up crime.

4 There are many legal issues surrounding privacy—for example, telephone conversations; reading someone else's e-mail; caller I.D.; the use of cellular or cordless phones in public; searching through a person's trash; or reading someone's diary or other personal material. What's legal and why? Hold a discussion on "privacy matters" in your troop or group. Invite a lawyer or police officer to attend.

5 Learn about scientific methods, such as DNA testing, fingerprinting and hair analysis, used in criminal investigations. How can they be used as evidence in solving crimes? Find two newspaper or magazine articles that discuss these methods in criminal investigations. Share your findings in a troop or group meeting.

Service Projects

1 Invite a police officer, judge, or attorney in to explain the law to teens and to answer questions. You might want to make it a multimedia event by including video clips, etc.

2 Help with a voter registration drive for the next election in your community.

3 Write a letter to an elected official or newspaper editor expressing your opinion on any "hot" issue, from school budget reforms to the rights of former convicted felons. Review several newspapers or magazines for information on the topic you've chosen.

4 Organize a "Safe Rides" club that offers rides to teens who feel they can't drive safely or are unwilling to get into a car with a driver who is impaired by drugs or alcohol. Ask your local police station for suggestions. Volunteers may answer phones, provide rides, or coordinate assignments.

5 Write a play, skit, or story, or produce a video for a young audience, dramatizing what can happen to a juvenile who breaks the law by shoplifting, driving while intoxicated, or using an illegal drug. Research the details so that they are accurate. If possible, read your work or show your video to a group.

Career Exploration

1 Research careers in law enforcement by interviewing two of the following: a judge, police officer, state trooper, criminal lawyer, civil lawyer (in a field that interests you, like entertainment law or product liability). What was their education and training? What are their personal or financial rewards?

2 Make a list of related law-and-order careers, such as crime writer, children's advocate, probation officer, forensic technician. Write a detective or "whodunit" story or play in which one of the main characters has such a career.

3 Participate in an internship or community service program that deals with a law-related or political career. Keep a journal of your experiences.

4 Hold a mock trial on an issue that affects teens. Include the roles of prosecutor, defense attorney, judge, jurors, witnesses, etc.

5 Read a book about or by someone involved in politics. What do you consider essential qualities to cultivate for a person embarking on a political career?

And Beyond

CREATE AND SHARE A BIBLIOGRAPHY OF books about crime and detectives.

Take a trip to Washington, D.C., and visit the Federal Bureau of Investigation, the Supreme Court, the Capitol, and/or the White House.

Use your sleuthing skills and investigative eye with these related interest projects:

- Why in the World?
- Inventions and Inquiry
- Writing for Real
- Digging Through the Past
- Your Best Defense

Leadership

I s there a burning issue in your life, such as the need to help feed the homeless or reduce illiteracy? You can translate your unique vision and voice into action. The key is leadership and teamwork. A leader is someone who can accomplish great things with others. On a successful team, each "player" can contribute her strengths to common goals.

Skill Builders

1 Observe leadership in action: visit meetings of at least two different groups, such as members of a city council working on a piece of legislation, or a group of volunteers developing plans for an event. Before your visit, talk to the group leader about the group's purpose and agenda. Find out how the group seeks to accomplish its tasks and what role the leader will play. Ask the leader for her tips on running a meeting. Take notes, and make your own one-page tip sheet on how to run a meeting. Refer to it when you're a group leader.

2 In a group meeting, observe how people interact. Who talks and why? Is there a person who helps move the group along or blocks progress? How does the setting (room, tables, lighting, etc.) affect the group? How does the leader get everyone involved? Are goals stated clearly, and are they achieved? If so, how? If not, why not? Share your observations and conclusions with at least two people.

3 What leadership skills do you bring to a group? What leadership skills do you need to add to your repertoire? For some ideas about leadership skills, read the relevant chapters in either the *Cadette Girl Scout Handbook* or *A Resource Book for Senior Girl Scouts*. Pick one of the skills that you want to develop and devise a plan that will help you become better at it. Follow your plan for at least one month.

4 Read about leadership styles and figure out your dominant style. Ask other girls in your troop or group to do the same. Discuss how all of you differ in the ways you lead and what things you have in common. Then, each girl role-plays a leadership style different from her dominant one.

5 Name and discuss two or three examples of "negative leadership," such as political leaders who used their power in ways that were harmful or illegal. Come up with a group vision or checklist on how to recognize and prevent the destructive aspects of negative leadership.

Technology

1 Presentation skills are important for public speakers and leaders. Have someone videotape you speaking in front of a group. With an adult, such as a teacher, professional coach or trainer, or public relations professional, analyze what worked and what could be improved based on the tape.

2 Watch a variety of television shows and read newspapers and magazines to see how leaders are represented in the media. Which people, besides politicians, are represented as leaders? What are some of the issues facing leaders? How do leaders deal with those issues? What kinds of ethical issues do leaders confront?

3 Talk to two or three educators, business people, consultants, or other leaders about how changing technologies affect leadership. Does a telephone conference call require different leadership skills than an in-person meeting? Ask about video conferences or forum discussions on the Internet.

4 Help organize an online forum to discuss an issue affecting older girls. Establish rules for the discussion to make sure all participants are made to feel welcome and have the opportunity to contribute.

Or observe an online forum. How is leadership determined and consensus reached? Compare and contrast the dynamics of a cyberspace forum with a real-life forum. What are the advantages and disadvantages of online leadership?

people with disabilities, or celebrating diversity. Recruit or join others to work together on a project that addresses the needed change through outreach posters and presentations, news items, a speakers' bureau, or other means.

4 Organize a youth meeting through your school, religious community, or Girl Scout organization to identify projects that can improve your community as a whole. Plan your work by identifying general goals and specific action steps to accomplish them.

5 Lead a group of younger girls by volunteering to be a coach for a sports team in your neighborhood. Younger girls look up to teenagers and you will have an opportunity to help girls have a happy, healthy sports experience.

Talk with a teacher, academic adviser, or professional in one of those careers to learn about ways to develop and practice the needed skills. For example, practice listening to others or making speeches.

3 Create a résumé that highlights your leadership experience and the skills and qualities you possess.

4 Start a club or after-school activity, such as a debating, drama, computer, or sports club. Enlist the aid of teachers or advisers.

5 Get involved in the election process. Help arrange a candidate forum, issues night, or voter registration drive. (Be aware that you cannot campaign for a candidate or advocate partisan issues while representing Girl Scouts.)

Service Projects

1 Volunteer to help coordinate your school elections or participate in a planning committee for a school event. Or run for an office or take the lead on a project like managing the set design for your school play.

2 Help to organize an ongoing service project, such as a community literacy program highlighted by a yearly book fair. Create follow-up activities for the project, such as a weekly reading program using community leaders, school tutoring programs matching older students with younger students, or a poster contest with the theme of reading.

3 Identify a need in your community like recycling, building school spirit, preventing child abuse, ensuring accessibility for

Career Exploration

1 Compile a multimedia leadership resource list. Go to a public library, bookstore, video store, school library, or your Girl Scout council office to look for books, newspaper and magazine articles, videotapes, and audiotapes to create your leadership bibliography. You might search the World Wide Web for resources as well. Organize your materials in categories, such as definitions of leadership, new trends in leadership, leadership skills, ethics in leadership, and issues for women in leadership. Share your resource list with others.

2 List the careers that you are interested in pursuing and identify leadership skills that you will need to succeed in those fields.

And Beyond

ATTEND A LEADERSHIP INSTITUTE SPONsored by GSUSA or your local council. If your council does not offer one, ask about how you can organize one.

From selling cookies to saving the planet, improve your leadership skills with these related interest projects:

- Cookies and Dough
- Your Own Business
- Law and Order
- Planet Power
- A World of Understanding

Travel

All aboard! Your "super-sonic" metro is about to depart. Experience different cultures, photograph breathtaking vistas, and try exotic foods. Your ticket to ride is courtesy of your own personal travel service—your imagination. Unlimited mileage. Frequent flyer rewards. No cost restrictions.

This interest project is designed for those who want to explore the world—even if your dream trip may not happen right away.

Skill Builders

1 Sample two modes of travel that are unfamiliar to you, or that you'd like to learn more about. Consider a ferry, mountain bike, horse-drawn wagon, sleigh, canoe, or horseback ride. Photograph your adventures and share them with your troop or group.

2 Plan and take a day or weekend trip to any U.S. city. Read pages 132–134 in *A Resource Book for Senior Girl Scouts*, and answer the questions on pages 133–134. With the help of a travel agent, tour guide, or other adult, research transportation options and fares, accommodations, restaurants, activities, and tourist attractions. Check on special and seasonal events. What type of clothing is appropriate and what other gear might you need? Get a reasonable estimate of costs. Keep a trip diary and write in it for at least 10 minutes a day.

3 Which country, state, or city captures your fancy? Read travel guides, magazines, and travel sections of newspapers. Contact chambers of commerce, tourist boards, information centers, and travel agencies. Talk to experienced travelers. Keep a file and plan that trip for sometime in your future!

4 Getting away from it all starts with organization. Create a master luggage list so you can pack effectively. Prepare a "Before Leaving Home" checklist that includes making arrangements for mail and newspaper delivery, plant and pet care, phone messages, and bill paying.

5 Find out how to say hello and good-bye in 10 different languages. Find a way to use this information in an activity with a younger group of girls, such as during an international flag ceremony conducted in your troop or group, at a wider opportunity, or at a council-sponsored event.

6 With your troop or group, produce a simulated talk radio show on a particular travel subject, like the solo traveler, winter getaways, the student traveler. You may first want to listen to similar shows on the air. Invite a travel agent, a travel writer, a hotel or restaurant manager, or a few experienced travelers to be on your show.

7 Read about Girl Scout wider opportunities in the *Cadette Girl Scout Handbook* or *A Resource Book for Senior Girl Scouts*. Find out what events are going on this year. Which ones might you want to apply for? Send away for an application, and start the process going!

Technology

1 Check out your local computer store and locate software on geography or travel. Make a list of resources for your troop or group.

2 Collaborate with your local cable company, historical society, museum, library, or chamber of commerce in making a video or brochure that describes your community or town.

3 Find an online computer bulletin board for travelers and/or travel writers and chat with them about their experiences.

4 Learn to read two of the following: a topographical map, nautical chart, subway guide, street map, road map, or CD-ROM map.

5 Find out about recent technological advances in airport security. What mechanisms are in place now to help ensure safety?

3 Volunteer for about five hours with a group that works to help people who have recently arrived in your community.

4 Plan a neighborhood walk or tour for a younger Girl Scout troop. Include interesting places like a bakery or toy store. Ask a local merchant or restaurant if you can see the behind-the-scenes operation.

5 Bring a faraway place to those who cannot travel long distances. For example, organize a slide show with music to give nursing home or rehabilitation center residents a chance for armchair travel to a distant land.

3 Find out about careers in two other countries, including educational requirements, working conditions, and salaries.

4 Write a piece about a recent interesting trip you've taken or about a fantasy vacation, and send your article or story to a suitable travel magazine.

5 Compile a list of jobs in travel and tourism: for example, tour operator or guide, pilot, flight attendant, interpreter, cruise ship activity planner, hotel musician. What types of skills, such as speaking several languages, would you need? Make a presentation or visual display for a career night event.

Service Projects

1 With a community group or organization that helps people with disabilities, volunteer to assist a person with special needs take a short day trip. Find out about special facilities she may need, such as moving walkways or wheelchair ramps. Ask about travel agencies or organizations that cater to individuals who have disabilities.

2 Enjoy a travel adventure with someone who finds it difficult to travel on her own. Discuss her needs and concerns ahead of time. Ask what she would like to do and work together to arrange for transportation, dietary needs, and additional help, if needed.

Career Exploration

1 Explore careers in the travel industry by organizing a travel fair. Choose from travel agents, tour guides, hotel managers, travel writers, restaurant personnel, airline employees, car rental agents, social directors, and ship officers. Ask them to set up booths and be willing to give short talks about the nature of their jobs, education and training requirements, and financial and other rewards.

2 Invite a travel writer or photographer to speak to your troop or group. How does she come up with story or picture ideas? What research and travel are involved? Can a writer or photographer use material from her own vacations? What are the benefits and demands of being a travel writer or photographer? Look at her work samples.

And Beyond

READ *THE TIME MACHINE*, BY H. G. WELLS, *A Wrinkle in Time*, by Madeline L'Engle, or other books exploring time travel. Or see some classic movies that take place in other lands: for example, *Lawrence of Arabia*, *Casablanca*, *Out of Africa*.

If you love to travel, become a true citizen of the world by trying these related interest projects:

- Folk Arts
- Invitation to the Dance
- Once Upon a Story
- The Lure of Language
- Heritage Hunt
- Museum Discovery
- Space Exploration

Understanding Yourself and Others

Are you curious about other people, and do you want to learn more about yourself? You'll have the opportunity to reflect on your unique self, set and work on personal goals, and develop helpful ways to influence others. You'll also learn how to shape attitudes, share beliefs, and help younger Girl Scouts deal with peer pressure. Understanding Yourself and Others can make your world a better place, so proceed with enthusiasm!

Skill Builders

1 You can learn a lot about people by watching them—in school, in a public place, at a party. Observe body language (gestures, facial expressions, posture, etc.) and listen to what people say. Share at least five observations in a troop or group meeting.

2 Set a personal goal that you can reasonably accomplish in one month. For help, review the *Cadette Girl Scout Handbook*, especially chapter 5, "Skills for Life," or *A Resource Book for Senior Girl Scouts*, chapter 5, "Skills for Living—The Amazing Balancing Act." Both books offer tips for managing your money, time, etc.

3 Every culture develops social norms or ways of interacting with people (such as how close to stand to another person). Observe what happens when you break these norms. Do one of the activities that follows:

■ Go to a public place, and sit right next to a person at a relatively empty table.

■ During a conversation with a friend, stand closer to her than you usually do.

■ Ride an elevator facing the back instead of the front.

■ Treat someone whom you're usually friendly with in a formal manner.

How difficult was it for you to do the activity? How did the other people react? Why?

As an alternative, act out one of your choices with a friend if that would make you feel more comfortable. Afterward discuss how you think you and the other person would have reacted in a real situation.

4 Write your autobiography. Interview your relatives for help in remembering events from when you were younger, or look at a family photo album to help recollect them. How have these events from the past shaped who you are today? Draw pictures or use photos to illustrate your autobiography.

5 With friends, or in your troop or group, role-play at least two of the following situations:

■ A girl is being pressured by her friends to try drugs at a party.

■ A girl makes a prejudiced remark about a classmate who is not there.

■ A girl's parents tell her she can't go to the school dance.

After your role-play, share any new insights you have gained from this activity.

Technology

1 With the help of friends or other members of your troop or group, create a video or presentation that focuses on building self-esteem or awareness about a particular issue that affects teens. Topics to consider: violence prevention, substance abuse, or pressure to be successful.

2 Some people, perhaps your older relatives, did not grow up using computers. As a result, they may feel intimidated by all the new technology. Create a plan to introduce these beginners to a computer system or other technology.

3 Accidents are often caused by "human error" (for example, pressing the wrong pedal in a car). If tools and machines were easier for people to operate, some of these mistakes could be avoided. Change the design of a tool or a machine (such as a car, a computer, or a garden tool) to make human errors less likely. People who do this type of design work are called "human factors engineers." If you come up with a really good suggestion, send it to a manufacturer.

4 Find out how well television and other media represent the elderly, women, and people of color. For a one-week period, keep a record of three shows (including the commercials) that you watch regularly. Pay attention to what each character is doing (cooking dinner, working in a lab, etc.); their personal attributes (intelligence and attractiveness, for example); their roles at work, in school, or within the family; and how each character is treated by others. Share your observations and conclusions with others.

Service Projects

1 Design and carry out a project to change attitudes, and hopefully behavior, about an important issue, such as drunk driving, the use of seat belts, or racial or religious prejudice. Remember, attitudes are often emotional and deeply ingrained. Presenting a good, logical argument may not be enough to change people's attitudes. What else could you do?

2 Peer pressure can be a powerful influence in a girl's life. With some friends, put on a play for younger girls that demonstrates both the benefits and harmful effects of peer pressure.

3 Teenagers often say, "Nobody understands me." Put together a booklet to help parents, teachers, and other adults gain a better understanding of what it means to be a teenager today. Use cartoons, photographs, poems, stories, etc., to get your points across. Share your booklet with adults close to you!

4 How do you feel and act when you wear different types of clothing: for example, a fancy dress or your Girl Scout uniform? Do the people you know or strangers treat you differently? Keep a record of reactions as you change your style of clothing during a two-week period. Also keep track of how you react to people wearing unusual clothing.

Career Exploration

1 In many instances, people get hired for jobs because of their "people skills." Employees also get fired because of personality conflicts with others. Observe different types of people at work. What personal characteristics make them good (or bad) at what they do?

2 Psychologists work in a huge number of professions and settings. Compile a list of 8–10 possible jobs for someone with a psychology background; gather in-depth information about two of them.

3 Everyone plays many roles. You're a student, a Girl Scout, a friend, and so on. Create a list of your roles. Do the same for an adult you know. Spend a day with that adult and see how she plays out her various roles: for example, bank manager, mother, and so on.

4 Design a dream job of the future based on your interpersonal skills. For instance, if you have a "good ear" for listening to your friends' problems, you might succeed in the field of counseling. Describe the responsibilities of your dream job, and the training necessary for it. Ask an adult you know in a related career for help.

5 Sports psychology is a growing field. Find out about some of the techniques that are used and try out a couple of them.

And Beyond

PARTICIPATE IN A FOCUS GROUP (TASTE-test soft drinks in a store, for example) or complete a survey in a magazine.

Observe human nature wherever you can to better understand yourself and others. These related interest projects will help:

- Conflict Resolution
- A World of Understanding
- Child Care
- Family Living
- Leadership
- From Stress to Success
- Law and Order
- Public Relations

Your Best Defense

Karate kicks and elbow uppercuts may come to mind when speaking of self-defense. But self-defense involves using brains as well as brawn. Quick thinking and being alert will help you protect yourself.

Learning to defuse conflict before it starts is also a great self-defense tool. Planning ahead, good communication skills, and a sincere effort to work out a solution can go a long way toward squelching hostile encounters.

Skill Builders

1 Explore several philosophies of self-defense. Learn about several martial arts such as karate, tae kwon do, jujitsu, and akido. Participate in classes or interview a martial arts master.

2 Take a self-defense course designed for women and girls. Once you've completed the course, sponsor your own "mini" self-defense workshop for your friends and family, or for your Girl Scout troop or group.

3 Your body language and tone of voice can play a role in stopping a hostile or violent encounter from happening. Recite the following sentences—once with an angry voice and again in a gentle manner. Think about the effect each version would have on the listener. How can you express your displeasure with someone without putting them on the defensive?

■ "Shut the door now, please. I'm trying to study."

■ "When are you going to return my sweater?"

■ "I'm angry that you continue to lie to me."

Make up three more emotionally charged discussions and role-play them.

4 Increasing your self-confidence can increase your sense of personal safety. What can you do *now* to increase your self-confidence? Speak up more often in class? Learn a new sport? Stand up for your beliefs on an issue? Make your own list and select one or two items to begin working on today. Keep a journal of your feelings and experiences as you practice new behavior.

5 Avoiding an attack sometimes means having to act unfriendly. Role-play two of the following situations with a partner:

■ Walking home, you notice that a car going in your direction has slowed to match your pace. You feel uneasy. How would you feel about quickly turning to run in the other direction, or "making a scene"? Would you worry about what the driver thinks?

■ You're in an apartment building elevator and a well-dressed man enters. He positions himself "too close for comfort" and begins to ask you very personal questions. Would you respond? Why or why not? How could you "defend" yourself from this stranger's approaches?

■ Coming home on a bus, you realize you've traveled past your stop to an unfamiliar neighborhood. A passenger insists on walking you in the right direction. How would you decline her or his help?

Technology

1 How do images of women on television and in the movies influence the way you feel about your own personal safety? Over the next two weeks, record every aggressive act you see on television or film committed against women or girls and their responses. Arrange a discussion group to share your findings.

2 Many teen magazines give girls conflicting messages about interacting with boys. Take an inventory of several current issues of popular teen magazines. How many articles send mixed messages on issues such as date rape, beauty, body image, and self-esteem? What about advertisements? Cut out and compile your examples in a booklet to share with your classmates or arrange to hold a "Messages in the Media" night at your troop or group meeting place.

3 Explore the pros and cons of pepper spray, stun guns, and other personal protection items. Research your state's laws regarding the legality of carrying these and similar items. Ask a self-defense instructor for a lesson on everyday items that can be used to fend off an attack. Invite the instructor to speak at a meeting of your troop or group.

4 Guns, carried by many teens for protection, are responsible for a staggering percentage of teenage deaths. Take a survey of your peers. Ask this question: "Is carrying a gun for protection ever justifiable and, if so, when?" Write an editorial for your local or school newspaper summarizing the results of your survey and giving your perspective on gun use among teens.

5 Watch your favorite police drama with a group of friends. Have the group select a violent scene from the drama. Role-play a new ending in which the perpetrator and victim avoid using violence to "solve" their conflict.

Service Projects

1 Invite a law-enforcement officer to speak to a group of your neighbors about crime patterns and threats to safety in your neighborhood. Discuss activities you and your neighbors can take to make your streets safer, then assist in implementing a neighborhood project to tackle one of your community's biggest safety concerns.

2 Volunteer to teach a group of elementary school students skills for dealing with strangers, walking home alone, handling emergencies, and other personal safety issues. After your presentation, have them demonstrate what they have learned using role-plays.

3 Offer to be of service in a place for victims of violence—a battered women's shelter, for example. Perhaps you can arrange a recreational activity or assist in tutoring. Or help with a community "hotline" that offers assistance to victims of violence.

4 Develop a directory of helpful resources for women and girls who are the victims of violence. Provide copies for local libraries, religious institutions, community centers, and businesses.

Career Exploration

1 Our society needs professionals who physically and emotionally "repair" victims of violence. Interview at least one of the following professionals or another of your choosing: social worker, therapist, health-care provider, police officer, counselor, volunteer in a battered shelter, 911 operator. Try to find out:

■ What training and certification they received.

■ How they help victims.

■ How they handle the stress brought on by continually helping others in crisis.

2 Interview an employee or volunteer who develops projects related to domestic abuse. Find out how you can implement a project in your community.

3 Job-shadow or interview a police officer (at her or his headquarters or precinct, not on the beat) or a social worker. Interview the person about the skills needed in relating to people in crisis and in dealing impartially with victims and offenders.

4 Find out and discuss the laws and policies that exist to protect children, women, and elderly victims of domestic abuse. In what capacity would you best work with victims of crime? Why? What skills do you have—both technical and interpersonal—that make you suitable for such work?

And Beyond

PUT FORTH YOUR BEST DEFENSE WITH YOUR newfound skills. Consult the interest projects related to sports, health, and dance for ways to keep physically fit and "people smart." These include:

■ Law and Order
■ From Stress to Success
■ Understanding Yourself and Others
■ Conflict Resolution
■ Do You Get the Message?
■ Sports for Life
■ Women's Health
■ Invitation to the Dance
■ High Adventure
■ Emergency Preparedness

Your Own Business

Are you an independent thinker who loves to generate ideas and find ways to make things happen? If so, you may have the makings of an entrepreneur. An entrepreneur organizes and manages a business from fashion to sporting goods. Can you think of some local or world-famous entrepreneurs: for example, in the fields of fast food or ice cream? If you would like to start your own business, this interest project is for you.

Skill Builders

1 Analyze several advertisements in magazines and newspapers, as well as radio and television commercials for the same product. What do you like or dislike about these advertisements? Do they make you want to buy the product? With a friend, brainstorm an advertising campaign for an imaginary or real product.

2 Market research is used to check consumer responses to a new product. Invent a new product and conduct your own informal market research. Interview five potential customers. Do they like your product? Why or why not? How might they improve it? Redesign your product using information from your market research.

3 Visit your library, chamber of commerce, or other service organization to research what support and resources exist at the city, state, and federal agency levels for small-business owners. How do you join an association for business owners? Are there associations for women or special-interest groups? Compile a list and save it for future reference.

4 Do you know anyone who runs her own business? What qualities make her a good businessperson? Interview her or invite her to speak at your troop or group. Ask her for tips on getting started, how to deal with customers, what kinds of business practices can ensure a degree of success, and the types of marketing techniques that work best.

5 Develop and implement a plan to turn a hobby into a business venture. For instance, design and sell greeting cards or jewelry, or start a dog-walking service.

Technology

1 Find out how technology has changed the face and pace of business. Interview three people who are self-employed and find out which technological advances have benefited them.

2 Draw "before and after" posters depicting a few of the changes in business practices, equipment, or technology over the last few decades. Can you predict any future changes in the workplace?

3 Investigate new techniques for presenting products. Find out about holograms and computer art and virtual reality. Design a three-dimensional ad or draw a two-dimensional ad.

4 Survey several small businesses in your community to find out about the equipment and technology considered most essential in their fields.

Service Projects

1 Help develop a proposal that will explain to businesses in the community the importance of contributing to a special project or a worthy cause.

2 Create a project to help parents educate their children to be knowledgeable consumers. Emphasize critical thinking skills that children can use when being bombarded with advertisements.

3 Arrange for "women in business" to be the theme for a meeting of your troop or group. Invite female entrepreneurs and ask questions about the challenges and rewards of their work.

4 Develop and implement a marketing plan to obtain volunteers for a Girl Scout council or community project (such as a camping trip for younger girls).

Career Exploration

1 Create a brochure to market your talents and skills as a consultant to a prospective client. Ask your friends and families for their suggestions. Look at sample business brochures before writing your own.

2 Consult a professional and learn how to prepare yourself for a job interview. What do you wear? Should you bring samples of your work? What questions should you ask? Then role-play an interview with that person.

3 Organize a career fair for your class. Invite representatives from the business and professional communities to discuss careers in marketing, public relations, journalism, and the law.

4 Shadow a business owner for a day. Learn about the skills she needs in her field. What per-

sonal qualities, such as patience and humor, and special abilities are needed on the job?

5 Explore the careers of three women who began with small businesses and became millionaires. What qualities do these women share? What qualities would be useful to you if you were an entrepreneur?

And Beyond

ROUND OUT YOUR BUSINESS SKILLS WITH these related interest projects:

- Public Relations
- Cookies and Dough
- Dollars and Sense
- Leadership
- Understanding Yourself and Others
- Exploring the Net
- Desktop Publishing
- Graphic Communications

Nature, Science, and Health

All About Birds ▪ Build a Better Future ▪ Creative Cooking ▪ Digging Through the Past ▪ Eco-Action ▪ The Food Connection ▪ From Shore to Sea ▪ Inventions and Inquiry ▪ It's About Time ▪ Math, Maps, and More ▪ Pets ▪ Planet Power ▪ Plant Life ▪ Space Exploration ▪ Why in the World? ▪ Wildlife ▪ Women's Health

All About Birds

I f it has feathers, it's a bird! Birds are an "indicator species" for environmental health, meaning that if a species of birds gets sick, there is something wrong in the entire ecosystem. Birders often become involved in environmental issues, such as rainforest destruction or pesticide use, that threaten the survival of birds. So, invite a friend, grab your binoculars and field guide, and go birding!

Skill Builders

1 Have you ever wondered how birds fly? Find out about the mechanics of flight. Compare the anatomy and flight patterns of birds with the design, construction, and aerodynamics of airplanes or gliders.

2 Birds can be identified by size, shape, color, flight patterns, vocalizations ("bird calls"), and behavior. Field marks or distinctive features of the bird such as a stripe over the eye, bars on the wing, or a bright rump patch are often used for identification purposes. Differences between male and female birds are often very dramatic. Observe and make notes about five birds in your community. Use a field guide to identify each bird.

3 Birders learn to identify birds by sound as well as sight. This is especially helpful when a bird is hidden in dense foliage or perched high in a tree. Birds are usually most vocal early in the morning and at dusk. Learn to identify five birds by their songs or call notes.

4 Birds have fascinating life histories. Many travel great distances in yearly cycles of migration. Do a detailed study of three different types of birds: for example, a songbird, a bird of prey, and a waterfowl. Include in your study vocalizations, flight patterns, nesting and feeding habits, and threats to survival. Take notes and/or draw what you see. If the bird migrates, draw a map tracing its migration route.

5 Set up a bird-feeding station. Attract a variety of birds by providing different types of food, feeders, and watering devices. A trash-can lid on a post or a flowerpot saucer on the ground can be used to hold water. List and describe the birds that come to the feeding station. Note diet preferences.

6 In addition to watching birds, many enjoyable hours may be spent capturing birds artistically. Visit an art museum, natural history museum, or wildlife art gallery in which paintings or other depictions of birds are on display, or look at illustrations of birds in field guides. Next, create an original work of art, such as a woodcarving, drawing, or painting, or take a series of photographs of birds.

Technology

1 Most birds are watched from a distance. Practice using binoculars, an important tool for birders, until you become comfortable locating perched birds and birds in flight. Visit a store that carries binoculars. Compare the features—such as weight, design, and magnification—of several pairs of binoculars. Find out the meaning of center focusing, alignment, and field of view.

2 Specially designed traps or mist nets are used to capture birds for banding. A captured bird is identified for age, sex, and physical condition. The bird is carefully fitted with a numbered leg band and released. Find out the name of a professional who bands birds' legs to learn about migratory routes, etc., or visit a wildlife refuge or nature center to learn about banding birds.

3 There are approximately 800–900 species of birds that have been seen in North America. Serious birders keep a diary or life list of birds. Design a life list database or use a commercial birding software program to keep track of each species of bird you see. Record the name of the bird, date and location seen, and any other data such as the weather conditions, names of birding companions, and whether this is a rare sighting.

4 Serious environmental problems such as the use of pesticides and loss of habitat have been responsible for nearly destroying a variety of species, including the bald eagle, peregrine falcon, whooping crane, and California condor. Find out through research or at a bird sanctuary/habitat how captive-breeding programs have helped to restore the populations of these endangered species.

5 A spotting scope and tripod enable the serious birder to observe birds at a greater distance. A spotting scope is an excellent tool for watching waterfowl and nesting or perched birds. Find a person who is willing to teach you to use a spotting scope in the field. Use it to focus in on at least five species of birds.

Service Projects

1 Loss of wildlife habitat, competition with non-native birds, and pesticides have threatened many birds. Work with a local Audubon chapter or other wildlife protection group to help restore an endangered bird species in your area.

2 Introduce a group of younger Girl Scouts to birding by taking them on an early morning or late afternoon bird walk or bird-watch. Share your knowledge about ways to identify birds and how to use binoculars and field guides. Make a list of the birds seen by the group.

3 Ornithology is the branch of zoology dealing with birds. Amateur birders have contributed to this field for many years by participating in organized bird surveys designed to count numbers of individual birds or species. Join with your local Audubon chapter or bird club to participate in a bird count or survey. Keep track of the birds you have seen.

4 Birds need food, water, nesting places, perches, and places to hide. Develop a guide or poster with planting and feeding information for local property owners.

5 Volunteer at a local zoo or nature center that offers opportunities to work directly with birds as an assistant keeper or indirectly by educating the public about birds.

Career Exploration

1 Birds suffer injuries from being shot, poisoned, flying into buildings or radio towers, or even being hit by cars. Licensed wildlife rehabilitators work with animals to nurse them back to health and return them to the wild. Find out where the nearest wildlife rehabilitator might be found. Interview her about her work. If possible, work with her to restore a bird to health.

2 Veterinarians work with sick and injured animals, including birds. Visit a local veterinarian and ask about the education and experience you would need to become a veterinarian.

3 Investigate which colleges offer programs in ornithology, wildlife biology, wildlife management, or related fields of study. What are the admission requirements? Basic course requirements?

4 Spend several hours shadowing an ornithologist, naturalist, or wildlife biologist at a nature center, zoo, or wildlife refuge. Learn about the training needed, hiring process, and tasks of the job.

5 Find a local artist or woodcarver who specializes in birds. Arrange to observe her at work. Ask questions about who commissions and displays her work, what her training was, and her artistic techniques.

And Beyond

BIRDING MAY LEAD TO A PARTICULAR career or may become a fulfilling hobby. To find out more about the animal and plant kingdoms, try these related interest projects:

- Wildlife
- Plant Life
- Pets
- Museum Discovery
- Collecting

Build a Better Future

W hether talking about building a space station or the plumbing for a sports arena, building a better future involves problem solving on the part of many professionals, including engineers. Engineers take ideas and turn them into reality by applying math and science. The activities in this interest project will stimulate your imagination. And who knows, you may come up with a better bridge, baker's oven, or bite plate!

Skill Builders

1 Learn about some of the things engineers must consider when designing amusement park rides, including how electrical circuits are used in bumper cars, what the safest maximum speed for a carousel is, and how many people can ride a roller coaster in an hour. Then, with the guidance of a science teacher, engineer, or mentor, design your own ride. If possible, construct a model. (Amusement parks often have kits available for school groups.)

2 Study at least two different types of blueprints that are created in the design of a building: floor layout; diagrams of electrical, heating, ventilation, and air conditioning units; and specifications for fire protection, plumbing, etc.

3 Tour a manufacturing plant. Find out what types of machines are used in the manufacturing process and why, and what measures are taken to improve product safety, productivity, and quality.

4 Compare several brands of one mechanical product. Look for differences in their external design and features. Which brand looks easiest to use and why? Which is the most attractive? Why?

Now design your own version of a product, making it both practical and artistically appealing.

5 Select one item that is recyclable, such as paper, plastic, glass, or metal, and find out how it is converted into a new product. Draw a simple diagram of the steps involved. Try to name two or three more products into which this item can be recycled. Where and how is this done? Find out if chemicals or heat must be used for the recycling process.

Technology

1 Learn about computer-aided design (CAD) programs. Observe a demonstration of how CAD is used to design items. Then create your own design using CAD. (CAD programs can be found in local industries, high schools, or colleges.)

2 Make a list of 8–10 items that did not exist 25 years ago, such as cellular phones or CD players. Find out how three of the items work today and imagine how they might look in the future. Improve upon their function and design.

3 Find out about five devices used to assist people with disabilities, describing how they work and how they improve the person's life. Hospital rehabilitation departments, rehabilitation centers, or organizations focusing on particular disabilities provide good information. Brainstorm ways in which devices are adapted, or design a device to help someone who has a particular disability perform a function that is difficult for her.

4 Learn about the infrastructure in your community, such as traffic lights or the water system. Make an in-depth investigation of one community. Describe the technology needed to ensure continued safety and efficient service to the public.

5 Investigate how three changes in car design have enhanced safety in the past 10 years.

repairs, or assist with building something at camp or in your community. Learn to use basic tools of construction, plumbing, or electrical work under the guidance of a skilled and knowledgeable mentor. See *Safety-Wise* for recommended safety precautions.

4 Plan an exhibit of engineering fields for your school, council, or community, perhaps for a career day. Invite women engineers to speak and exhibit. Include a design contest or hands-on activities.

her work? Present what you have learned in a class discussion or meeting of your troop or group or club. Or invite the engineer to make a presentation.

3 Find out about the engineer's contribution to advancing medical technology in the design of implants, CAT scans, etc.

4 Use a computer simulation program to practice making the kind of decisions engineers make.

Service Projects

1 Volunteer at a local science center that highlights technology. Assist in building an exhibit during a special event or act as an exhibit interpreter.

2 Plan or help facilitate an "engineering" activity day with hands-on projects for younger girls. Address at least three different areas of engineering. This might be in conjunction with National Engineering Week (February) or National Science and Technology Week (April).

3 Spend a day volunteering in construction or in improving the environment through a local group effort. Perhaps you can paint, garden, help with minor

Career Exploration

1 Learn about careers in various fields of engineering by using your local library, by writing to engineering societies or to the Junior Engineering Technical Society (under the National Society of Professional Engineers), or by using the Internet to do additional research. Find out the requirements for training for mechanical, electrical, or civil engineers.

2 Shadow an engineer for a day. Ask her what tools she uses in her job. What is most and least satisfying about her job? What challenges does she encounter and how does she overcome them in

And Beyond

CONTINUE TO BUILD A BETTER FUTURE WITH these related interest projects:

- Inventions and Inquiry
- Why in the World?
- Math, Maps, and More
- Digging Through the Past
- Space Exploration
- Planet Power
- Architecture and Environmental Design

Creative Cooking

Creative cooking is a great way to express yourself. Meals can be prepared to reflect the color, climate, and "flavor" of a place. If you can't visit a faraway place now, you can still take a "taste-full" journey by enjoying international cuisine right in your own kitchen. Here's your chance to be a creative cook.

Skill Builders

1 Become familiar with the United States Department of Agriculture's (USDA) Food Pyramid or Vegetarian Food Pyramid. You can write to the USDA in Washington, D.C., or find this information in a nutrition textbook. See also pages 60–62 in the *Cadette Girl Scout Handbook*. Compare your own daily diet to the dietary recommendations of the USDA models. Is your diet lacking in some nutrients? If so, what changes would you make?

2 Learn how to select the freshest and most healthful foods at the store—fruits, vegetables, meats, dairy, eggs, prepared foods, etc. Check the labels to find food that is low in salt, low in fat, and low in chemical additives. Look for color and firmness in fruits and vegetables.

3 Find a food, canned or fresh, that is *not* native to your area. Find out what region of the U.S. or other country it is from, and where and how it is produced. Use this food as an ingredient in the preparation of two different recipes.

4 Go to the cookware section of a store and familiarize yourself with the tools of the trade. When would you use such items as a mortar and pestle, peelers and choppers, mashers and ricers, spatulas and other "flippers," knives, food processors, juicers, bread makers, pressure cookers, and various pots and pans? What is the difference in cost of items designed to do the same thing (knives, choppers, and food processors, for example)? Is the extra cost worth it?

5 Choose a recipe that can be easily prepared while camping or hiking. Review the information on this topic in *Outdoor Education in Girl Scouting*. Test that recipe while hiking or camping.

6 Pick a cuisine (Mexican, Caribbean, Indian, vegetarian, etc.) and prepare two meals using recipes that include appetizers, entrees, and desserts. Familiarize yourself with the basic ingredients and seasonings of the cuisine you choose.

7 Adapt a standard recipe for someone with special dietary needs: low fat, low salt, low sugar, lactose intolerant, vegetarian, etc.

Technology

1 Look at the technology used in cooking. Examine the advantages and disadvantages of different heat sources: electric or gas stoves, microwave ovens, pressure cookers, grills, crock pots. Name two foods that cook best in each of these.

2 There is a lot of chemistry behind many cooking tips and recipe directions. Questions to consider: What items serve as thickeners in a recipe? As leavening? What would happen when baking a cake if you left out or changed one ingredient? For instance, lemon juice will curdle milk. Take a recipe and substitute similar ingredients such as currants instead of raisins, or walnuts instead of almonds. Does the substitution improve the recipe, or not? How about the texture?

3 Visit the Web site of a cooking school or food company. Compare the recipes that you find with those that appear in older cookbooks. What has changed? How do these changes reflect the eating and health habits of today's consumers?

4 New scientific discoveries have brought a lot of change to cooking, from how we create and store food to how we cook it. Investigate a new procedure that affects food in some way such as irradiated food, genetically engineered food, plants grown by hydroponics, or freeze drying. Describe the advantages and disadvantages of two such foods to your troop or group.

Service Projects

1 Volunteer at a soup kitchen for at least two weeks for several hours a week. Find out how food is prepared and served for a large number of people.

2 Organize a basic cooking class for a community center or homeless shelter with some friends.

3 Organize a food drive for a local shelter. Consult the proper nutritional guidelines or a professional dietitian for a list of recommended foods.

4 Work with a local service that helps provide nutritious meals to people who cannot leave home. Help prepare at least three different meals. Make sure your meal meets the dietary needs of these homebound people.

5 Using the Food Pyramid or other guidelines, evaluate the food service in a local facility you use (school, camp, or activity center). Discuss your evaluation with the personnel in charge. Offer alternative food suggestions and your reasons for them.

6 Plan a menu for a full, festive meal. Cook and serve it to a group as a celebration of a cultural heritage, a holiday, or other event.

Career Exploration

1 Interview a food critic at your local newspaper. Ask about her experience, education, and work history. Or read several newspaper restaurant reviews. Then, write two reviews of popular restaurants in your area.

2 Find out how institutional cooking differs from restaurant cuisine or home-cooked food. Take a poll in your school cafeteria and ask people what they like/don't like about school lunches. See if you can come up with one or two suggestions based on the poll to improve the choices or quality of the school lunches. Share them with school personnel.

3 Visit a local cooking class or culinary school. Talk to an administrator or instructor about the types of jobs their students are prepared for.

4 Arrange to job-shadow a chef, baker, caterer, pizza-maker, etc. Write down the skills and techniques that you've observed, as well as lifestyle pros and cons: for example, flexible hours, late night hours, etc.

5 Get a part-time job in a restaurant or working for a caterer.

And Beyond

EXPLORE THE FANTASTIC WORLD OF FOOD with these related interest projects:

- The Food Connection
- Home Improvement
- From Fitness to Fashion
- Women's Health
- Travel
- A World of Understanding

Digging Through the Past

What do searching for dinosaur bones and unearthing artifacts of an ancient culture have in common? These exciting pursuits revolve around the physical history of our planet. Today, people from all walks of life are coming together to study the history of the earth: its extinct creatures, ancient peoples, volcanoes, or vanished ecosystems. Embark on an adventure into the earth's past as you do some of these activities.

Skill Builders

1 Go on a day hike and examine the geology or archaeology of the region: for example, streams, fossils, and rock formations. Make sketches or take photographs of the major environmental features.

2 Grow your own crystals. Keep track of the crystal formation with sketches, descriptions, or photographs. Here is one crystal-growing method to try. Dissolve an ounce of table salt or sugar in a half pint of boiling water. Pour the solution into a saucer or low dish. Place a string in the solution and over the edge of the dish. Let the solution evaporate for one or two days. Use magnifying instruments to analyze the crystal structure.

3 Make a collection of at least 20 specimens of rocks, minerals, and fossils. Before you collect anything, make sure you have the landowner's permission to do so if you are on private property. Also, in many places, such as national parks and nature preserves, the removal of artifacts, fossils, or any natural material is against the law, so check before you collect! The best sources for collecting are excavations in bedrock, road cuts in solid rock, and cuts made by streams. Be able to tell about the mineral composition of at least five specimens and how each was formed. Accurately identify and label each specimen.

4 Find out how archaeologists and anthropologists make discoveries about past cultures. Learn what skills and scientific aids are needed for an excavation, and what different objects reveal about the past. Find out about one recent archaeological discovery.

5 Find out about different types of fossils, including how they are formed and the clues they give us about the history of the earth and the life it has supported. Try to observe actual fossil samples.

Technology

1 What technology is used to map the ocean floor or the surface of the earth? Try making a simple topographical map of a local area. Pages 106–109 of *Outdoor Education in Girl Scouting* will provide you with helpful information.

2 Put together a geologist's adventure kit that includes the equipment and tools geologists need in the field. Keep handy a list of the items in your kit for easy reference. Consult *Safety-Wise* for safety rules when using tools or equipment. For example, wear protective goggles if you use a hammer or a chisel to crack open rocks.

3 Investigate how modern technology (photographic equipment, microscopes, computers, lasers, chemicals, etc.) assists archaeologists and paleontologists in recreating art and artifacts from the past. Arrange to speak with scientists or natural history museum personnel about how ancient artifacts or fossils are dated and preserved. Or talk to an artist who makes models of prehistoric animals. What research must she do to reconstruct these animals?

4 Find out about earthquakes and the frequency with which they occur in your state. Learn about faults and plate tectonics. Visit a facility where earthquakes are monitored, or find out how a seismograph works. Learn the safety precautions to take during an earthquake.

Service Projects

1 Set up a rock and mineral search for younger Girl Scouts at their meeting place. Buildings have many things in or around them that are made from minerals, rocks, petroleum, or coal. Make sure to include items on your list that fall into any of these categories.

2 Do a project to reduce erosion in your area. Devise a method to show that your project has halted or reduced erosion. The project might include planting trees, shrubs, or dune grasses. You might reduce trail erosion at a natural area or campsite by relocating the trail to avoid steep grades or wet areas, or adding steps and barriers in appropriate places.

3 Find out how weathering occurs and what effect it has on rocks and soils. Visit places in your area where you can observe the effects of weathering. Possibilities include cemeteries, old stone buildings, and areas with severe soil erosion. What effects do heat, freezing temperatures, wind, plants, water, and acid rain have on weathering processes? Take part in a pro-

ject that will offer protection from or repair the effects of weathering.

4 Collect some objects, such as a tooth, a shell, or a cleaned (boiled) chicken bone, to use as mock fossils with younger girls. Make the "fossil" by mixing plaster of Paris, gravel or sand, and water. Pour the solution into aluminum baking pans coated with petroleum jelly. Embed one or two fossils in the mixture in each pan and let dry for 24 hours. Find an area with soft soil or sand (you may have to import some for the activity) to use as a fossil bed and hide each of the fossils you created in it so that younger girls can find them. Take along the tools that the girls need for digging and demonstrate their use. To make fossil prints with the girls, see the Outdoor Happenings Try-It on page 240 of the *Brownie Girl Scout Handbook*.

5 Find out about an environmental issue in your area, such as agricultural, mining, foresting, or irrigation practices. Devise a plan to raise public awareness about the issue and, with the help of other Girl Scouts, present it in a public forum.

Career Exploration

1 Invite someone who works in a geology-related field to speak to your troop or group. Ask the speaker to discuss the local geology of your area. What geological hazards are faced by your local area and your state? What schooling is necessary to become a geologist? The speaker can also highlight specialty careers within geology, such as marine geology or hydrology. What other fields are involved and how?

2 Read about an individual who has done work in one of the earth sciences. Some names to start with are Mary and Louis Leakey and their son, Richard Leakey; Donald Johanson, and Tim White. What has been the significance of their work?

3 Geology and related sciences offer a wide variety of careers to explore, including fields such as engineering, geophysics, petrology, hydrology, geochemistry, paleontology, planetary geology, and oceanographic geology. Select an area of each science that interests you and interview someone who has made a career in that field. If possible, spend a day with that person to learn more about her area of expertise.

4 Do a college search to find out which schools offer programs in any of the fields related to earth history or geology. Write to one or more colleges that interest you to find out about their course offerings.

And Beyond

DIG UP YOUR OWN BACKYARD! THAT IS, find out what's beneath the surface of your soil, from rubble to ruins. You may want to dig up more facts and fossils with these related interest projects:
- Plant Life
- Wildlife
- Eco-Action
- Heritage Hunt
- Women Through Time
- It's About Time

Eco-Action

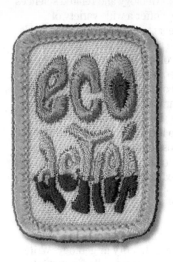

Eco-action is the Girl Scout name given to efforts to sustain and improve the quality of the environment—air, food, water, land, people, and animals. Eco-action informs you on ways to "walk the talk" for a quality of life that includes caring for the earth.

Skill Builders

1 Learn what you and your family can do to be more environmentally aware. Investigate recycling, composting, reducing water consumption, energy conservation, and "precycling" (purchasing products with less packaging and buying some things in bulk). Find alternatives to the use of chemicals and pesticides that harm the environment. Incorporate eco-action steps into your lifestyle for one month. At the end of that time, evaluate your actions and make adjustments as needed to continue your commitment.

2 Choose an environmental issue that affects your community, such as water quality, land-use planning, or use of pesticides. Gather information on all sides of the issue, and evaluate it scientifically on the basis of short-term and long-term effects. Share your findings with others through a presentation, "hands-on" activity, debate, or display.

3 Record some pleasant, relaxing sounds and some sounds that make you feel tense. Share your findings with others and exchange ideas with them on ways to minimize annoying or harmful sounds. Find out how loud sounds affect human hearing. Does your community have a noise ordinance? Does it need one?

4 Trace the contributions of someone deeply concerned with environmental quality. Find out how this person became interested in environmental problems and how she pursued her interests. Or find out how different cultures such as the Navajos in North America, the Yanomamos in the Amazon Rainforest, or the Aborigines in Australia viewed their relationship to the earth. Ask your librarian to recommend a recent book about one or more of these groups.

5 Monitor a stream for pollution sources. Learn to identify the plants and animals that are typically found in clean water and in polluted water, if any, in your area. What happens to the plants and animals that cannot adapt to the changes caused by pollution? Find ways you can improve conditions for wildlife and recreation. Use this information to develop a plan to improve conditions and put your plan into action.

Technology

1 Find out about an alternative source of energy (such as solar or wind power) that can cut down on personal consumption of nonrenewable resources and demonstrate to others how this energy source is tapped.

2 Find out about how new technology is used in testing air, water, and soil quality.

3 Participate in an online discussion about one worldwide environmental issue to get different perspectives on the issue. Find out if there are any networks or bulletin boards used by young people for environmental action.

4 Visit a store or look through a catalog that advertises "environmentally friendly" products. Determine if "high-tech" items can be and are included among these products. Develop personal criteria for selecting products that are "environmentally friendly."

5 Recycling has become a major effort in many communities. Find out about one recycled resource and how it is recycled. What products are made from the recycled materials?

Service Projects

1 Create and display posters on energy-saving actions at a mall or other public place and have people sign energy-saving pledges.

2 Volunteer to work on an ongoing environmental project. Or work as a docent, or interpretive guide, at an aquarium, botanical garden, zoo, nature center, or museum that addresses environmental issues.

3 Collect information from an organization concerned with environmental issues of particular interest to women and children (for example, birth defects related to pesticide exposure). Create a display or make a presentation to your troop or group on the organization and the issue.

4 Create a directory or display of local, state, or national groups concerned with environmental issues and actions. Include groups that provide materials and opportunities for young people to get involved. Distribute this information to others.

5 Combine arts and environmental action. For example, form a theater group that addresses current environmental topics. Perform in your community.

Career Exploration

1 Do a computer search for careers related to the environment. Follow it up by contacting an organization, business, or individual for information on a specific career in this field.

2 Attend a career fair that gives you the opportunity to speak with individuals working in professions related to the environment.

3 Learn about careers related to the environment and the law. Find out the educational requirements and nature of work in those fields.

4 Identify three past and present environmental activists in your community, nation, or the world and learn more about the work of at least one. Using photos, excerpts of speeches, media clips, etc., arrange a display or special ceremony honoring their contributions.

5 Identify three or more degree programs in fields concerned with the environment. Compare the course requirements and list the career possibilities with each of these degrees. Try to visit or speak with someone enrolled in the program or a faculty member.

And Beyond

CONSIDER OBTAINING A COMMUNITY Service Bar by working at a nature center, zoo, or botanical garden. Opportunities also exist with organizations such as Habitat for Humanity or the Student Conservation Association.

Commit to conserving, preserving, and enhancing your environment. Take action with these related interest projects:

- All About Birds
- From Shore to Sea
- Plant Life
- Wildlife
- Architecture and Environmental Design
- Build a Better Future
- Home Improvement
- Planet Power
- Museum Discovery

The Food Connection

*C*heeseburgers. Milk-
shakes. Potato chips.
Sound familiar? Even
though there is a move-
ment toward healthy eat-
ing, many people still
eat fast food on the run.
It's not always easy to
make smart food choices.
It's easier to pop and
crunch. Learn more
about making healthy
food choices in this
interest project.

Skill Builders

1 Familiarize yourself with the
food pyramid found on page
61 in the *Cadette Girl Scout Handbook*. Plan a menu for your family
for two weeks, choosing foods from
the food pyramid. Substitute healthy
foods, such as fruits, yogurt, and
juice, for foods high in fat, sugar,
salt, and caffeine. Discuss the menu
with your family prior to trying it,
then again at the end of the first
week. Incorporate changes into the
following week's menu.

2 Water is the perfect drink.
Your body absolutely needs
water and you get it in many forms.
Almost all foods and beverages
contain water. However, equip
yourself with a water bottle and
make a conscious effort to drink
eight cups of water a day, the recommended daily amount. Do this
for a two-week period. Do you
notice a difference?

3 Find out about the role cho-
lesterol plays in health. Learn
about the difference between HDLs
(high-density lipoproteins) and
LDLs (low-density lipoproteins).
Make a list of foods high in choles-
terol or high in fats that are favorite
foods for teens. Develop a list of
substitutions. Find out how to read
labels for fat content. Share your
findings with friends and family.

4 Collect recipes on a theme of
interest, such as vegetarian
soups or sugar-free desserts. Illustrate the recipes and organize them
into a cookbook. Share copies with
interested people.

5 Vitamins and minerals are
essential to your well-being.
They are in food and also available in vitamin supplements.
Make a poster or chart that lists
vitamins and minerals, their functions, and which foods contain
them. Present your display at a
troop or group meeting.

Technology

1 How large a role do media
and advertising play in defin-
ing our body image? How might this
create a climate for eating disorders? Discuss female body images
and their relation to bulimia and
anorexia nervosa (see pages 31–34
in *A Resource Book for Senior Girl
Scouts*). Learn about these eating
disorders. What are some of the
symptoms? What should you do if
you know someone who seems to
have an eating disorder? Create a
poster or awareness campaign to
promote healthy body image.

2 Find at least five resources
online to help maintain a
healthy lifestyle. Key words might
be *women's health, nutrition, food
pyramid,* and *exercise.*

3 Learn to see beyond food
packaging by understanding
content labels. Look for such information as serving size, fat content,

and the presence of vitamins and minerals. Visit a grocery store and compare the packaging, contents, and price of at least four different products. Share what you learn with others.

4 What is insulin? What function does it have in your body? Having diabetes means that your body doesn't make enough insulin or is unable to use the food you eat in the proper way. Learn about the two major types of diabetes, juvenile (Type I) and late (Type II). What are the warning signs of diabetes? Talk with someone who has diabetes or works with diabetics. Find out about tests that determine blood sugar levels and about diet.

able to justify recommendations for changes based upon dietary needs and healthy alternatives to present fare. Consider cost per serving, government guidelines, and labor in planning these menus.

5 Learn about different foods that are eaten and not eaten for strongly held religious or dietary beliefs. This might include, for example, people of the Jewish, Muslim, Hindu, Buddhist, or Sikh faiths, as well as vegetarians. Determine if events you attend are being inclusive or exclusive when it comes to food options. Work with a group to broaden food options for an organized group or event, such as a day camp, resident camp, school potluck gathering, or cultural festival.

3 Dietitians work in hospitals, nursing homes, schools, or on their own as consultants. They promote healthy eating habits to prevent illness. Arrange to shadow a dietitian and see how she impacts people's lives. Find out about the training required for becoming a dietitian.

4 Interview two women who work in a health- or food-related career. If possible, choose someone who is working for herself, such as a nutritional consultant or the owner of a health food store, and someone who works for others, such as a chef or trainer at a health club.

5 Get firsthand experience in a food-related field by working part-time or during the summer in a food business.

Service Projects

1 Volunteer to help with a communitywide health fair. Or work as a volunteer for a fitness walk or run. Ensure that first aid, water, and high-energy, healthy snacks are available.

2 Create a puppet show or presentation for younger girls or the elderly that addresses healthy eating habits. Learn about nutrition needs for these two age groups.

3 Organize or participate in a food drive. Contact a local food bank, or see if your local Girl Scout council has an annual food drive and volunteer to be on the planning committee. If not, organize one with the help of a mentor.

4 Serve on a committee to make recommendations for school cafeteria or camp food. Be

Career Exploration

1 Make a list of four to six careers related to food and then find out the following for two of these careers: skills and responsibilities; working conditions; training and education needed; earnings.

2 Agricultural science includes food science, plant science, animal science, and soil science. People with careers in these areas work to increase agricultural productivity, as well as to meet the nutritional needs of consumers. Write to a school specializing in one of these areas or visit its Web site. If possible, communicate with a student at the school. Find out what specific jobs are available upon graduation.

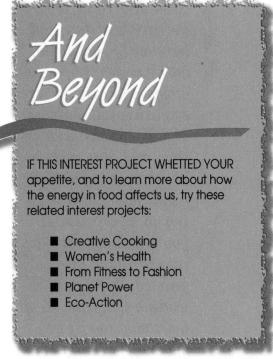

And Beyond

IF THIS INTEREST PROJECT WHETTED YOUR appetite, and to learn more about how the energy in food affects us, try these related interest projects:

- Creative Cooking
- Women's Health
- From Fitness to Fashion
- Planet Power
- Eco-Action

From Shore to Sea

The oceans of the world cover over 70 percent of the earth's surface and have an impact on the entire planet. Important ecosystems exist in river estuaries, salt marshes, and along coastal shore-lines and coral reefs. Whether eating a tuna fish sandwich, or reading about an oil spill, you are connected to a resource often taken for granted. So get out your wading shoes and see an awesome sunrise or gulls in splendid flight as you set off to sea.

Skill Builders

1   Learn about the creatures that inhabit ocean tide pools and the rocky shoreline. Discover these creatures firsthand or at a saltwater aquarium exhibit. Find out which creatures are filter feed-ers, grazers, predators, or scav-engers, and observe their feeding habits. Compare and contrast the methods of protection, camouflage, and movement of each organism. Compare the rocky coast plants and animals with those of the sandy beach and salt marsh.

2   Become a geological detec-tive. Using a magnifying glass or microscope, study a handful of sand. With the help of a geologist or earth science teacher, or a geology book about the region, identify at least three different kinds of rocks, particles, or minerals in the sand. If possible, learn about the history of the sand by consulting a geological map or book about the area.

3   The oceans and large bodies of water such as the Great Lakes influence global weather and climate patterns. Determine what effect the major bodies of water have on the weather, including hur-ricanes, cyclones, and tsunamis.

4   What are some of the envi-ronmental concerns about the extraction and mining of ele-ments from the sea? What kinds of safety precautions should be or are being taken? Describe and illustrate your findings or discuss them in your troop or group.

5   Investigate global warming. What role do oceans play in the process? Find at least two dif-ferent studies going on regarding global warming and two actions taken by world governments to deal with causes and/or concerns. Con-sult your science teacher, group leader, or another adult for help. Present your findings in a discus-sion, using visual aids as needed.

6   Create a piece of art, a collec-tion of poems, a slide or video show using pictures and music inspired by the ocean, or something else water-related. Share your work with family members or your troop or group, and explain to them the role the ocean played in inspiring you.

Technology

1   Tour a boat used in deep-sea fishing or in marine biology studies. What kinds of equipment are used to navigate, to find the depth of the ocean, or to perform studies?

2 Find out how scientists use sonar, satellites, and super-computers to explore the deepest reaches of the oceans without getting wet.

3 From water wheels to hydro-electric plants, people have been using water power for centuries. Pick one of the following technologies to learn how modern scientists continue to explore ocean energy to meet the growing demand for power:

■ Ocean thermal energy conversion.

■ Wave and tidal power.

■ Ocean currents.

Keep the following questions in mind as you explore: How does this technology work? Can it be used anywhere in the world? Are there any potential health or ecological risks associated with it?

4 There is a tremendous need for fresh water in countries all over the world, yet the majority of the world's water is found in oceans which contain salt. Research and then try out one way to distill fresh water from salt water.

5 What kinds of technology are being used to predict the tremendous storms that can devastate coastal regions? Each year, tsunamis, hurricanes, cyclones, tidal waves, and storm surges cause many deaths and destroy property. Find out about a storm that might impact your area or one in which you have an interest. Find out how the storm is tracked, how warnings are issued, and what the procedures are for safety and evacuation.

Service Projects

1 Assist with a local project that involves ecological studies of aquatic species. Work with a scientist or researcher to interpret your data.

2 Volunteer time with a marine conservation or education organization, such as a nature center or aquarium. Help educate the public about the importance of marine ecosystems.

3 Assist with a clean up of a water habitat. Volunteer to publicize a clean-up day by designing and/or distributing fliers.

4 Create an educational game for younger girls that will help them learn more about the oceans.

Career Exploration

1 Develop a list of 8–10 careers in the field of oceanography. Include a brief description of each. Interview or read about someone in one of these fields and find out what her work entails.

2 Investigate at least two Sea Grant institutions concerned with research, education, and exchange of technology regarding coastal, marine, and Great Lakes issues. What kinds of research, career training, or community concerns are being addressed by the universities? Describe two of these concerns.

3 Visit with someone who earns a living from the sea. What are the issues about sustaining ocean harvests? Find out what training, apprenticeships, and education are required for careers in fishing, aquaculture, food production, or mining from the sea.

4 Investigate two tourism careers that are associated with an ocean environment, such as working in an aquarium or on a cruise ship. What kind of training, skills, and education might be needed?

5 Capture the ocean's beauty on camera, sketch pad, or by writing a poem or song about the sea.

And Beyond

FIND INTERESTING INFORMATION AND freshwater and saltwater activities in the Girl Scout book *Exploring Wildlife Communities with Children*.

If you want to dive into the waters further or navigate the scientific seas, try these related interest projects:

■ Paddle, Pole, and Roll
■ Water Sports
■ Smooth Sailing
■ Wildlife
■ Plant Life
■ Eco-Action
■ Photography

Inventions and Inquiry

*L*ook around you. Can you imagine life without stereos, microwave ovens, cars, or your favorite soft drink? From pencils to computers, inventions begin with someone asking some very simple questions: "How can I solve this problem for myself or others?" "How can I make this better or easier to do?" Learn about the stages in the creative process with this interest project. Put on your thinking cap and start your inventor's journey!

Skill Builders

1 Do you feel that sometimes your brain is idling in neutral? There are actually many activities that you can do to put yourself in a creative frame of mind. Try at least one of the following warm-ups or develop some of your own:

■ Brainstorm a list of 10 inventions you would like to see.

■ Take two objects and list all of their uses. Then visualize the two objects combined as one. What new uses could this object have?

■ Imagine people as musical instruments, animals as machines, or any other paired categories. This is a mental warm-up exercise. Be creative and free-floating with your ideas.

2 Spend a week listing problems that need to be solved at home, at school, or in your community. Be a detective and brainstorm a lot of solutions. Record and date your ideas in a journal. Next, focus on *one* of your problems and the list of solutions you have written out for that problem. Has this problem been addressed already, and how? To find out, you will need to do some research. Do you have a better solution? Will this be something people will want to use?

3 Create an invention. In a journal, make a detailed sketch of the invention. Label all the parts. Go on to develop a three-dimen-sional model of your invention. Then develop a prototype, or working model, of your invention. Do a final sketch, including the dimensions. Add a description of the materials. Give your invention a catchy name that suggests its function. The right name can help you to market your invention. Brainstorm possible choices of names with family and friends.

4 Find out about the patenting process. What does it mean when a patent is pending? What is the difference between utility, design, and plant patents? What are trademarks? What are trade secrets? Where do you look up patents?

5 Develop an advertising campaign for your own or someone else's invention. Complete two of the following: write a radio or TV ad; write an ad for a newspaper; or make a video. Present your advertising campaign to others and ask them to give you feedback. Did they want to buy the product? Why or why not?

Technology

1 Survey resources for inventing on the World Wide Web. (Key words include *inventions*, *inventors*, and *patent*.) Look for an online chat group for inventors and talk with others interested in inventing. Visit the National Inventors Hall of Fame online and find information on women inventors.

2 Explain how changes in technology have altered at least two inventions in terms of function or design: for example, eyeglasses are now made with thin plastic lenses and have lightweight frames. Do some research in order to compare old and current models.

3 Investigate the role of research and development ("R and D") in creating a new product. How long does it generally take for a product to get from the drawing board to the consumer? How much of a successful company's budget is devoted to R and D? Which kinds of projects are funded by the government? Discuss these and other questions about product development in a troop or group meeting.

4 Attend a new products exposition, a science and engineering fair, or an inventions fair. Look for new or improved products. If possible, interview the inventors and find out as much as you can about their inventions and the processes of inventing, patenting, and marketing.

5 Ask people in five different fields what they foresee as the most valuable inventions for the years beyond 2000, that is, what are the most important problems that need solutions in the future? Take one problem that someone suggests and, in a group, brainstorm the kinds of training and knowledge a person might need in order to address the problem and "invent" a solution.

Service Projects

1 Start an inventors' club through your school, troop, or group. All it takes is you, two or three friends, and a lot of good ideas! Put together an inventors' "fair" at which members of your club and others can highlight their inventions.

2 Many women have made scientific discoveries and have come up with inventions in this and previous centuries. Create a show, play, or visual display to celebrate women inventors for an audience of young women.

3 With the help of an expert or consultant, invent or improve something that addresses a problem that a person with a disability has to face in her life. For example, for a child who has difficulty writing, create a pencil with a special grip. Perhaps ask her teacher for ideas. Get feedback from the people you are seeking to serve by testing your product with them.

4 Create a toy for young children. It can be educational or may just appeal to their sense of fun. First, visit local toy stores and see what's available. Be sure to consider safety issues for young children. Then make a prototype of your toy and with adult help test it with children. Does the toy appeal to the children? Do you need to refine the idea? Get some friends together and build several more models to donate to the program or center.

Career Exploration

1 Read about inventors in at least two books. Find the answers to questions such as: What started them in the invention process? What career choices did they make and how did they succeed? How did they turn "failures" into successes?

2 Investigate courses to take in high school and college to help you with a career direction in inventing. Try to set up, with your school counselor's help, an appropriate internship experience. Draw

a one-, five-, or ten-year time line for yourself. Look at it once a week. Add to it or revise it as you get new ideas and information.

3 Think about the kinds of careers that may relate to inventing: patent attorney, product designer, graphic artist, researcher, chemist, engineer, film animator, computer game designer. Select two that interest you and find out more about them.

4 Frequently, inventors specialize in a field of interest. For example, if you like sports, you can interview someone who designs sports equipment, such as tennis rackets, in-line skates, or snow boards. How do they redesign equipment? Have they ever designed equipment for a new sport? What was that experience like? If new materials were used, how were they made?

And Beyond

READ *GIRLS AND YOUNG WOMEN Inventing*, by F. A. Karnes and S. M. Bean (Free Spirit Publishing, 1995). It's a great book about the inventing process and girls who are inventors.

If you enjoyed stretching your mind with Inventions and Inquiry, try these related interest projects:

- Build a Better Future
- Math, Maps, and More
- Architecture and Environmental Design
- Graphic Communications
- Your Own Business
- Exploring the Net
- Digging Through the Past
- Why in the World?

It's About Time

*D*o you have time on your hands? How about on your side? Explore the nature of time, calendars, ways to manage and master time, and how to use "prime time" in order to get the most out of the day. Take the time to appreciate your surroundings, activities, and experiences.

Skill Builders

1 Many cultures mark the passage of time with the observance of important religious, political, and social events. Illustrate or describe how three ancient civilizations kept track of the passage of time. Or compare the Hebrew, Mayan, Chinese, and Gregorian calendars with one another. What themes do different calendars have in common: for example, time, seasons, or celebrations of the New Year?

2 There are many devices that keep track of time, such as an hourglass, sundial, or atomic clock. Someone even made a flower clock, based on the times at which various flowers open. Construct your own timekeeper by using regularly occurring events you see or experience, or by using sand, water, shadows, etc. Other things you may want to use are plastic soda bottles, pots, cups, rulers, tape, cork stoppers, cardboard, Ping Pong balls, marbles, or toys.

3 Can you name three regular time cycles in nature (such as the lunar cycle)? Remember that humans are part of nature, too! Devise a system for keeping time based on one of these cycles. Investigate three ways in which animals respond to changes in the time of year.

4 Compare the ages of rites of passages in three or four cultures. Determine what you think was or will be your most significant rite of passage.

5 Compare the use of rhythm and time values of notes in four styles of music (such as reggae, rap, calypso, waltz, polka, flamenco, and salsa). Does how long a note is held or the beat affect how we feel or what we do?

6 Are you feeling as if there isn't enough time in the day? Read pages 118–120 in *A Resource Book for Senior Girl Scouts* for helpful hints on time management or complete the activities on page 87 of the *Cadette Girl Scout Handbook*. To help you make the most of your time, create a time clock of all of the activities you do on a weekly basis. To make the clock, draw a "pie" with twelve slices. Color in all the times that are taken and label them: for example, 11 p.m.–7 a.m. for "sleep." Any time left is "free time." Make sure that your extracurricular time includes "prime time" to plan, organize, relax, and exercise. Know that you have limited free time, so use it well!

Technology

1 Use a library's resources, such as its computer search program or microfiche collection, to help you find fashion pictures in magazines and newspapers of another era. Pick a decade and create a theme event (a retro fashion show, a costume dance or party, etc.) that illustrates the dress and music of that time.

2 Use camera equipment to take a time-lapse photograph. Try photographing in different light and settings.

3 Find out about the technology of quartz crystal timepieces. Consult a watchmaker or watch repair person, a mineralogist, or a book on the subject.

4 List four ways in which time-keeping devices have been used in medicine. Draw a picture of these devices to display at a troop meeting or a special event.

5 Find out about the principles behind an atomic clock. Why and how is an atomic clock used?

Service Projects

1 Has technology lived up to its promise of freeing us from drudgery, or have advances in machines and communications systems simply meant more time in which to do more work? Interview people of different generations and compare how much time each spent/spends on work and leisure activities. How do people of different generations feel about their quality of life?

2 Set up and manage a "time bank" to provide services for people in your community who have special needs. Here's how it could work: Girls "deposit" hours in the "bank" that can be "withdrawn" by those in need of their time. For example, hours can be withdrawn by an elderly or homebound person who needs someone to shop for groceries or walk a pet. You may have to open various "accounts" (such as reading, chess playing, letter writing) to match a girl's interest with the persons in need. The girls receive "interest" in the form of smiles, hugs, friendship, and appreciation from the people using their services.

3 After consulting with teachers, family members, or reading about the subject, make a time line or chart of two or three of the developmental stages a child goes through, such as learning to talk or read. Include the kinds of activities and toys that enhance development, and the approximate age at which a child reaches a particular milestone. Donate the chart to parents you know, a day-care center, a community center, a school, etc.

4 Organize a call-in service for the elderly of your community to help them to keep their appointments and take their medications on time. You might want to call them once a day at the same time.

Career Exploration

1 Design two to three articles of clothing for a woman of another era, such as the Roaring Twenties or the Victorian era. Do your research through books, magazines, museum displays, or by contacting a local college's history department.

2 Find out what a time management consultant does by interviewing one or reading about one. Check psychology or business magazines and journals. Write a job description that you think fits the consultant's title based on your research or your own ideas.

3 Interview four people (an educator, health professional, musician, scientist, etc.) who have different careers and find out how they make use of time in their work. Questions to consider: How do self-employed workers such as business people or artists deal with challenges such as deadlines? How do workers affected by the seasons, such as a restaurant owner or

tour guide, manage their time and finances?

4 Women who work both outside and inside the home may feel as if they are working at least two jobs. Workers of all types may feel they have too much to do. Create a time management plan that incorporates exercise and leisure activities for today's busy women, and ask at least three women you know to try the plan for a week. Have them share the results with you at a troop or group meeting.

5 Create your own personal time line. Chart where you'd like to be and what you hope you will have accomplished one, five, and ten years from now. You can use a graph, a chart, or even a photo collage to illustrate your time line. Share it with your family or with your troop or group members.

And Beyond

USE YOUR IMAGINATION TO LOOK INTO the future. Write a short story, play, or cartoon strip that describes the inventions, architecture, or fashions you envision.

Look at time's many facets in any subject of interest, and in these related interest projects:

■ Women Through Time
■ Inventions and Inquiry
■ Digging Through the Past
■ Generations Hand in Hand
■ Writing for Real
■ On a High Note
■ The Play's the Thing
■ Math, Maps, and More

Math, Maps, and More

Have you ever thought about the connection between math and other areas of your life, like money, space, and time? Discover why people in all walks of life—from chefs to geographers—need to know some math to succeed at their jobs. After completing these activities, the probability is good that you'll further explore the fascinating world of mathematics.

Skill Builders

1 Use your math skills to create a budget for something that you would like to do or own. You could plan a dream trip or create a savings plan to buy a new computer. Choose tools for the task, such as a calculator, price lists, maps, or computer software. Be sure to list all the costs involved. For example, if you are planning a trip, include all the costs of accommodations, food, and ground and air transportation.

2 Math is a vital part of maintaining a healthy lifestyle. Percentages of fat, protein, starch, and fiber in your daily diet change as your age, health, and activity levels change. Determine the total calorie intake for someone of your age, height, and activity level. Put together a menu for yourself, keeping in mind the need for balanced nutrition.

3 Many indicators of health and fitness require math computations. Do a complete profile of yourself using numbers. For example, use math skills to determine resting, target, and recovery heart rates. Find your pulse and count how many times your heart beats in 10 seconds. Multiply that number by 6. This is your resting heart rate. Be very active for at least 15 minutes. Take your pulse and compare this rate with your resting heart rate. See how long it takes for your pulse to return to your resting heart rate. Other things to check are height, weight, blood pressure, and respiration.

4 Find out about the statistics used to determine how well a player and team in a particular sport are doing. Local papers carry many statistics on a variety of teams. Select a team or single player to follow for a month. Determine how your team or player did. Try this with a friend who tracks another player or team. See whose team comes out on top.

5 Geographers and cartographers use math skills to make and read maps. Use symbols to create a key for buildings, parks, and other features of interest. Draw your map to scale: for example, 1 inch = 1 mile or 1 cm = 1 km.

Technology

1 Use graphs to illustrate an issue that you feel is important, such as U.S. population shifts, acid rain patterns, or endangered species. Show comparisons, changes over time, and your projections for the future. If possible, use a computer to organize the data to create graphs or charts and then analyze them.

2 Use online resources to search for and explore several math-related Web sites. Find out about at least three women mathematicians, and visit a news group to discover what's being discussed by people interested in math.

3 Learn to play a computer game that uses math skills. Practice during several sessions to improve your skill level. For example, play a flight simulation game on a computer and try to get your plane safely to its destination without running out of fuel.

4 Technology is changing the field of medicine, and math plays an important part in the new advances in equipment and treatment. MRI and CAT scans are diagnostic techniques that can give a visual mapping of the body. Talk with a medical professional who can show you how MRI and CAT scan images are created and used to diagnose and treat diseases.

5 Learn how to read a thermometer, a barometer, a psychrometer, and an anemometer.

Service Projects

1 Create a math activity kit to use with children. You can write a weird and wacky math story or a detective story with math "clues." Or develop a math play focusing on one particular math concept such as factors, fractions, or percentages.

2 Host a Girl Scouts' Game Night. Use *Games for Girl Scouts* to find math-based games or collect board games from your friends and neighbors. Make sure they are age-appropriate! You may also want to consider creating your own board game. You will need to devise not only the board and the pieces, but also a method of scoring.

3 Volunteer to help collect data that could be used to assist an organization. You could do pro-

gram surveys for your Girl Scout council or you might do something like assist the National Audubon Society with a bird count or help a local environmental group monitor water quality.

4 Volunteer to be a treasurer for an organization and keep records in a ledger for a period of at least three months.

5 Help younger girls develop arithmetic skills by using simple computer math games.

Career Exploration

1 With two friends, create a list of eight "traditional" math careers like accountant, engineer, or statistician. Talk with adults and add another 10 careers which, while not math-based, rely heavily on mathematical skills. Then find out which of these 18 fields are "very easy entry" (high school education only is needed) and which are "delayed entry" (graduate school and internships are required).

2 What does math have to do with being a chef or restaurant owner? Find out by creating and running your own restaurant for a day. Select three dishes to feature on your menu and then estimate how many of your customers will wish to order each dish. Calculate how much of each ingredient you will have to purchase to provide each dish for your customers. Compute how much money you will have to spend to purchase these ingredients and what you will need to charge to make a profit. Figure out what profit you made (if any). What changes would you make for the next day? Or interview a restaurant owner, a caterer, or the banquet manager of a hotel. Ask questions

such as how forecasts are made, how quantities are controlled, and how inventories are kept.

3 Use online resources, personal interviews, or the resources of a career education center to investigate college programs in mathematics. Determine which programs are best for undergraduate and graduate studies.

4 Imagine that you have your own small business. How would you need to use your math skills? Come up with a product or service you can provide and sell. How much capital is required to order supplies and equipment to start your business? List these start-up costs. Estimate your total number of customers. How much will you charge? Why?

5 For a week, keep a log of all the people you interact with who use math in their work. What types of math skills do they need?

And Beyond

IF YOU LIKE USING MATH IN DIFFERENT WAYS, from mathematical puzzles to brainteasers, try these related interest projects:

- Games for Life
- Home Improvement
- Build a Better Future
- Inventions and Inquiry
- Space Exploration
- Creative Cooking
- Cookies and Dough
- Dollars and Sense
- Your Own Business

Pets

Hamsters, dogs, birds, cats, rabbits, fish, horses. Can you think of other animals that can be pets? Humans have always depended on animals for assistance and companionship. While people benefit from this relationship, they should not forget that it carries responsibilities as well. Work on the following activities to provide the animals in your life with all the advantages of a healthy home!

Skill Builders

1 Prepare a care chart for a particular pet (yours or someone else's) that a pet-sitter, boarding kennel, or family could use to raise and maintain that animal in a healthy and happy manner. Be sure to include information on diet, exercise, training, grooming, activity preferences, medical history and care, and emergency information.

2 Become an expert on some aspect of a particular type of animal or species: its evolution, history, or anatomy. Where did it originally come from? Is it related to any species of wild animals? Is this animal known for a specific use or characteristic?

3 Learn how to train and socialize a specific animal. Learn the reasonable behaviors to expect, and the appropriate types of exercise and discipline for that animal. Put these skills to work with a specific animal.

4 Talk with a veterinarian, breeder, or animal supply distributor about special diets for a specific type of animal. What health conditions are affected by diet? How do dietary needs change as the animal gets older? Share this information with a fellow animal lover or your troop or group.

5 Discover the types of laws that your community has to protect animals (licensing, leash laws, health laws, anti-cruelty laws, etc.). Find out which animals are legal to keep as pets and which are not. Create a booklet or poster to illustrate the legal information you have found.

Technology

1 Talk to a veterinarian about the types of illnesses to which a particular animal might be susceptible. Ask about vaccines and ongoing health maintenance for that animal. Learn the symptoms of three specific illnesses and the treatment for them.

2 Talk to a veterinarian about the environmental hazards for a particular type of pet. Be sure to ask about both people-produced as well as natural hazards. Learn how to identify and prevent three to five hazards. Create a chart, a photo display, a video, or a poster campaign to educate others about these hazards.

3 Investigate the types of animal-containment devices that are available for a specific type of pet. What types of fences, cages, and carriers are on the market today? Talk with an animal trainer, staff at a boarding facility, transportation company employee, and/or veterinarian to learn the pros and cons of two different devices.

4 All animals need exercise to be healthy. Talk to an animal breeder, animal supply distributor, or animal trainer about two or three devices available for safely exercising your pet. What technological changes have there been in these devices in the last 5–10 years?

5 Locating lost or stolen animals can be difficult. However, there are now a number of organizations and devices available that make locating animals easier. Learn about these devices or design a new one. Or write an ad about one of these devices.

Service Projects

1 Volunteer at a kennel, animal shelter, or veterinarian's office for several hours a week over the course of a month. Be sure to get training by the organization or the veterinarian before you start your service.

2 Volunteer to provide exercise, grooming, or transportation to a veterinarian for the pet of a homebound person. Provide the service at least once a week for a month.

3 Volunteer to raise an animal such as a seeing-eye dog for a service organization. You and your family should be aware that this may involve a one- or two-year commitment.

4 Work with an agency or organization dedicated to animal care and protection. Determine how you can help, and volunteer to serve the agency or organization for at least one day.

5 Work with a humane society, an animal shelter or clinic, or a veterinarian to help find homes for homeless animals.

6 Organize a pet visiting day for people who are in institutional settings such as a nursing home or a rehabilitation center.

Career Exploration

1 Learn about the training and job responsibilities of a police department's canine team. What types of crimes are these dogs used for? Why? How are they used? Are certain breeds required in some fields? Why? Take what you've learned and create a comic book, coloring book, story, essay, or article to teach others about this field.

2 Interview a professional animal-care worker such as a local veterinarian or assistant, a kennel owner, or a zoo worker about the training and education she has had to complete to do her job. Find out about the essentials of animal care. If you do not know a professional in this field, contact local professional organizations like the American Boarding Kennel Association, the American Animal Hospital Association, or the American Society for Prevention of Cruelty to Animals and ask for a local contact. Or go online and join a discussion group that focuses on animal care. Many times professionals contribute to these discussion groups. Write an article for your community or school paper using the information you have learned.

3 Learn about the field of animal-assisted therapy. In this therapy, companion animals assist the blind or people with specific disabilities with functional tasks. Read articles, participate in online discussions, or interview people who are trained in the field. What is the history of this field? Why did it develop? What kind of training/certification is required to practice in this field? What benefits do people get from this therapy? Why?

4 Learn about three different types of animal handlers, people who care for and groom animals at competition sites, circuses, zoos, boarding kennels, etc.

5 Interview the owner or an employee of a local pet-supply store. What training, if any, did she have to go through? How have pet products changed over the years?

And Beyond

IF YOU'D LIKE TO FIND OUT MORE ABOUT animals, or depict them through the arts, try these related interest projects:
- All About Birds
- From Shore to Sea
- Wildlife
- Horse Sense
- Photography
- Visual Arts
- Writing for Real

Planet Power

Flick on the lights, switch on the stereo, and turn up the heat. These actions, which people do every day, require energy, something often taken for granted. Scientists say that as demand for energy increases around the world, fossil fuels such as coal, oil, and gas will eventually be depleted. If this happens, how will people operate their cars, heat their homes, and attend to their daily business? Do this interest project to learn more about energy and energy conservation.

Skill Builders

1 Conduct an energy audit of your home or troop or group meeting place. Check the windows and doors for drafts, which cause loss of hot or cool air. Make a checklist of inefficient uses of energy. Your local fuel or electric company can provide a consumer brochure that you can use as a guide. Recommend improvements. Carry out at least one of your suggestions.

2 Go to a building supply store to learn about insulating materials. Find out the meaning of the term "R-values." Learn what the recommended R-values are for ceilings, outside walls, and floors in your area. Try to find out what type of insulation is used in your home or school. If possible, watch insulation being installed or help to insulate a house, apartment, or building.

3 Create a game that shows how energy moves within a particular habitat such as a deciduous forest. Are there more producers than consumers? Why or why not?

4 Figure out how much electricity each of the appliances you use at home consumes. First, look on your family's electric bill or call your local utility company for the current charge per kilowatt hour (this is how energy use is measured). Next, use the formula below to calculate how much electricity each of your electrical appliances uses.

Involve your family in making a list of things it pledges to do to conserve energy consumption for a week. Find out if your family successfully conserved energy by checking your meter, utility bill, or using the formula below.

5 Arrange to visit your local electric company or one of its power plants. Ask about the problems that utility companies face today in having to provide energy to more and more people. Is the company using any alternative energy sources?

Technology

1 Search via the library or Internet for names of solar energy information services and companies. Then proceed with an activity from the list below:

■ Build a solar cooker and cook at least part of a meal in it.

Wattage of the Appliance	X	Hours Used	X	Number of Days Used	÷	1000	=	Amount of Kilowatt Hours Used

- Build a model solar water heater that works and demonstrate its use to your troop or group or camp director.

- Design your own solar energy collector and explain how it works.

- Visit a building that uses solar energy and find out how it works.

2 Review at least three sources of energy, including nuclear power, and hold a debate in your troop or group over which source is the most environmentally sound, safe, efficient, and cost-effective.

3 Suppose there is a severe oil (petroleum) shortage and the government requires you and your community to cut back on the use of oil to conserve the available supply. Prepare a plan to help your family and community respond to this emergency. Find out how oil is used in your daily life—for example, heating your home or running your school bus. Then decide how people can reduce oil usage.

4 Choose two of the following energy sources: oil, nuclear, hydroelectric, gas, solar, and coal, and determine steps involved in transporting this form of energy from its production site to the consumer. How does your chosen energy source impact the environment? For example, dams that generate electricity can cause flooding. Display your findings.

Service Projects

1 Visit a recycling center and consider:

- What options are available for recycling glass, paper, aluminum, plastic?

- Can food waste be recycled, and how?

1 Can you avoid purchasing items that are overpackaged? Devise a recycling project for your home or troop or group meeting place. Set it up and help keep it running. Or volunteer your services at a recycling center.

2 Make plans for the possibility that your home might be without electricity for two days. How will you keep warm or cool, cook food and keep it fresh, and do your homework? Include plans for cooperation with neighbors.

3 Teach Brownie or Junior Girl Scouts how to make recycled paper out of newspaper or other discarded paper. (See the Artistic Crafts interest project.)

4 Put on a puppet show or skit for a group of younger Girl Scouts that shows the connection between recycling and energy conservation. Try to represent different points of view. Hold a question-and-answer session at the end of each "show." Invite local officials to your presentations.

Career Exploration

1 Invite a panel of speakers—from representatives of traditional and alternative energy companies, to ecologists and dietitians—to discuss with your troop or group career options in the energy field. Encourage the audience to ask questions. Then, as a group, put together a pamphlet or report, such as "Careers in the Energy Fields." Distribute it to other troops or groups in your council.

2 Become an "expert" in one area of alternative energy. Compare its advantages and disadvantages. What careers would be open to you? Contact an expert in

the field for advice and information, or research it at your library.

3 Shadow an ecologist and see what an average workday is like for her. People in this career are interested in how energy is obtained by plants and then converted for use by animals. Ask questions you prepared, or about what you are observing.

4 Create a time line of events in the history of nuclear science that includes a few of the people mentioned below. Describe their key contributions:

- Neils Bohr
- Hans Geiger
- Marie and Pierre Curie
- Otto Hahn
- Albert Einstein
- Lise Meitner
- Enrico Fermi
- Wilhelm Roentgen
- Paul-Ulrich Villard

And Beyond

EXPLORE WAYS YOU CAN MAKE THE MOST of the planet's powers and energies with these related interest projects:

- Plant Life
- Eco-Action
- The Food Connection
- Home Improvement
- Architecture and Environmental Design
- Build a Better Future
- Car Sense
- Travel
- Inventions and Inquiry

Plant Life

Growing and caring for plants are enjoyable and productive ways to beautify and enrich the environment. Explore the plant world through this interest project.

Skill Builders

1 In order for plants to absorb nutrients well, the soil has to have the proper pH, or acid/alkaline balance. Before you plant, figure out if your soil is acidic or alkaline by using a pH test kit. This kit can be found at garden centers. Find out how to adjust the soil if it is too acidic or too alkaline for the type of plants you wish to grow.

2 Rich soil that drains well is especially important to plants that grow in a confined space. Some plants, such as cacti, grow best in loose or sandy soil that drains quickly, while others, such as geraniums, need richer soil that will hold onto water a little longer. Determine how well your soil drains water and what you need to do to improve the soil if it becomes waterlogged or loses water too quickly.

3 Plan and plant a garden with at least three kinds of food crops (vegetables, fruits, and herbs). If you can only plant indoors, improvise by using pots, hanging baskets, or other containers. Prepare the soil before planting to ensure proper pH and adequate drainage. Arrange your garden "plot" for maximum sunlight or partial shade, depending on what your crop needs. Follow a garden maintenance schedule that includes watering, fertilizing, weeding, and pest control, using organic methods when possible.

4 Visit a supermarket produce section or a local distribution point for fruits and vegetables. Find out where selected fruits and vegetables came from (sometimes they are stamped or labeled with the name of a state or country). Create a geography game or scavenger hunt for younger girls linked to the products in a supermarket. For example, have them find fruits from at least three different states or countries.

5 Start three new plants without using seeds. Consult with a gardener or use a basic gardening manual to learn about tubers, runners, "eyes," rhizomes, spores, grafting, layering, and cuttings.

6 Compare traditional chemical pest control methods with natural ones. What are the advantages and disadvantages of growing things organically? If possible, interview a gardener or farmer who uses each method. Or contact your local cooperative extension agent and ask for information about integrated pest management, a program that combines chemical and natural pest control methods.

Technology

1 To do any job right, you need the proper tools and materials. Make a list of gardening tools and materials that you will need to grow your own plants. Find out what these tools and materials are used for, what each is made of, and why.

2 Visit a Web site, library, or botanical garden for information on growing plants hydroponically (in water). Grow a plant hydroponically at home or at school.

3 It used to be that you could only find tofu (soybean curd), juice, and milk cartons in the refrigerated section of your grocery store. Now, you can find these items sitting right on the shelf. How can this be? Discover the technology used to keep items packaged in aseptic (germ-free) containers from spoiling.

4 Learn about different kinds of watering tools and equipment. Find out which methods and equipment waste the least amount of water. Learn about different kinds of drip irrigation that work best for the amateur gardener.

5 Scientists are trying to "improve" on nature all the time through genetic engineering, the manipulation of plant or animal genes to produce a desired result. Find out how plants are genetically altered. Select three fruits or vegetables and find out why they have undergone genetic engineering. If possible, buy one of these food plants and compare its taste to the regular kind. Compare the advantages and disadvantages of producing food plants that have been genetically engineered.

Service Projects

1 Help turn a vacant lot or other public space into an "oasis" by volunteering to landscape it. Or help start or maintain a community vegetable garden for a season.

2 With a partner, or your troop or group, plant an area with native vegetation that will provide food or shelter for birds.

3 Plant a community butterfly garden. Find out which flowers attract different species of butterflies and plan a garden that will bloom over an extended period of time.

4 Grow or help harvest food for a community food bank. Or organize local gardeners to contribute their surplus produce to a community food bank.

5 In cooperation with your parks department, plant trees or plants to help prevent erosion. A state or federal agency, such as the U.S. Forest Service, or a nonprofit organization such as the National Arbor Day Foundation or Global ReLeaf, may be able to provide you with free saplings.

Career Exploration

1 Find out about at least one career related to plants. Arrange to interview or shadow a person in that career. Careers to consider: groundskeeper, landscape architect, florist, greenhouse owner, botanist, forester, tree pruner, researcher, farmer, agricultural consultant, or botanical illustrator.

2 Visit a garden that was especially created for people with disabilities (for example, those with visual impairments). Find out what factors were considered in designing this space.

3 Have you ever admired the plant displays at office buildings and indoor shopping malls? They are taken care of by professionals in the plant maintenance business. To try your hand at this career, volunteer to take care of the plants in one or more of these places: a friend's or relative's home, a neighborhood business or medical office, your Girl Scout council office, or your place of worship. Find out the name of each plant and look up its water, light, soil, and feeding requirements. Make a portable plant maintenance kit to use "on the job" by placing a spray bottle, watering can, trowel or large

spoon, sponge or wash cloth, etc., into a basket or plastic container.

4 Flower arrangements add a beautiful touch to any home or business. Many professional flower arrangers got their start from making gifts for friends and family members. Look through home decorating magazines or books about flower arranging to get ideas and to find out what equipment you will need. Then try your hand at creating botanical art by making flower baskets, accessories, or special occasion gifts out of dried flowers.

5 More and more health-related facilities such as nursing homes and rehabilitation centers have developed horticultural therapy programs. Under the guidance of a trained adult, assist in a program of this type and find out how and why it works.

And Beyond

YOU MIGHT ALSO BE INTERESTED IN earning your Cadette or Senior Community Service Bar by becoming a docent for a botanical garden, nature center, or community gardening program.

If botanic gardens and growing things excite you, why not explore the indoor and outdoor worlds of plants, with these related interest projects:

- Eco-Action
- All About Birds
- From Shore to Sea
- Creative Cooking
- The Food Connection
- Wildlife
- Outdoor Survival
- Reading
- Museum Discovery

Space Exploration

For centuries people have looked to the skies with awe and wonder. Today, astronomers, physicists, and other scientists use sophisticated instruments to gather and analyze data collected from earth and space. Join in this exciting quest to understand the universe.

Skill Builders

1 Find out about at least four of the following astronomical phenomena: *quasars, pulsars, novas, supernovas, black holes, dwarf stars, giant stars, proto-stars, neutron stars, variable stars, cosmic clouds,* and *globular clusters.* Can you observe any of these with the naked eye?

2 Visit a museum, planetarium, observatory, or space center to learn about the history of space exploration, or visit the National Aeronautics and Space Administration (NASA) site on the Internet to find out about projects currently in progress. Make a file of your findings and develop a list of Web sites for others to explore.

3 Learn more about the sun and the moon and their relationship to earth. Do two of the following:

■ Mark your calendar with the phases of the moon for a month.

■ Learn to read an ocean tide chart.

■ Make a poster illustrating why and how seasons change.

■ Demonstrate what happens during a solar or lunar eclipse.

■ Identify a tale or superstition about the sun or the moon. Discuss whether or not this is a valid or even measurable belief.

4 With a group, discuss "the case for space," addressing issues such as: Who owns space? Who owns the moon? Who should fund space travel or research? What are priorities for research in space? What happens if we find other life in space? Come up with charts and posters depicting your questions and answers.

5 Science fiction often predicts future developments. Read science fiction written in the 1960s or earlier, or view an old science fiction film from the sixties or earlier. How do they appear today in light of the new information people have about space? Or try your hand at writing science fiction. Incorporate technological or social changes brought about by space travel.

6 Develop your own space exploration activity. Here are some of the things you might do:

■ Explore what countries around the world are doing in space exploration.

■ Using a telescope, monitor an object in the night sky for a month.

■ Visit NASA and, if possible, view the launching of a space vehicle.

■ Develop a space exploration resource file. NASA has many educational materials available to the public.

■ Keep a scrapbook of news clippings on items related to astronomy and space exploration.

Technology

1 Find out about the capabilities of today's telescopes. If possible, visit an observatory or a site on the World Wide Web to learn more about these telescopes.

2 Investigate the role of mathematics and computer simulations in developing theories about the universe. Talk with someone knowledgeable in astronomy or physics, if possible.

3 Design a human space colony. Decide whether it is a station in space or one that will be set up on a planet in this solar system. Determine what conditions will need to be considered as well as the purpose of the vehicle/structure, living arrangements, special equipment, health and safety needs, and environmental protection or danger. Share and explain your design or model with others.

4 Build an accurate scale model of a space exploration vehicle. Find out about its design, function, and basic operation. Be able to help others learn about your vehicle.

5 Construct a "flying object"—something that is capable of flight. Be able to explain the scientific principles that governed your design. Determine which actual flight vehicles operate on the same principles.

Service Projects

1 Help sponsor an event, such as a space exploration activity day or science career day. Incorporate hands-on and creative activities, such as acting in a play about women who have studied or explored space in some way.

2 Develop a booklet or display that highlights women who have played an important role in the history of flight and space exploration.

3 Help Brownie and Junior Girl Scouts learn about space exploration. Do two of the following: Conduct a night-sky exploration, put on a play about life on a space station, tell a story about a woman astronaut, including her training and achievements, or share stories from different cultures about the night sky.

4 Design a library exhibit about space and astronomy for your school, library, or town recreation center. Include books, an activity box, and a list of resources in your display.

5 Using glow-in-the-dark paint, stars, or reflector tape, make an accurate constellation map on a ceiling. The map should include a minimum of twelve constellations in any season. Create a guided tour of the ceiling.

Career Exploration

1 Check out at least two of the following careers and show how they are linked to the space program: biomedical engineering, meteorology, ceramics, chemistry, industrial engineering, materials science, metallurgy, optical engineering, physiology, and photography.

2 Plan to attend a "space camp" or astronomy camp to get more hands-on experiences.

3 Contact two science societies for professional women related to astronomy or space exploration. Find out what careers are related to space exploration. Also, find out what benefits members of the society receive and whether they have any special programs for young people.

4 List five ways that you can maintain your interest in space and/or astronomy. Investigate and list space-related places to visit or activities to pursue in your community or on the Internet.

And Beyond

TAKE A VOYAGE TO WORLDS BEYOND your own in these related interest projects:

- From Shore to Sea
- Travel
- A World of Understanding
- Inventions and Inquiry
- Build a Better Future
- Folk Arts
- Fashion Design
- Once Upon a Story
- Creative Cooking

And take the time to gaze upon the stars!

Why in the World?

*S*cience is the search for understanding and knowledge about people and the universe, and technology is the application of science to life. In this interest project, you will be the scientific investigator, exploring the world from weather to watch parts, and from microbes to minerals.

Skill Builders

1 Why does the weather often change from day to day and from one season to the next? What makes a "bad hair day"? Investigate weather patterns by talking with a meteorologist, visiting a meteorological Web site, or watching a television weather station. Find out what happens when a warm front meets a cold front, a cold front meets a warm front, or the jet stream shifts north or south in the winter or summer. What is El Niño and how does it affect weather? What causes global warming and holes in the ozone? Learn to read three weather instruments as well as the weather map in your local newspaper.

2 Have you ever asked yourself how something works? To find out, start by observing an item while it is in use: for example, a radio, a telephone, or a bicycle. Identify its purpose, its parts, and its energy source. Using resources found in the library, a science museum, or on the World Wide Web, draw a diagram to show how it works, or make a model of it.

3 Visit a science museum, rock shop, or the gem and mineral collection at the Smithsonian Web site to learn more about gems and minerals. Learn how to identify at least 10 minerals. Start a collection of common rocks and minerals found in your area.

4 Investigate how new synthetic materials play an important role in two or more of the following: clothing, cars, homes, toys, sports equipment, media equipment, and medicine. What materials were previously used? What are the advantages of the new materials?

5 Find out about modern techniques used in food production, processing, or preservation. Select one area and identify some of the key issues relevant in your community. For example, does the use of pesticides need to be more carefully monitored? Hold a debate on the pros and cons of the issue. Share the results of your debate.

6 Be a creative cook. Learn the chemical properties of carbohydrates (sugar, starch), microbes (yeast), acids and bases (lemon juice, baking soda, and baking powder), oils, proteins (eggs, gelatin, meat, and milk), and other substances. Create a recipe from scratch that involves a chemical reaction, using at least two items from the above list. Share your tasty creation with others.

Technology

1 Ergonomics is a growing field of study that analyzes the human body in relation to physical space. The objective is to create suitable work, products, and work environments for people. Investigate the design that is best for an office. How can computers be set up to prevent back, eye, and wrist strain for the users? What is the best kind of chair for long periods of use? Evaluate your own study area. Make two "ergonomically correct" changes in the position of your desk and other study-related furnishings and equipment: for example, is your chair at the correct height for your desk? Share this information with others.

2 Tour a manufacturing or food processing plant. How are different machines used to make and assemble a product, from start to finish? What are the roles of workers in the production process? Are robots used? What kinds of laws govern the manufacturing process to ensure quality and safety? How was this product produced 50 years ago? Share your information at a meeting, club, or career fair. If possible, show slides, photographs, or diagrams of your findings.

3 How have science and technology affected the arts? Talk with a musician, sculptor, actor, photographer, or other artist. What new materials and tools do they use? What new art forms are being created that use advances in technology? Experiment with one of these new art forms.

4 Name the manufactured parts that can be implanted in the human body. Consult with a biomedical engineer or surgeon, and look at medical textbook illustrations. Discuss reasons that body parts may need to be replaced or strengthened. Then draw an outline of the body. Label the parts that can be replaced now. What materials are used to create these artificial body parts, and why? What are the scientific challenges and the ethical considerations in this field?

5 Take a common household appliance such as a refrigerator, stove, TV, CD player, or telephone and think forward 20 years. How will it look? What might it be able to do? Will it be the same appliance or will it be combined with something else? Draw or design and display a model of an appliance of the future. Or read a magazine or

find a Web site that predicts new developments in science and technology. Present your findings through a creative medium: for example, paint a mural, make a poster, or write a poem. Share it with others.

Service Projects

1 Help organize a school or Girl Scout science fair that encourages participation by girls.

2 Help a Brownie or Junior Girl Scout troop or group earn a science Try-It or badge and/or use activities from the National Science Partnership science kits. Or develop a series of science and health activities for girls in a homeless shelter or after-school program.

3 Volunteer in an ongoing program to educate others about breast cancer or osteoporosis, or other diseases that affect many more women than men.

4 Work with an organization to inform other teens about sexually transmitted diseases (STDs), drug use, smoking, anorexia, or bulimia.

5 Host a forum to generate greater interest among girls in science and math. Invite teachers and women scientists to participate.

Career Exploration

1 How do women get involved in science? Interview at least two women in science fields. Find out how they got started. Did they have mentors? While in high school,

did they have to contend with negative stereotypes about girls who like science or girls who are smart? How do they feel about the future for women in science?

2 Identify at least three women scientists who have won the Nobel Prize and report on or write about their contributions in your club, science class, or troop or group meeting.

3 Participate in a scientist pen-pal program through an established mentor project or through a professional organization. Ask your librarian or guidance counselor for assistance.

4 Volunteer as a demonstrator at a science exhibit, science museum, or nature center.

And Beyond

BECOME A PROGRAM AIDE WITH A concentration in science or environmental education, or work on your Community Service Bar in conjunction with a science/technology lab or museum.

If you love investigating the why and how of things, continue to do so with these related interest projects:

- Wildlife
- Plant Life
- Planet Power
- Space Exploration
- Build a Better Future
- Computers in Everyday Life
- Digging Through the Past
- Exploring the Net
- Inventions and Inquiry

Wildlife

Have you ever watched a hawk soar over a meadow, caught a glimpse of a fox while hiking, seen wildflowers rustle in the breeze, or watched a fish break the calm surface of the water? You can make wildlife observations in your own backyard, a town wood lot, a city street, a national park, a forest, or a field. You can study animals and their habitats with binoculars, a camera, a tape recorder, or a sketch pad, or simply relax and feel the peace that comes from being in the outdoors.

Skill Builders

You will find the Girl Scout book *Exploring Wildlife Communities with Children* very helpful as you work on the following activities.

1 Find a natural area such as a forested park, a meadow, or a pond that you can use as a field ecology study site. Visit the site and take time to conduct some observations. What did you see, hear, smell, or feel? Record the date, time of day, temperature, and weather conditions.

2 Identify as many of the flowers, shrubs, and trees at a field ecology study site as you can. Sketch some of them in a field notebook. Use a field guide to identify them; record their names alongside your sketches.

3 Identify and record the names of animals you see, or find signs of, at a field ecology study site. Look carefully for and learn to recognize animal tracks. Be able to name at least three. Try to follow the trail of an animal in mud, sand, or snow and see if you can tell what it was doing (walking, running, etc.). You may wish to photograph the tracks or make plaster casts so you can show them to younger girls. For help in identifying insects and their relatives, see page 19 of the Girl Scout book *Fun and Easy Nature and Science Investigations*.

4 Select a specific animal to observe at a field ecology study site. Record the date, time, location, and weather conditions at the time of your observation. Create an ethogram, a detailed record of animal behavior, by putting down categories of behavior on a chart: for example, walk, run, rest, play. Observe for about 20 minutes. Note when the behaviors occur at regular times (for example, 30 seconds or one minute). Also note how the animal interacts with others of its kind and with other species of animals.

5 Put up several bird houses. Find out the box dimensions and entrance hole sizes for the species you wish to attract. You can either make them yourself or purchase them. Discover why it is beneficial to have birds living nearby.

6 Conduct an experiment to show how a plant reacts to its environment (either at a field ecology site or in your home). Think carefully about what environmental conditions you want to test. Record and/or illustrate what happens during your experiment. Be careful not to injure the plant.

Technology

1 Learn about how wildlife biologists study animals in the field. What types of equipment do they use and how? Is different equipment used for animals of the land, air, or water?

2 Choose three species from any of the following categories for in-depth study: birds, mammals, insects, reptiles, amphibians, fish, trees, herbaceous plants. Use current computer technology (CD-ROMs, online encyclopedias, Web sites of wildlife organizations, etc.) to help you answer the following questions: What are the species' habitat requirements? What is its life history? How does it fit into the food chain? Is it threatened or endangered? If so, why?

3 Research how documentaries about wildlife are produced. Discuss ethical and practical issues related to photographing, filming, or recording animals in their natural surroundings.

4 Find out how insecticides, herbicides, and fungicides travel through an ecosystem. Create a visual display that shows the hazards of using these chemicals for both wildlife and people. Investigate alternatives to these products and suggest their use to family or friends who have a garden.

Service Projects

1 Teach the meaning of the following italicized words to younger Girl Scouts by creating a game that uses the words: *predator, prey, plant life, herbivore, carnivore, omnivore, scavenger, decomposer, wildlife community, food web.*

2 Contact a local wildlife agency, bird club, or nature center to volunteer your services. You could participate in a project to restore a wildlife habitat by planting trees, erecting wood duck nest boxes, building dens, or cleaning a section of a stream or vacant lot. Involve other Girl Scouts in the project. Record your results as you carry out the project.

3 Help make a nature trail at your Girl Scout camp or local park accessible to more people. For example, design a set of trail markers with information about a plant, animal, or rock formation that can be easily read by someone in a wheelchair. Another idea is to produce an audiotape that a visually impaired person can use along the same nature trail to help inform her of the special feature each marker highlights.

4 Examine your own values and beliefs related to wildlife and the environment and evaluate possible actions you could take. With a group of Girl Scouts, discuss an environmental issue important in your area or a broader issue, such as hunting, acid rain, or the logging of forests.

5 With the cooperation of your Girl Scout council, survey one campsite. Inventory the property by listing the kinds of plants and animals found there. Highlight threatened or endangered species and the problems they face. Organize a group of Girl Scouts to create an endangered species bulletin board at the campsite to raise awareness among other Girl Scouts about the plight of the species on the property and elsewhere in the country or world. Read page 106 of the *Cadette Girl Scout Handbook* to find out about setting up a Lou Henry Hoover Memorial Sanctuary at your campsite.

Career Exploration

1 Brainstorm five career choices involving wildlife and the environment. Contact government agencies and other organizations that might employ people in such careers and inter-

view one of them. How did she get into this field? What does she do on a daily basis?

2 Investigate what it means to be an ethnobotanist or cultural ecologist. Or explore another career that combines knowledge of wildlife and people. Arrange to interview someone and ask her what species she studies, what her background and training are, etc.

3 Arrange to shadow a wildlife biologist or naturalist for part of a day to learn about the job.

4 Investigate laws that protect wildlife around the world. How effective are these laws in regulating trade? Which group of people benefits from the sale of wildlife products? Pick an animal species affected by the trade in wildlife products (for example, the African elephant hunted for its ivory or the snow leopard hunted for its fur) and write a story or a play about it. Share it with or show it to younger Girl Scouts.

And Beyond

ONCE YOU DISCOVER THE FANTASTIC variety of wildlife, from butterflies to grizzly bears, you'll want to go further by trying these related interest projects:

- Pets
- Plant Life
- Outdoor Survival
- All About Birds
- Eco-Action
- Digging Through the Past

Women's Health

Positive health habits and practices that start in adolescence can help you experience a vibrant and healthy adulthood. Many books, magazines, videos, clinics, and other resources concentrating on "wellness" for teens and women are available. Completing this interest project will help you become informed about your body so that you can enjoy good health today and tomorrow.

Skill Builders

1 Evaluate the stress in your life. Stress isn't always negative. It can motivate, challenge, and propel you to achieve your visions and dreams. What are the positive stresses in your life? How do they keep you going? What are the negative stresses you might want to reduce? Read "Life Success Skills #2: Handling Stress," on pages 88–90 in the *Cadette Girl Scout Handbook*. Complete the Teenage Stress Scale. Look over the "Stress Reducers" on page 61 of *A Resource Book for Senior Girl Scouts*. Try some of the stress-reducing activities.

2 Learn about the harmful effects of drugs, such as alcohol, caffeine, tobacco, amphetamines, marijuana, cocaine/crack, or steroids, on the body. Become an expert on one substance and the consequences of using or abusing it. Then participate in a project to prevent substance abuse.

3 Investigate the importance of a healthy diet. Research major threats to good nutrition in females, including anorexia and other eating disorders and fad dieting. Design a poster or draw a storyboard to depict your findings.

4 Read the information on breast cancer awareness in *A Resource Book for Senior Girl Scouts* and other sources. Help develop or promote a workshop that focuses on both prevention and education for peers.

5 Bones are the framework upon which your body is built. Find out what bones are made of, what part calcium plays in forming healthy bones, and what foods or nutritional supplements ensure bone health. Investigate the role of exercise in bone health. Osteoporosis is a disease that causes bones to become fragile and break easily. Share your findings on bone health.

6 With the help of experts, design an exercise program to promote cardiovascular fitness. Include vigorous aerobic activities, including warm-up and cool-down exercises. Incorporate monitoring the pulse rate of the participant before, during, and after the exercise program.

Technology

1 Visit a cardiac rehabilitation center. Find out about technology used to detect cardiac problems and promote cardiovascular fitness. Share this information with others.

2 Today the study of DNA has become central to medical research, and is dramatically changing the ways in which diseases are understood. Online or at a specialized medical library (try your hospital or a university), research and discover what female health issues are related to genetic factors.

3 Find out how advances in technology have changed the detection of breast cancer and other diseases over the past 25 years.

4 At a gym, health club, or store, try out three types of fitness equipment. Which features help to maintain or increase your motivation? Teach a friend or family member how to use the equipment.

Service Projects

1 Create and monitor a health-care program for an older relative or neighbor. Help her choose three goals to achieve over a two-month period, such as exercising three times per week, eating healthier foods, and attending a senior hobby group once a week. Be sure that the individual you are working with has her doctor's permission to follow your program.

2 After researching the effects of smoking, create an anti-smoking campaign for your school or community. Contact local or national organizations for materials and information. Use various media, such as posters and films, to present your message.

3 Create a program for younger children (puppet show, game, coloring book, or other activity) to help them understand healthy habits, such as choosing good foods and handling stress.

4 Sleep is one of the components of health and fitness that people most often neglect. Yet inadequate sleep can adversely affect your whole day. Present a workshop on sleep to a Girl Scout troop or group. Issues to address might include how sleep can affect your ability to exercise; how exercise can impact on sleep; how lack of sleep can affect reaction time, memory, logical thinking, and the immune system. Include information about the sleep needs of adolescents.

5 Participate in a councilwide "Be Your Best!" or sports-day event. For example, volunteer to coach younger Girl Scouts in a game.

Career Exploration

1 Volunteer at your local hospital or rehabilitation center. Record your experiences and feelings in a journal. Develop your own long-term and short-term goals concerning working in the medical and health-care fields.

2 Visit at least two training programs or schools in the health care field in person or online. Find out about entrance requirements, recommended courses, and career options. If possible, interview someone enrolled in one of the programs.

3 Investigate opportunities and issues in scientific research in the area of women's health. Visit a laboratory or online chat room, or attend a professional meeting of scientists so that you can talk with women doing research.

4 With a team, organize a panel discussion at school or in your Girl Scout troop or group on the topic of careers related to women's health concerns.

5 Read two biographies or autobiographies of women who have worked in a field related to women's health.

And Beyond

TAKE CARE OF YOUR BODY AND MIND with specific goals and action plans. Boost your spirits by taking up a new hobby or trying any of the interest projects related to the arts, science, or sports.

Expand your health knowledge with these related interest projects:

- Understanding Yourself and Others
- The Food Connection
- From Fitness to Fashion
- From Stress to Success
- Family Living
- Child Care

Communications

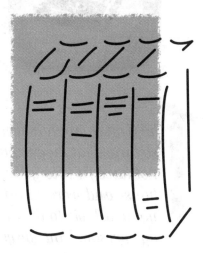

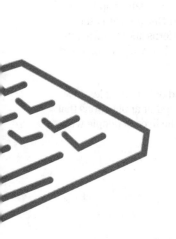

Computers in Everyday Life

*T*he first computers were so large that they would not have fit into your house and were certainly not available to the average person. Nowadays computers fit on your desk, in your bookbag, or in the palm of your hand. They can be found at school, in libraries, and at most places of work and play. This project will introduce you to everyday functions of using the family PC as well as computers at school, at work, and in the community.

Skill Builders

1 Find out about personal computers and their capabilities. Visit a computer store or consult computer magazines. Investigate the hardware required to run today's software and to gain access to the Internet. Compare costs and add-on capabilities, including CD-ROMS, faxing, and audio and multimedia capabilities.

2 Learn how to use a word processing program. Become proficient in formatting, editing, spell-checking, cutting and pasting, inserting page numbers or symbols, and creating columns and boxes. Be able to take shortcuts by customizing the toolbars. Write a paper for school, publish the minutes of your troop or group meeting, or design a flier using this program. Or if you already know how to do the above, select a software program that allows you to do something totally new. Apply the program to an activity: for example, redesigning your bedroom, creating party invitations, or keeping track of a month-long project.

3 Learn to use a desktop publishing software package that allows you to create a newsletter or informational brochure for your troop or group.

4 Learn to use a software program that allows you to create spreadsheets. Master basic functions such as formatting and editing a worksheet, entering and organizing data, using formulas, and creating a chart or graph from your data. Use the spreadsheet to keep a personal or family budget for a month, to keep records of an event's income and expenditures, or to keep track of your troop or group finances. Or try a personal finance software package for a personal or family budget.

5 Play three or four computer games, or visit an Internet or Web site that previews computer games, trivia, or murder mystery contests. What games appeal to you? Why? Discuss with others some concerns about playing these games, such as violence or sexist stereotypes.

6 Find out about at least two computer applications that enhance the lives of people with disabilities.

Technology

1 Read reviews of hardware, software, and Web sites in at least two magazines that address products and applications for home computer use. Interview at least three or four computer users of different ages and find out what they look for in these products. Develop your own checklist of criteria and share it in a meeting of your troop or group or at your school.

2 How many times is your life affected by the computer? Keep a log for yourself covering a week, noting all the times your life is touched by a computer. Share this log with others, perhaps in a discussion group.

3 What amazing things are happening in the movies now? Compare early special effects in the motion picture industry with the computer-assisted effects possible today. Find out about the costs and the advantages of using computer graphics. Host a video night for friends and show movies enhanced by computer effects, or arrange to go with a group to one such movie.

4 Find out how computer technology has changed common household appliances (for example, ovens and clothes dryers). What are the advantages and drawbacks?

5 Investigate how information is stored on credit cards, medical emergency cards, and other kinds of cards. Find out about protecting against criminal use of this information.

Service Projects

1 Work to help set up a computer, modem, and online service for a community in your area. Assist in teaching residents how to use the online services. For instance, show them how to use e-mail.

2 Set up a directory of community resources, scan a photo collection onto a computer, organize a recipe collection, or develop some other computer application for your own family, someone else's, or a service organization.

3 Use a computer to produce an informational brochure or newsletter for a community organization, or your troop or group.

4 Design a flier for families on Internet and World Wide Web use, including safety and "netiquette" tips and a list of great Web sites for family exploration. Share your flier with your council, school, or community group.

5 Set up a neighborhood software library or computer game exchange.

Career Exploration

1 Compile a directory of Web sites that contain information about careers. Create some major categories, such as technology, medicine, law, and education. Share your directory with friends.

2 Investigate careers that are possible from the home with a computer, technical support, and access to online resources. Interview at least two people who work at home (at least 50 percent of the time) and use a computer. What are the advantages/disadvantages of working at home for them? What special hardware and software do they use, if any?

3 Investigate a computer-related career: computer salesperson, computer programmer, software developer, graphic designer, computer analyst, systems developer, systems programmer. Arrange to interview at least two professionals in person or online.

4 Identify three types of businesses or industries which, while not computer-based, rely heavily on computers for documentation, data collection, or production. Create a means of sharing your findings.

5 Find out how your school, Girl Scout council, or another community group creates fliers, newsletters, brochures, and invitations. Who does what, such as editing, design, production, and circulation? Assist in some stage of the creation of flier, a newsletter, a brochure, or an invitation.

And Beyond

THE RELATED INTEREST PROJECTS BELOW allow you to put creativity and technology together for great results.

■ Exploring the Net
■ Desktop Publishing
■ Graphic Communications
■ Media Savvy
■ From A to V: Audiovisual Production
■ Games for Life

If all this technology is getting to you, take up a recreational hobby as found in All About Birds, Collecting, High Adventure, Rolling Along, or Water Sports, and unwind with From Stress to Success, On a High Note, or Reading.

Desktop Publishing

Ever think about creating your own flier for an event or creating a business card, personal letterhead, or troop newsletter? Computers and good desktop publishing software can make this possible. You can really create a customized product. With access to resources on the Internet and a scanner, the options for desktop publishing are spectacular. Learn about a field that is growing every nanosecond.

Skill Builders

1 When you are desktop publishing, you don't have to be an artist, but it does help to have an eye for design and layout. Collect samples of newsletters, stationery letterhead, logos, business cards, fliers, résumés, or other materials produced through desktop publishing. Take at least one category, such as newsletters, and decide which samples appeal to you the most, and why. Consider format, size, use of color, or space, choice of paper, fonts, graphics, and photographs.

2 Learn to use one desktop publishing program. Design a card, stationery letterhead, or a newsletter format. If possible, print your piece with a color printer.

3 Review different résumé formats. Write a résumé using a template form in your word processing software. Create your own design, or use a résumé form available on desktop publishing software.

4 To be a good home desktop publisher, you need editing skills as well. Learn how to use spell-check and grammar check on computer software. Learn how to proofread everything that you produce. Learn standard editing symbols for manuscript work: for deleting copy or letting copy stand, capitalizing and lowercasing words, reversing letters, and marking copy to be set italics or boldface. Find out what to do about single words or very short lines at the top of a page. Learn how to format paragraphs and add page breaks when doing a newsletter. Develop your editing skills by trying to tighten your copy.

5 Find out about the following in relation to desktop publishing: copyright laws, public domain, plagiarism, and use of trademarks. Find out how to copyright your own work.

Technology

1 Visit a computer store, graphics center, or desktop publisher and find out about the different kinds of computer hardware available for desktop publishers, including their cost. Compare the features of various monitors, keyboards, scanners, and color printers. Find out how much hard drive is recommended to run industry standard desktop publishing and art software programs.

2 Arrange for a tour of a local print shop or copy center. Find out about the basics of desktop publishing in the business world: equipment, services, ink colors, paper stock, pricing. If possible, follow a project in progress and observe several of the steps in developing a finished project.

3 Find out about desktop publishing on the Internet and the World Wide Web. Visit several Web site publishers and compare their work. Find out about online files of clip art, pictures, and fonts, and how to download them for your use. (Be sure that the files are marked for the public domain and are not copyrighted material!)

4 Learn how to use a scanner to transfer photos into your computer program and onto the page.

5 Find out about the changes in desktop publishing that have happened in the last 10 years because of innovations in technology. Are there differences in production time, quality, and costs between the earlier and present methods?

Service Projects

1 Help write, edit, and design at least two issues of a newsletter for a nonprofit group, senior citizens' center, or neighborhood youth center.

2 Design a logo for a group or a patch for an event using a desktop publishing or a drawing software package. Present your design ideas to a selection group. If possible, be involved in pricing the cost per unit of the finished product (for example, stationery, fliers, T-shirts.)

3 Create cards, invitations, or programs for a special observance for a community group. Present the product to the group for approval after developing a model. Work with the group or a sponsor. Choose paper that complements your design.

4 Compile a booklet of poems and illustrate it with your own graphic arts. Use type, layout, and paper that enhance the theme.

5 Teach what you have learned about desktop publishing to a group of Junior Girl Scouts. Help them to create a newsletter or publication of their choosing.

Career Exploration

1 Investigate two careers that relate to desktop publishing, such as a freelance desktop publisher, desktop publisher in a large organization, printing shop owner, graphic artist, fabric designer, logo designer, editor, production manager, publisher, or computer programmer. Find out the daily responsibilities involved in these careers, and what kinds of training are needed. What volunteer or apprentice experiences are available for teens that might lay the groundwork for such a career?

2 Investigate courses at a community college or university that would lead to careers in desktop publishing or computer-generated design.

3 Keep a portfolio of your best work. If you plan to go into this field, you will need to show others what you can do. Speak with an art or business teacher to get some ideas for presentation.

4 Start your own business in home desktop publishing. Decide what you want to specialize in, develop a portfolio of your work, and make business cards with your own logo. Develop a flier or advertise in a community newspaper. Keep track of your expenses and earnings.

5 Spend time with a printer or a designer. Make note of the hardware, software, and techniques that she is using in her job.

And Beyond

WORK ON YOUR COUNCIL'S CADETTE and Senior Girl Scout newsletter for your Girl Scout Community Service Bar, or assist with another organization's newsletter for your Community Service Bar.

Desktop publishing comes in handy in school, service, and career pursuits. Enhance your skills with these related interest projects:

- Exploring the Net
- Graphic Communications
- Public Relations
- Writing for Real
- Visual Arts
- Your Own Business

Do You Get the Message?

A scowl, a laugh, a shout, or a hug—all of these things send a message. How proficient are you at sending and receiving cues to and from your friends and family? Do you sometimes feel like you have a sixth sense that allows you to finish a friend's sentence or to understand someone's problems without a lot of explanation? In this interest project, you'll learn how to account for what you say and don't say.

Skill Builders

1 Learn some words in another language. Be able to communicate at least five short phrases in your new language. For example, try Braille, sign language, Morse code, or a foreign language.

2 Develop your debating skills. With a group of at least four people, form two teams and take opposite sides of an issue. For example, consider the pros and cons of "free speech." Prepare for and then debate the issue before an audience.

3 How does someone's appearance or clothing influence your impression of that person? Observe current fashion trends in magazines and catalogs. Make a collage or display board with advertisements for clothing that send a message without words. Do these ads send biased or sexist messages? What messages are they sending?

4 Which is more important, what you say or how you say it? What effect do tone of voice and mannerisms have on verbal messages? Do the following with a group. Choose a neutral sentence, such as "I'll see you on Friday," and say it in five different ways: with anger, sadness, nervousness, love, and impatience. Include body language, facial expressions, hand motions, etc., that will help convey the emotion. Ask others for their reactions. Then, over the next week, analyze your messages. Are you "saying" what you mean?

5 Use humor to convey a message. For example, write a funny caption for a picture or poster, create a cartoon, or tell a joke or a funny story to a group.

6 Something that may be acceptable in one culture may be considered offensive in another. For instance, in some cultures, it is considered respectful to look down or away from a person when speaking with her. In other cultures, failure to maintain eye contact might indicate that you're lying or hiding something. Discuss regional and cultural differences in communication in a meeting of your troop or group, at your club, or in another public forum.

7 How does a particular physical environment affect you? Analyze the surroundings in several places: for example, your dentist's or doctor's office, a hair salon, or a bookstore. What do the colors, textures, and furnishings in these places tell you? Share your observations with friends or family members.

Technology

1 Design a costume display to communicate each of the following messages: "I want to be noticed." "I want to blend into the crowd." "I want to relax." "I want to impress someone." The costumes may include illustrations or actual garments.

2   Develop an advertising campaign targeted for a specific group of people. Look at print, television, and radio advertising. Create an ad campaign for one product or service.

3   Technology plays an important role in creating a model's "look." Learn about some of the techniques that can be used to improve or enhance a model's appearance. You might want to investigate air-brushing photographs, the use of special lenses when taking pictures, and the ways in which computers can be used to modify photographs. If possible, go to a photo-finishing store that offers computer enhancement and make a recent school picture of yourself "picture perfect."

4   Listen to the lyrics of several popular songs and watch several music videos. How are girls or women represented? Select female recording artists of different ages and from different ethnic groups. Share your observations with others.

Service Projects

1   Develop and administer a survey to girls in your school or council related to the way females are portrayed in the media. Here are two sample survey questions. Check the box that best represents your feelings.

■ How concerned are you about the way women and girls are portrayed in the media?

❏ Very concerned   ❏ Fairly concerned

❏ Not very concerned   ❏ Not at all concerned

■ The amount of violence shown in movies, television shows, and popular music is a serious problem.

❏ Strongly agree   ❏ Somewhat agree

❏ Somewhat disagree   ❏ Strongly disagree

Come up with three or more of your own questions, and try your survey out on a group of girls. Then analyze and share your results.

2   With a partner or a group of friends, arrange a self-defense workshop that includes demonstrations by experts.

3   How can you improve messages in the media? Design a positive media campaign or reword several news reports to convey a positive message. For example, emphasize the number of teenage girls who have quit smoking in a given year rather than the number who have begun the habit.

4   Create a game that helps younger girls sharpen their communication skills.

Career Exploration

1   Interview someone older than you about significant school or work experiences that that person experienced at your age.

2   Find out the differences between a speech pathologist, a speech coach, and a speech teacher. Read about or interview one of the above. Share what you have learned with your Girl Scout friends.

3   List three careers in which language skills are particularly important: for example, a customer service representative, a salesperson, or a politician. Describe the language skills they need to be successful.

4   Write a résumé that accurately describes your education and work experience. Do a practice job interview with a friend.

5   Design your own business cards. Include your name, your title, and the name, address, and phone number of your business.

And Beyond

PRACTICE MAKES PERFECT, SO PRACTICE "getting the message" every day with any of these related interest projects:

- ■ Public Relations
- ■ Law and Order
- ■ Your Best Defense
- ■ Leadership
- ■ Conflict Resolution
- ■ Understanding Yourself and Others
- ■ Family Living
- ■ Media Savvy
- ■ From A to V: Audiovisual Production
- ■ Once Upon a Story
- ■ Writing for Real

Folk Arts, Invitation to the Dance, On a High Note, The Performing Arts, Photography, The Play's the Thing, and Visual Arts show us how to communicate through the arts.

Talk to the animals in Pets, All About Birds, and Wildlife. Communicate with nature in From Shore to Sea, and beyond your own backyard in A World of Understanding, The Lure of Language, and Travel.

Exploring the Net

Visiting an art museum, finding out about what plants grow best in your part of the country, investigating a career, shopping for custom-made jeans, reading a movie review, or chatting with a friend half a world away—these are just a few of the infinite possibilities open to you when you explore the Internet. Surely Juliette Gordon Low would have been one of the first to have her own home page.

Skill Builders

1 Learn about the options for accessing the World Wide Web. Can you use a computer through your school, library, community center, or Girl Scout center? Is one available through a computer club business or nonprofit organization? Perhaps you have a computer at home. In addition to the big-name national commercial online services, there are many other local Internet providers. Find out who they are and compare costs and services offered. (Don't forget to include telephone costs as well!)

2 Develop family and/or personal guidelines for use of online services and exploration of the Internet. Discuss issues such as costs, amount of use that is reasonable, parental guidance, shopping by computer, best times to use the phone line, sharing of the computer and phone line by family members, and safety on the Internet.

3 Find out about URLs (Universal Resource Locators), the addresses by which you can access files, news groups, and Gopher ftp sites using a Web browser. The three letters at the end of an address generally give a clue as to the type of site—.com (commercial), .gov (government), .org (nonprofit organization), or .edu (educational). For example, Girl Scouts of the U.S.A. can be found at "http://www.gsusa.org". Find two Web sites in each of the following domains—.com, .gov, .org, .edu—and visit two Web sites in countries other than the United States. How are countries identified in an address? Develop your own "hot list" of 10–12 sites for friends to visit.

4 Learn how to use key words in searching for information on a specific topic when using an Internet information browser or a search engine. Find out if there are shortcuts to narrow the field of inquiry. Do a search that will give you answers to a specific question, such as finding out about college scholarships, your favorite sport, a museum you would like to visit, or information for a school report. Visit several Web sites and explore related topics from those Web sites. Keep a log or use bookmarks to mark sites you wish to revisit.

5 Find information on "netiquette," "nethics," and "Net jargon." Determine what the guidelines are for using materials you have accessed (how to cite sources, what copyright means); sending e-mail; and participating in forums. Learn some of the jargon.

6 Learn how to send e-mail to someone. Find out how much it costs to send e-mail through the service you are using, as compared to sending information by fax or calling directly. Learn to attach a document from a file and send it as part of your e-mail message, if your server and software will allow you to do this. Keep a list of favorite e-mail addresses.

7 Become an Internet tourist by "visiting" a major metropolitan area in the U.S.A. or abroad. Access maps and information about weather. Visit art and science museums, universities, and other places of interest. Share your tour with others. Or use the Net to plan a family or Girl Scout trip.

Technology

1 Learn to evaluate computer hardware. How many megabytes (MBs), megahertzes (MHz's), and other features does a computer need to use the software you are interested in? What are your options for connecting to the Internet, browsing the Web, sending faxes, and using a CD-ROM? Learn computer terms: for example, RAM, memory, byte, modem speed, PC- or MAC-compatible, graphical interface, and point and click. Review at least two different magazine articles that rate new products and discuss issues related to using the Internet and other computer services. Share your information with others.

2 Discover three major trends in technology, business, or law that will affect the way the Internet is accessed, and learn about hardware and software. You might visit a computer store and talk with a knowledgeable salesperson, read some online news about the Net, or read computer and Net magazines.

3 Has computer technology been responsible for community building, or has it contributed to isolation of the individual? Has it widened the gap between social classes in the United States and abroad? Or is the verdict still out? Develop a presentation, display, debate, or computer forum on these issues to share and discuss with others.

4 Learn how to assemble a presentation that uses video, audio, and computer graphics. If possible, create a short presentation and show it to a group of people.

Service Projects

1 Develop a scavenger hunt for peers or younger Girl Scouts that teaches them how to use the Internet. Include questions that take girls to different sites. Asking them to find out specific information about science, art, sports, music, and geography.

2 Host an online chat with Cadette and Senior Girl Scouts on issues facing older girls.

3 Help to develop a community service Web site for teens. Facilitate the linking of people who want to offer materials or their time to public or private agencies.

4 Volunteer your time with a "homework" help line or offer computer assistance at a community center or library dedicated to helping kids access resources for their homework.

5 Open some doors. Teach adults who have never been around a computer how to surf the Net. Learn about their interests so you can design a grand tour for them.

Career Exploration

1 Explore three careers you might be interested in and research how using the Internet might be of value in these careers. If possible, interview people in these careers in person or by e-mail. Find out how they are using computers and the Internet in their work.

2 Use the Internet to access information about a career you are interested in. Find out what the educational requirements are for that field. Then locate two schools in two different parts of the country that meet those requirements.

3 Discover the many careers based on the Web: for example, Web designers, Web managers, e-mail postmasters, zine writers, and publishers. Make a list and interview at least one person who is working on the Web.

4 Find out about skills needed for Web-based careers such as HTML (hypertext markup language) design, Web site design, Web research, and online zine publishing. Use the Internet to contact at least two businesses, schools, or universities, and find out what kinds of courses or experiences are available and/or recommended for people wanting to work in these areas.

And Beyond

HELP YOUR GIRL SCOUT COUNCIL OR another organization develop and staff its Web site.

Explore the compelling world of cyberspace with these related interest projects:

- Computers in Everyday Life
- Desktop Publishing
- Graphic Communications

Research any other topic of interest by exploring the world at your fingertips on the Net.

From A to V: Audiovisual Production

Have you watched a TV show or presentation and thought, "I could do better!" Are you interested in computer graphics and design elements? Can you operate a still or video camera, a tape recorder, or a slide projector? Would you like to write a script? If the answer to any of these questions is "yes," then you are ready to use your talents to create a fun and useful audiovisual project.

Skill Builders

1 The production of movies, television, and videos involves the creation of storyboards. Storyboards, which read like comic strips, illustrate the key sections of specific scenes. The frames present what the camera would see during that particular scene. Create a storyboard for a scene from one of your favorite movies, videos, television shows, or for a story you've written.

2 Listen to a favorite song and develop a video for it. What images come to mind as you hear the song? At what speed do these images change? What colors and angles are present in the shots? Keeping these questions in mind, create your own music video, or a slide or illustration presentation set to music.

3 Public service announcements (PSAs) are "advertisements" that address social issues like dropping out of school or substance abuse. Look at how the PSAs are presented in each of the different media. Using video or audio equipment, create your own PSA on the topic of your choice and share it in your community.

4 "Foley artists" add sounds to movies and television programs to make them more realistic. Watch a movie or TV show and see if you can catch the foley artist in a slip-up. For example, is the actor sneaking around silently in leather boots and jacket? Is the knock at the door too soon or too late? Then tape a scene from a favorite show with the sound off and try to add your own soundtrack. Substitute your interpretation of the sound while showing the video with the original sound turned off. You may need some friends to help out with the dialogue!

5 Explore the world of sound recording. Learn how a tape recorder, microphone, or mixing board work. Tape-record, with permission, an "event" in your family: a group sing, a birthday party, or even a dinner-time discussion. Replay the tape and find five things that you would need to address in future taping: Are the people speaking clearly enough? Are background noises getting in the way? etc. Tape another "event" (perhaps your Girl Scout meeting) and address these issues.

Technology

1 Find out how a video, movie, or a still camera works. Explore the uses of the different settings, speeds, exposures, and special effects offered.

2 Find out how slide projectors work. Observe two different slide presentations at your school, library, local museum, or theater. Without changing the topic, how would you change the presentations to make them more interactive and interesting? Or give a slide presentation to a group.

3 Digital technology is revolutionizing the audiovisual field. Find out how slides and projections are created and used in

presentation software like Power-point, Harvard Graphics, or Aldus Persuasion. What equipment is needed to create a presentation using these software packages? How are computers used to create multimedia presentations? Watch a computer store "demo" presentation of multimedia software.

4 Visit a camera store and learn more about one of the new digital cameras. Then explore the uses of digitized pictures. Look at how photos are used on Web pages and other online resources, how they are used on CD-ROM, why the publishing companies need them, or how artists can change them to create new types of art.

5 Learn the difference between regular and DAT tapes. If possible, go to a music store and listen to both a traditional and a DAT tape, exploring the difference in the quality of sound between the two mediums. Or explore the quality of sound that's available via the Internet. Are music concerts as good online as they are in person? How is digital technology enhancing the quality of sound in online resources?

6 Visit a television studio. Take a tour and see how video, sound, and editing techniques are used to create TV shows. How different is the sound system from the one you have at home or school? How different is the TV camera from a video camera? Find out how film, text, and sound are edited. What other machines are used? If possible, observe the taping or producing of an entire show, focusing on what goes on "behind the camera." What happens prior to production? What work remains for post-production?

Service Projects

1 Create an audiovisual (AV) presentation to highlight the benefits of Girl Scouting. Make sure that you work with someone at your council to ensure the accuracy of the information. Use it to help your council recruit new volunteers, get funding, or encourage girls to join Girl Scouting.

2 Work with others in your community to record the history of your community. Find out what the town was like 30, 50, even 80 years ago by recording people who lived then. Use old maps and photos to illustrate your presentation. Don't forget to include background music.

3 Videotape an event in your community for people who cannot get there. For example, is your town honoring a notable resident, or staging an original dance or theatrical presentation? Make the tape available for viewing at your local or school library.

4 Volunteer to be a member of your school's AV team or squad.

5 Volunteer to create, maintain, or index an organization's photo or slide library.

Career Exploration

1 Talk with someone at a local camera or sound equipment store. Find out the requirements to be a camera or sound equipment salesperson. What training does the person get? What is the beginning pay? What career options could such a position lead to?

2 The work of many different inventors has contributed to the advanced technology presently available in the field of audiovisual production. Read a biography or watch a video about one individual whose invention had a resounding impact on the media and on society.

Read up on the invention this person created and imagine how it will change in the next 10–20 years.

3 Find out what kind of education and training is required to be a camera operator for film or television. Gather information about one person's experience in the field from magazines or books, or by going online.

4 Get online and chat with the Web manager of your favorite Web site. Find out what her education is, how she was trained for her job, how she uses multimedia in her site, and the concerns she has about the ability of others to copy things directly from the Web. What advice would she give someone starting out in this field?

5 Create a comic book or picture book to teach younger girls about careers in AV production. Use the skill of storyboarding to help you plan out your book. Make the characters realistic and positive role models for girls in your community.

And Beyond

FOR THE MEDIA-MINDED, TRY THESE related interest projects:

- Media Savvy
- Writing for Real
- Graphic Communications
- The Play's the Thing
- Do You Get the Message?

Or mix and match media by doing audiovisual activities in any other interest projects.

Graphic Communications

The newspapers, magazines, and books you read, the stamps you place on envelopes, even the words or logos on the pens and pencils you write with are products of the graphic communications industry. Everywhere you turn, you'll see visual and printed messages in the form of printed text, illustrations, and photographs. As you work on this interest project, visualize the messages you wish to share with your family, friends, and community.

Skill Builders

1 Look through a newspaper or magazine to find different examples of the following: an illustration, a photograph, an advertisement, a headline, and the text. Create your own newspaper or magazine pages.

2 Look at posters and fliers in your community. Analyze how designers use art, words, fonts, color, and "white space"—the area that contains neither art nor text. Design a poster or flier to be used as an announcement or invitation to an event, party, or family gathering. Share your creation with others.

3 Look at some food products in a store. What's printed on the packaging? What color is most dominant on the package? Sharpen your graphic designer's eye. What colors or typefaces are pleasing? Visit your local market and make a list of five product designs that you like and five that you don't. What do you or don't you like about them? Now, design your own "package" for a favorite food.

4 Learn a printmaking skill, such as silk-screen, linoleum cut, or woodcut. Create an original design and make at least three copies of it.

5 The logo or trademark of an organization can reflect the mission or purpose of the company. After looking at the logos of several organizations, create two of your own. How well do they reflect the products or services of the organizations you have selected.

6 Design your own greeting cards or note paper using a computer or your own photographs or artwork. Present the card to someone on a special occasion.

Technology

1 Find out how photos or artwork can be placed in magazines and on T-shirts and jigsaw puzzles. Talk with a professional photo finisher and ask her to explain the process. Share this information with two other girls.

2 Compare two to three computer graphics programs for use in desktop publishing. To accomplish this, read newspaper or magazine articles that rate or critique the programs; or compare the descriptions on the packages; or try your hand at the programs by asking for a "demo" at a computer store. Make a list of three skills each program will let you do, three hardware requirements of each program, the cost of each program, and one strength and one weakness of each program. Make a recommendation to your council as to what type of graphics software it should purchase.

3 Computers have revolutionized the publishing field. Find out what role they play in writing, designing, illustrating, and printing books, magazines, and newspapers.

4 Find out how the technology in print shops, newspapers, or publishing companies has changed in the last 25 years.

5 Calligraphy is the ancient art of fine handwriting or penmanship. View an exhibit of calligraphy or look at samples of it in library books. Learn some lettering styles by taking a calligraphy class or studying an instruction manual. This may require that you use special pens. You can buy a beginner's set or individual pens. Or you may experiment with felt-tip pens of different thicknesses. Write a letter, invitation, quote, or your favorite poem in calligraphy. Identify at least four different styles of calligraphy.

6 Web page design is a growing field. Look at five different Web sites and identify three specific design components used at each site. Then visit GSUSA's Web sites (http://www.gsusa.org.) and compare design differences when the audience changes from adults to girls.

Service Projects

1 Volunteer to work on your school newspaper or yearbook, your Girl Scout newsletter, or the bulletin or newsletter of another organization.

2 Volunteer to help younger girls record their experiences in Girl Scouting. You can help them illustrate a story, document a special event, or create a graphic depiction of the year.

3 Help your Girl Scout council or another troop or group design a Web page. Work with adults and other girls to decide on the critical issues of design (color, format, type font, photos, illustrations, etc.). Collect materials that will need to be incorporated in the site. If possible, digitize the artwork and text for them.

4 Design a letterhead for yourself or for your troop or group. Use the letterhead for invitations, requests for information, and thank-you notes.

5 Help your council or other girls advertise a special event. It can be an overnight training, special sports program, or even the Girl Scout cookie sale. Design fliers, posters, or brochures, etc., using three to five elements of design, such as composition and choice of colors.

Career Exploration

1 Talk with a lawyer who specializes in copyright law. Find out about copyright rules, regulations, violations, and infringement. What issues are affecting copyright protections today?

2 Job-shadow or interview a designer or commercial artist. Why did she go into this field? What was her training or education? What is a typical day like? Write up your experience and submit it to your school or community newspaper. Or create a graphic representation (picture book, coloring book, cartoon) of the profession for younger girls.

3 Arrange to visit a local college or technical school that offers a program in graphics or communications. Talk to advisers or students in that program. What are the benefits of attending such a program? What are the drawbacks? What other options are there for people interested in this field? Ask if you can sit in on one of the classes.

4 The field of Web management/ designing is relatively new. Get online and locate two or three Web sites that interest you. E-mail two or three questions to the Web manager or page designer about her field, her training, and her future plans.

5 Get a part-time job in a printing shop or photocopy shop. You'll have an opportunity to examine and compare lots of different graphic designs.

And Beyond

IF GRAPHIC COMMUNICATIONS SPEAKS to you, try these related interest projects:

- Photography
- Paper Works
- Artistic Crafts
- Visual Arts
- From A to V: Audiovisual Production
- Media Savvy
- Public Relations
- Computers in Everyday Life
- Desktop Publishing
- Do You Get the Message?

The Lure of Language

Language is the foundation of communication and opens the door for self-expression. The languages by which people communicate vary the world over. Whether spoken, written, or signaled, language links us all.

Skill Builders

1 People who share common activities or professions, like sports, computer science, medicine, and the law often use specialized languages. Tennis, for example, uses terms like *ace*, *love*, and *foot fault*. Some terms may not be known to people outside these fields. Create a small dictionary of specialized words for a particular activity or profession and share them with your troop or group.

2 Using an unabridged dictionary or encyclopedic dictionary, identify five of your favorite words and trace their origins. Ask your local librarian or language teacher for assistance.

3 Become familiar with American Sign Language. Learn a few simple phrases. Are there other ways deaf or hearing-impaired people communicate? If possible, attend a production for the deaf or hearing-impaired.

4 Even people who speak the same language pronounce some words differently, have different accents, and use different dialects and colloquialisms: for example, "pop" for "soda." If you know someone from another region of the country, compare some familiar expressions. Have an English teacher recommend some American authors who successfully used dialects in their writing. Read at least two books or stories by one of these authors. Write down five of your favorite expressions from each book.

Technology

1 Go online and surf the Internet. Identify at least five new words being used in cyberspace. Or learn how people from different countries can communicate with each other via computers and satellites. See if you can find an international pen pal.

2 Using your computer, listen to a foreign language CD and learn some phrases.

3 Explore how technology is used to help facilitate communication for people with disabilities: for example, software that uses voice controls for people who are unable to use a keyboard. Arrange to visit a school, clinic, or training site for people who have disabilities and speak to professionals about the latest advances in communications technology.

4 Use visual aids in a presentation to trace the progression of writing implements from stone tablets to recyclable paper, quill pens to laptops.

Service Projects

1 Learn the alphabet in American Sign Language and teach it to a group of younger girls.

2 Experience the power of words. Develop a letter-writing project to cheer someone: a child in the hospital, someone in the armed services, or a resident of a nursing home.

3 If you are fluent in a second language, try producing a one-act play in that language for children or senior citizens who understand that language.

4 If you speak and write a second language, offer your translation services to someone.

5 Thoughts and feelings can be conveyed not only through spoken or written words but through body language as well. Using a series of movement exercises, work with younger girls and show them ways that feelings and moods can be expressed nonverbally.

Career Exploration

1 A variety of disciplines follow the structure and development of languages. Contact a nearby college or university to investigate courses offered in the study of language.

2 Interview one or two teachers of English as a second language (ESL). Ask them about their backgrounds, required training, and greatest challenges. Or investigate a local program offered by a library or literacy group that helps immigrants learn English.

3 Public speaking skills can translate to careers as trainers, translators, or broadcast journalists. Invite someone with experience in one of these areas to discuss the skills she uses on her job. For example, you might invite a journalist to show your troop or group the basics of "air copy" and then draft several stories for a radio show with her help. You could even perform the show before a live audience with one person serving as a translator for the hearing-impaired or for a second language.

4 A speech therapist or speech pathologist works with individuals who have speech impairments (for example, stuttering), speech articulation problems (the sounds of letters and words), or language-processing problems (something is at the tip of your tongue and you can't remember it).

Talk to a speech therapist or pathologist who works with children and, if possible, arrange to observe her in action. What props and activities does she use? Does she play speech games? What advice can she offer to a young person interested in this career?

And Beyond

FOCUS ON LISTENING TO LANGUAGE TO appreciate its rhythm and the power of words. See a play, listen to a speech, go to a lecture, or attend a poetry reading.

Practice speaking the language of the heart. Speak clearly and with sincerity. Say what you think and think before you speak.

You can really "travel" with your love of language. Try these related interest projects:

- Once Upon a Story
- Writing for Real
- Do You Get the Message?
- Public Relations
- Reading
- Travel

You'll need to know the technical language of computers when doing Exploring the Net and Computers in Everyday Life. Learn to use sailor's jargon in Smooth Sailing, and conduct a tuneful conversation in On a High Note. Whether you're On the Court or On the Playing Field, you'll want to use the correct terms of the sport you are playing. And pay attention to the written and spoken language in The Play's the Thing.

Media Savvy

What constitutes "news"? How do the news stories you see on television, in newspapers, or in magazines get there? The media surround people in the United States and often influence action and opinion. Take a look around and begin to think critically about the media as you do the activities in this interest project.

Skill Builders

1 Watch or listen to a variety of promotional ads ("promos") for television shows or movies. Compare three promos with the actual movie or telecast. Note how the upcoming stories are presented. When you watch the actual show, determine whether the presentation matches what you were led to expect from the promo. If not, why do you think there's a difference? Prepare a more accurate promo for a show you felt had a misleading promo.

2 Research a trend in today's society and prepare a 5–10 minute video presentation by taping portions of shows and commercials to illustrate the trend you have chosen. Show your video to your troop or group, or your family. Follow this with a discussion addressing concerns about this trend.

3 Look at a variety of ads, movies, or TV shows with characters who reflect the diversity of American society. Are the characters well portrayed, or are the writers relying on stereotypes? Analyze how screenwriters depict one type of character, such as teenage girls. Note how they are portrayed in at least four different shows or ads.

4 How do movies, videos, situation comedies, docudramas, infomercials, talk shows, and news shows differ from one another? Create a graphic way to illustrate the similarities and differences among them.

5 Make a collection of ads designed to appeal to teenage girls. Get samples of print ads and record or write brief notes on them for TV or radio. What kinds of products are marketed? Identify those ads that you find appealing or unappealing. Why?

Technology

1 Innovations in cameras have had a great impact on what is seen on TV, in movies, and in videos. Do one or more of the following:

■ View an actual video production and note the number, placement, and types of cameras used.

■ Make your own video, using cinematographic techniques.

■ View at least three different types of shows: for example, live sports event, a prime-time action show, or an infomercial. Compare camera techniques for each show.

2 With the advent of the Internet, the explosive growth of cable television stations, and other changes, how do you envision the future of television, radio, newspapers, and magazines? Pick two of these media and share your vision with your troop or group, or with friends.

3 Critique several popular computer games. Survey at least five friends to find out what games they like and why. Select a game that you would revise and describe how you would do it. Or design your own video game.

Service Projects

1 Hold a panel discussion that focuses on the effects of television violence on children. Invite teachers, psychologists, community leaders, and social workers to speak. Encourage audience participation.

2 How have music videos influenced television and movie production? Tape segments from a variety of shows to illustrate this influence. Present your findings to your troop or group, or to your family.

3 Organize a video and audio library for a school, hospital, or hospice. Or arrange a collection for children in need. Make sure the resources are appropriate, in usable condition, and labeled well.

4 Do a review of television programming that is on at the prime viewing time for young children: early morning, early evening, and weekend mornings. Compile a viewing guide with recommendations about the acceptability of the programs, and why. You might work with a parents' group like the PTA to make a guide available.

5 Develop a project that would help vision- or hearing-impaired individuals. For example, volunteer at your local TV station to be trained in using closed-captioned technology or assist in putting books on tape.

6 Create a safety video to be viewed by children. Choose a topic such as bicycle safety, staying at home alone, or first aid, and make sure information adheres to *Safety-Wise* standards.

Career Exploration

1 Look at the masthead of your favorite magazine or newspaper, and identify five different media careers to explore. Find out more about at least one of these careers by contacting a professional and interviewing her.

2 Arrange to observe a video shoot, photo shoot, edit session, or the studio taping of a television show. Note all the different jobs on the site involving, for example, lighting and sound, computer graphics, or film or print editing. Which of these fields look interesting? Find out more about the field and what is required for a career in it.

3 Volunteer to be a media critic for a local or school newspa-

per. Focus on movies and on TV and radio shows that target a teenage audience.

4 Become media savvy. Find out more about how the public relations and communications industries use television to get across their messages. Share this information with others.

And Beyond

IF YOU LIKE LIFE BEHIND THE LENS, TRY these related interest projects:

- From A to V: Audiovisual Production
- Graphic Communications
- Photography

Also investigate:
- Public Relations
- Writing for Real
- Do You Get the Message?

Watch TV and films with a savvy eye. Use multimedia creatively when putting forth your messages. Invite experts to help you.

Once Upon a Story

Scene One: The Present
Main Character: You
Situation: You'd love to
write stories like the
ones you grew up with,
but where do you begin?
What can you write
about? How do writers
think up all that stuff?
In this interest project,
you'll have opportunities
to explore poetry, fiction
and nonfiction writing,
playwriting, and screen-
writing. Try several
activities to discover
and develop your talent.

Skill Builders

1 Read at least two novels or short story collections. Study the mechanics of plot and characterization and note the author's style. Keep a file or box of ideas, pictures, quotes, words, phrases, lyrics, or slogans you come across that you like. Add to it at least once a week for a month.

2 Write a science fiction story projecting what life would be like in the future. Create your own world with its own set of rules and unique characters. For example, imagine being on the planet Zan in the next galaxy during the year A.D. 3000. What conflicts would the main characters have to face there?

3 Write a historically based fiction story. To do so, you first have to learn about the time in history you plan to cover in your setting. Who were the famous people? What were the important events and politics of that time? What was daily life like for the average citizen? Most writers of historical fiction use real people and events to some degree in their stories, even though their plot is fictionalized.

4 If poetry is what you enjoy, learn three different poetic styles, and write at least three poems in any style you like: light verse, haiku, free verse, ballad, blank verse, sonnet, limerick. Identify instances of literary devices in your writing such as alliteration, assonance, consonance, simile, metaphor, personification.

5 Write a play. You can be serious or humorous, melodramatic or lighthearted. Formulate a premise or conflict on which to base the action of the play. What lesson will the main character learn? How will she learn it? What secondary characters will support or attack your main character? Remember, a play depends largely on dialogue, so write it carefully. Dialogue will direct the "rise and fall," the movement, of your play to conclusion. Or create a drama by adapting a children's story.

Technology

1 All writers have their favorite tools. Some like to write with pencils on legal pads, some prefer fountain pens and unlined journals, while others need a computer keyboard to compose and organize their thoughts. Try three or four different techniques. You might find that one type of writing works best in one medium, while another requires some other tool. Explain to someone what tools work best for you, and why.

2 There are lots of different writing, editing, and publishing software programs available for the professional and amateur writer. Look through catalogs, talk with both users and salespeople, and compare three different software programs. If possible, try out a couple of programs for yourself, by "demo-ing" them at a store or by running programs at school or at a friend's house. Which ones have the best editing options? Which would best fit your needs and budget?

3 Watch at least one TV show a night for a week, and take notes as you view any special video effects. For instance, how do the TV production people work with the TV scriptwriter to show a scene in a hospital emergency room or in a burning building? How could you find this out? In your club or troop or group, write the first scene of a TV program similar to one you studied.

4 Use a word processing program to write a fiction story. It may be on the topic of your choice. After you have completed the story, use computer clip art to illustrate your work.

Service Projects

1 Perform a play for an audience of your choice. The play can be an original play or a published play that you adapt to suit your needs. It can be performed for younger Girl Scouts, at a neighborhood gathering, or elsewhere.

2 Tutor a younger student in writing skills. Work with her or him once a week for at least a month. Help your student to write a book, complete with pictures, on a topic of special interest. It can be as short as eight pages.

3 Collect material about writing classes, workshops, or seminars in your community. Enlist the aid of your librarian, a teacher, or troop or group leader. Organize and share this information with at least three budding writers you know.

4 Write a humorous story, essay, or play based on a real-life experience. Think of some humorous incidents from your own life. Sometimes the use of exaggeration or something silly can make for humorous stories. Can you think back to a funny incident in your own life? Write it or tell it to a group of children in a hospital, day-care setting, etc.

Career Exploration

1 Attend a writer's conference or workshop.

2 Interview a writer. Talk about the full-time or part-time jobs she holds as well as the type of writing she does. How does she manage her time? What are the advantages and disadvantages of her work?

3 Find out from a writer about jobs in teaching, editing, or other related areas. Ask her how

these jobs can sharpen her writing skills or inspire story ideas.

4 Which jobs in publishing or entertainment employ strong writing skills? Consult any number of occupational handbooks in your library or review the resource list at the end of this book.

5 Watch or read interviews with fiction writers. What are their sources of inspiration? Strategies for staying motivated?

And Beyond

WORD LOVERS WILL BENEFIT FROM THESE related interest projects:

- The Performing Arts
- The Play's the Thing
- The Lure of Language
- Reading
- Writing for Real
- Public Relations

If technology and writing excite you, try From A to V: Audiovisual Production, Media Savvy, Desktop Publishing, or Graphic Communications.

One of the beauties of writing fiction is that you can write anytime or anyplace. You can write on your own or with a partner. Other people can keep you on track and motivated. Be prepared to rewrite a lot. Polish your prose until it sparkles!

Public Relations

f you've ever been spritzed with perfume by a glamorous department store model, or had your favorite book signed by its author at a special event, chances are a public relations (PR) professional arranged it all. These individuals aim to convince you that a particular product, client, or cause is worth your money, patronage, or support. In this interest project, learn more about the powers of persuasion in public relations.

Skill Builders

1 As they go about their work, PR professionals use a language all their own. See the chart on page 105. Test your knowledge of their jargon by correctly matching the terms on the left with the definitions on the right. If you need help, ask a teacher, librarian, or other knowledgeable person. (This Skill Builder may be useful to you in completing other activities.)

2 Create a press kit to publicize yourself! To find out what you should include in your kit, you can ask a public relations professional for help, request that several businesses or organizations send you sample press kits, or look in your library for books on public relations or communications.

3 Public relations professionals must be adept at writing for the printed page and spoken word. Try your hand at completing one of the following writing assignments:

■ A major food manufacturer hires you as a consultant to market its new line of low-calorie snacks. Write a sales pitch for supermarket managers to use to entice shoppers to buy a box of snacks.

■ The chief executive officer (CEO) at a large corporation asks you, the communications director, to prepare a speech for her to deliver to 200 of the company's largest shareholders. She has bad news — profits have dropped, and, as a result, so have the shareholders' earnings. What would you have the CEO say?

4 Public relations professionals must be able to relate to a wide range of people. Imagine being a spokesperson for your favorite cause. What would you say to your audience to get their support for your cause? Choose two of the following people or groups and role-play your pitches with some friends: a community association, your peers, a potential funder, or someone who opposes what you stand for.

Ask one or two of your friends to observe the role-play and critique your presentation. Try the role-plays again, this time incorporating the suggestions of your friends on how to improve your sales pitch.

Technology

1 "Image is everything," or so say those in the business of creating it. Host a roundtable discussion with your classmates, friends, or troop or group members about how the media influences consumer behavior. Select a moderator to facilitate the discussion, using the following questions as a guide:

■ To what extent does image influence your decision to buy a product or support a cause? Would your loyalty to a product or brand name be compromised if you found out something unfavorable about its manufacturer?

■ Brainstorm a list of celebrities for whom "bad" PR has been good. Do you think certain types of celebrities are more inclined to benefit from an unflattering public image? If so, which types and why?

2 What technology do PR professionals use to do their jobs? Find out how they track marketing trends.

3 PR professionals often use polls to find out how their target audience feels about a certain issue. Take a poll of your friends and neighbors to gauge their opinions about a locally controversial issue. Share the results of the poll—without revealing names—in a community newsletter or paper.

4 Every organization has a particular image it would like to project to the public. List five adjectives GSUSA and local councils use to convey messages about Girl Scouting. How do you think the public sees Girl Scouting? What misconceptions do you think people have about Girl Scouts? How would you go about clearing up those misconceptions if you were a Girl Scout public relations director? Create a poster, TV show, or radio ad or jingle to correct that misconception.

TERM	DEFINITION
___ A. Public Service Announcement (PSA)	(1) A set of characteristics that describes a target market (i.e., race, age, sex, occupation, etc.).
___ B. Press Release	(2) A magazine, journal, or newsletter that highlights current trends in a particular field or industry.
___ C. Premium, Freebie, or Giveaway	(3) A packet containing press releases, photos, timetables, and other pertinent information about a product, service, or event.
___ D. Target Market	(4) A series of activities designed to bring attention to a product, cause, or special event.
___ E. Demographics	(5) A short television or radio message created to promote a cause or point of view.
___ F. PR Campaign	(6) A one- to three-page "report" to the media about a product, service, or event.
___ G. Trade Publication	(7) The group to whom a promotion is directed.
___ H. Press Kit or Media Kit	(8) Special, no-cost Items to help consumers remember a particular product or project.

leader which organizations serve the needs of people with particular disabilities. Volunteer to work on a PR committee.

Career Exploration

1 Interview public relations professionals in three different sectors, from businesses to non-profit organizations. Compare their approaches to publicizing their products and/or clients.

2 Public relations professionals have many different titles. Call several organizations, businesses, or colleges to find out what some of them are. Ask for the name and title of the person who handles public relations for that organization. Interview at least two of these professionals. Present your information to your troop or group.

3 What public relations skills would be useful to someone looking for a job? With a partner, create a job search plan and help each other find summer employment or an internship. Help each other develop skills in listening, interviewing, and résumé writing.

4 Events planners organize events that are important for fund-raising and PR. Think about a special event you attended recently (a play or concert, for example). What tasks did the events planner or PR professional handle well to make the event a success?

Service Projects

1 Volunteer to help a local organization develop a PR campaign to publicize its services to the community or to youth.

2 Write an article about the recent activities and projects of your Girl Scout troop or group. Try to have the article published in your school or community newspaper.

3 Does your community plan to sponsor an event, such as a play, recital, or food drive? Spread the word by designing fliers, posters, or invitations. Or come up with other creative ways to publicize the event.

4 Find out from your school counselor or troop or group

And Beyond

PRACTICE WRITING AND SPEAKING SKILLS whenever you can, whether selling school raffle tickets or publicizing a Girl Scout event.

Join a music or drama club or perform in public. An accomplished PR person can't afford to be shy!

Further your flair for public relations with these related interest projects:

- Writing for Real
- Do You Get the Message?
- Cookies and Dough
- Leadership
- Desktop Publishing
- Media Savvy
- Your Own Business
- The Performing Arts

Reading

A journey through time and space—that's what reading can be. Whether you delve into the antics of a fictional character, the biographical account of an individual, or the events in an historical essay, reading will broaden your horizons and transport you to places far and beyond. This interest project reveals the pleasure that reading offers, so read on and turn the pages.

Skill Builders

1 Consider the following categories of books and decide which type is your favorite: fiction, nonfiction, poetry, or drama.
Prepare a creative project that illustrates why this is your favorite type of book. The project may be in the form of an oral presentation, illustrated panels, an "interview" with one of the characters, etc.

2 Learn the meaning of these literary terms, and find examples of at least five of them in your reading: allegory, alliteration, antagonist, blank verse, climax, conflict, comic relief, figurative language, flashback, gothic novel, haiku, irony, interior monologue, parable, proverb, protagonist, poetic justice, setting.

3 Have you ever read a book in which the author seems to be "reading your mind"? Think of a challenge or new event in your life, such as moving to a new home and changing schools, or trouble with a sibling. Find a book in the library that addresses a challenge like yours and read it. Analyze how the book's characters cope with their situations. What can you learn from them? Discuss the role of literature in enhancing life's experiences with your family or troop or group members.

4 Dramatize a scene from a book for an audience. For a biography, you might enact an event from the person's life. For a novel or short story, select a scene that provides good action or dialogue among the characters. Provide background information so that the audience understands the scene.

5 Form a book club with three or more people; family members can be included. All members should read the same work and come together at arranged times to share ideas and to exchange viewpoints.

6 Read literature from a culture different from your own. Compare the treatment of a common theme, such as coming-of-age for girls, by an American author with its treatment by a foreign author.

7 Read two or three magazines on any subject: for example, computers, gourmet cooking, car repair, fitness, current events, sports, fashion, nature, or health. Read each issue for at least two months, and discuss the most interesting articles with the girls in your troop or group.

Technology

1 What is electronic publishing? How does a manuscript become a book? How are illustrations, maps, and graphs inserted?

2 Use the Internet to hold a discussion about a book or author. Or use the Internet to help you conduct research for a term paper or project.

3 Write a synopsis of a book or book review and place it on the Internet. Call for correspondence from those interested in your topic.

4 Try out some educational computer games in a computer store. On your computer, create a word game that relates to a book of your choice. Ask others to play your game and get some feedback.

5 Visit a bookstore or exhibit that features old or rare books. Find out from the shop owner, curator, or librarian how old books and manuscripts are preserved.

6 How were books made in the past? Trace the development of bookmaking. You might start with illuminated manuscripts in the late Middle Ages. If you can, visit exhibits of rare books in museums or rare book shops in your community.

Service Projects

1 Entertain young hospital patients with fairy tales. You and your friends can dress up as, or make puppets of, characters from favorite childhood stories and fairy tales, such as: "Cinderella," "The Three Pigs," and "Little Red Riding Hood." Involve your young audience in the action during or after a presentation of the story. For instance, have them play with or make puppets.

2 Donate some time each week to read to someone with impaired vision. For example, you could help a senior citizen read her mail or newspaper. Find out if there is a local organization for the blind, and how you can volunteer your services through its programs.

3 Offer to read or be a storyteller in a Head Start or in an after-school program. Read dramatically, using different voices for each character, or read to focus on a skill area, such as building a better vocabulary.

4 Hold a book drive to collect used books. Advertise the dates of the drive and recruit volunteers, including adults, to help you. Redistribute the books either through a library or an organization of your choice.

5 Design bookmarks or bookplates for holiday gifts. Give them to hospital patients along with a new book. During National Book Week or Library Week, give them to younger Girl Scouts or students.

6 Work with an organization that provides tapes to people with visual impairments or learning disabilities. Tape one or two stories.

7 Organize a paperback book exchange in your community or school.

8 Find out more about local or national literacy efforts through your Girl Scout council. Become involved in a project or event in your area, such as serving as a reading tutor once a week to a younger student.

Career Exploration

1 Hold an event such as an author's tea, at which the author reads from her book and discusses it with the audience. Ask well-prepared questions about the author's writing process. Ask for any advice she can give to young people who like to write.

2 What are the roles of a book reviewer and a literary critic? Read at least three or four book reviews or essays of literary criticism. What skills and training do you think reviewers and critics need to have? Write one short book review.

3 Read a book that was made into a movie and then see the movie, or vice versa. What do you think the pros and cons would be for a writer who wrote the book *and* the screenplay? Which would you rather write? Why?

4 Learn about the career of a literary agent. What services do literary agents provide writers? How do they earn an income?

5 Investigate careers in library science. How has this field changed since computerized technology has replaced the card catalog system in many libraries? What work is handled at the Library of Congress? Try to shadow a librarian for several hours.

And Beyond

ARRANGE THE BOOKS IN YOUR HOME library. Select some to give away.

Create a book or magazine exchange with friends. Encourage young children to read by reading with them.

If you've enjoyed Reading and you love all things literary, try these related interest projects:

- Writing for Real
- Once Upon a Story
- The Play's the Thing

Continue to journey to other times and places in:

- Women Through Time
- Digging Through the Past
- Heritage Hunt
- Folk Arts
- Travel

A World of Understanding

Throughout the world, you will find a multitude of cultures, languages, foods, architectural styles, behaviors, and values. The result of all these differences is a fascinating but often conflict-filled world. Working on this interest project will help you gain an understanding and appreciation of your own and other people's cultures—the first step in creating a world of understanding.

Skill Builders

1 Plan what you would do to host a visitor from a different country. If you had the ability to transport this visitor across the continent, what would you show her that was typically "American" and that reflects the multiethnic nature of American society. Make a one-week itinerary for this visitor.

2 Choose a section of your town or your neighborhood and create a "walking tour." Identify the cultures of the people who originally settled in this area. Did any famous people live in the buildings? How has the area changed over the years? If possible, take a small group on the tour you have created.

3 Explore the cultural identity of your own family by tracing your roots. Create a family tree that includes at least your great-grandparents. Make sure to include any things of significance like changes in names or religions. You might want to create a chart that you can distribute to other members of your family, who will surely find your project interesting.

4 The Nobel Peace Prize has been awarded to military leaders and pacifists, diplomats and philosophers, and activists who protect human rights. If you were on the committee today, who might you nominate? Learn about at least one woman who has received the Nobel Peace Prize by reading or viewing an account of her actions.

5 Participate in mediation training, a peer leadership program, or a guided role-play focusing on a world peace topic. What are the connections you can make about mediation between individuals and mediation between groups or nations?

6 Plan and stage an event where each girl wears clothing representing a different country or ethnic group. Discuss what that clothing tells you about being female in that country or group. What roles and behaviors are expected of these women? How does their clothing affect everyday activities? Find out what clothing young women in a country of your choice wear to school, on the job, and on special holidays.

7 Pick a country and plan a trip to it. Use at least three different resources to find out about the country—such as the public library, a consulate, a travel agent, someone from that country, or special organizations that promote international understanding—and plan your travel itinerary.

Technology

1 Watch three different news shows that highlight world news. For each show, make a list of the topics and countries that are highlighted. What types of stories are selected to air about other countries? Discuss with a group of peers or your family what you have observed. How powerful a force has television become in shaping our impressions of and opinions about other countries? Can you list positive and negative aspects of this technology?

2 Search the Internet for information on a country or culture that intrigues you.

3 Learn about how computers are used for translating languages, especially those that use a different alphabet or characters.

4 Find out how technology is used to identify important information about artifacts from different cultures.

5 Use a shortwave or ham radio to listen to broadcasts from abroad. Perhaps you can find someone in your neighborhood with this type of equipment.

Service Projects

1 Work with an organization, religious group, or program that helps immigrants new to the United States settle into their communities.

2 Plan a dining experience with a foreign exchange student. Research restaurants in your community that serve ethnic foods or foods your guest would like to try. At dinner, compare how this food is the same as or different from the cuisine in the student's home country.

3 Volunteer with a local group or organization that teaches English as a second language or tutor someone in your school whose native language is not English. Exchange cultural information with that person.

4 Help organize an exhibit or celebration for World Peace Day, November 17.

5 Find out about a religion that differs from your own. You might choose to learn about the predominant religion of another country or about a religion in this country. If possible, visit a house of worship of this religion in your community and talk to someone of this faith. List adaptations you would make in living and eating habits if a person of this religion visited your home.

Career Exploration

1 Interview someone who has gone on an international wider opportunity through Girl Scouts or has been an exchange student in a foreign country. Find out what she did to prepare for the experience and what she learned about other cultures. Ask her if the experience she had while abroad will help her to choose a career.

2 Compare business customs in at least three different countries. If possible, interview someone who conducts business abroad and find out what customs they observe as a part of their job. How do these customs differ from those practiced in the United States?

3 Girl Scouting is dedicated to serving *all* girls. As a result, there are many people who do a variety of different jobs to ensure

that diversity flourishes. Explore the careers within Girl Scouting, especially those that include responsibilities that deal with pluralism and diversity, cultural awareness, and international affairs.

4 Learn about the Peace Corps. Find out what kinds of qualifications are needed to join. If possible, speak with someone who has been a Peace Corps volunteer or arrange for a Peace Corps speaker to address your troop or group or students at your school.

5 Investigate at least two colleges that offer degrees in political science, international affairs, or other fields that might lead to a position in the diplomatic corps.

And Beyond

READ THE POEM "DIVERSITY" ON PAGE 6 of *A Resource Book for Senior Girl Scouts*. What message does the poem convey about diversity? Do you have similar or different feelings?

If A World of Understanding has opened up whole new worlds to you, continue your explorations with these related interest projects:

- Travel
- The Lure of Language
- Creative Cooking
- Reading
- Games for Life
- Folk Arts
- Invitation to the Dance

Writing for Real

n your local newspaper, a headline reads: **"TEN-YEAR-OLD BOY SURVIVES CROCO-DILE-INFESTED SWAMP FOR FIVE DAYS."** The hair-raising details that follow are more exciting than the wildest fantasy tale. In this interest project, you'll explore journalism and nonfiction writing.

Authors of nonfiction write "for real." They write articles and books based on facts and observations. If you'd like to try your pen, tape, or laptop at writing for real, step right up!

Skill Builders

1 Write a short article on a subject that really interests you, such as horses, sports, or environmental science.

■ First, explore the subject you are writing about. Use the library, explore the Internet, and talk to people who have knowledge related to your subject. Take notes and jot down your ideas based on your research.

■ Develop an outline. Make certain you have the main story points you want to cover. Then add the secondary items that will increase interest in your story.

■ Designate a time and place to write. Establish a routine and stick to it. The discipline of a set schedule may help your writing the way physical exercise helps your body.

■ When you have written a first draft, have someone read it. Are her comments and suggestions helpful? If so, use them.

2 Write a short biography of a famous person or someone you admire. Begin by preparing a time line of outstanding incidents and events in the person's life. Include colorful anecdotes as well as important facts about your subject's achievements.

3 Read the poems in either the *Cadette Girl Scout Handbook* or *A Resource Book for Senior Girl Scouts*. Share your favorite poems with two or three others. Talk about how the poems convey important messages. Try your hand at writing a poem about a *real* event.

4 Be a "publishing entrepreneur"! Working with a small group, plan and create a literary newsletter or magazine. Include video and book reviews, essays such as "If Kids Ran Their Schools," cartoons, editorials, sports articles, and photographs and drawings. Assign a team to help fund and distribute your newsletter or magazine.

5 Cover an interesting event in your school. For example, if you choose to follow a class election for your school newspaper, you need to interview the candidates. Discuss with them their political platforms and the results they hope to achieve if elected to office.

6 Be a medical or scientific journalist! Select a medical or scientific topic to write about. Look into the new AIDS research, environmental links to illness, the return of rabies in some areas of the country, medical breakthroughs, etc. Read several articles in scientific or medical journals as preparation for writing.

7 Write for the government! Did you know that the U.S. government is the largest single employer of writers in this country? Many of these writing occupations are related to the boom in technology and telecommunications. You can look up government writing jobs in the *Dictionary of Occupational Titles* (DOT) at your library. Make a reference list of all the government organizations that use writers.

Technology

1 Compile a list of three to five online resources for writers. Include discussion or news groups, Web pages, and e-mail mailing lists. You might want to evaluate or rate each site as well, using a number scale or adjectives, such as fair, good, etc. Summarize the content of each resource to share with friends who like to write.

2 Use a tape recorder or camcorder to prepare a local news story.

3 Start a nonfiction book discussion group at school, in your troop or group, or online in a "chat group." You can participate in chat groups on computers at school or at your library. Check with a librarian or information specialist on key words to use to access other reading lists. Or attend a demonstration on using the Internet at your library or elsewhere.

4 Modern technology brings real-life stories to a world audience almost instantly. Select one "major" news story and follow it for at least one week. Note any changes in the facts or details that unfold as more information becomes available. What do you think the impact is on an unfolding news event to have reporters and state-of-the-art telecommunications equipment on the scene?

Service Projects

1 Help young people or adults who are not native English speakers to write or read in English.

2 Be an oral historian! Conduct interviews with senior citizens. Ask them where they were born, and what life was like when they were young, including favorite childhood games and songs. Use a tape recorder to record the interviews.

3 Can you write for real in many languages? Develop a multilingual news bureau for your school. Try to find students or writers who can write in diverse languages, such as Spanish, Japanese, Korean, French, Ukrainian. Suggest to your school administration that these translations be made available to parents or guardians who speak these languages.

4 Be a photojournalist! Hold an exhibition in your community on a special theme such as "Children Who Are Winners." Write a short text explaining the photos and display them at an opening.

Career Exploration

1 Find out in person or through interviews how journalists meet their daily, weekly, or monthly deadlines. What topics are newsworthy? What kinds of deadlines would you want as a journalist? Would you prefer longer "lead time" to write nonfiction articles, or the "rush" of daily newspaper deadlines?

2 Arrange to visit people at work in two of the following careers: data entry, desktop publishing, graphics design, book or magazine publishing, advertising, or newspaper reporting. Shadow them for a day to learn about the responsibilities and realities of these positions.

3 Through your school, arrange an internship that will give you real on-the-job writing experience. Note the tasks you enjoyed the most and the least on the job.

4 Reflect on ordinary life situations that can become the basis for hilarious stories. Turn a funny incident from your life into a news item or a cartoon for your school newspaper. Read the work of several cartoonists and analyze the topics they choose to address.

And Beyond

FIND WAYS TO MAKE WRITING FOR REAL A really exciting part of your life, whether you are starting your own business or reporting for your school paper. Arrange to share your prose with others, and be open to constructive criticism. And try these related interest projects:

- Photography
- Do You Get the Message?
- Media Savvy
- Desktop Publishing
- Exploring the Net
- The Lure of Language
- Once Upon a Story

The Arts
and
History

Architecture and Environmental Design

Stop reading for a moment and look around. Chances are you are sheltered overhead by a roof supported by surrounding walls. Most likely, an architect decided on the shape of the structure and the materials to be used. Architects design the buildings in which we live, work, learn, and play. They shape space and, therefore, indirectly shape the experiences we have inside those spaces. Try this interest project to find out more about creating buildings and designing space.

Skill Builders

1 Find out about the types of drawings architects make. Select a room or space and draw it architecturally, showing all the details, such as windows, stairways, closets, etc.

2 Freehand drawing translates mental images into pictures. Create three drawings of architectural spaces—a building from the outside, the interior of a room, and a view of the exterior as seen from the inside of a building. You may use pencil, pen, or a colored medium. Consider why these three different perspectives would be important to an architect. Share your sketches with someone.

3 Architectural models are an important way to translate designs into three-dimensional form. They show others how a proposed building will look. Make a model of an existing structure or one of your own design. You may use materials from home such as cardboard, lumber, or wooden sticks, or you may want to use a commercially packaged model that you purchase in a store.

4 Study your neighborhood to determine the predominant architectural styles. Compare these styles with some common architectural styles found in other parts of the country. Look at magazines, books, paintings, or illustrations of architecture for help. Do these styles reflect an adaptation to environmental conditions, locally available building materials, or cultural or spiritual beliefs?

Technology

1 Because of scientific advances in construction materials, some homes and buildings now have features that are technological marvels. Windows, for example, can turn from crystal clear to frosted with the flick of a switch. Explore three innovations that are currently being tested in the construction of buildings. Next, make a list of the benefits (lower cost, superior strength, etc.) and the drawbacks (higher cost, negative environmental impact, etc.) of each item.

2 In architecture, there is a growing concern about how construction practices affect the indoor air quality of buildings and impact upon the environment. Many products used in the construction of homes and office buildings may emit toxic gases for years, or may be obtained by means that are destructive to the land or produce toxic waste. Go to the library or call your local association of architects to find out how architects are using materials and designs to make buildings "environmentally friendly." Which materials would you use to design your own home if you were an architect?

3 Find out about computer drafting or drawing programs. Design something using one of these programs.

4 Design and build a small structure such as a birdhouse. Make sure your design has a real purpose, and monitor how it is used.

5 Landscape architects design outdoor areas—from plantings around office buildings and homes, to ski areas and golf courses. Investigate the technology that has become available in the last 10 years to facilitate the work of landscape architects.

Service Projects

1 The purpose of an environmental impact statement is to determine the effect a construction project will have on the environment *before* anything is built. You can determine the real impact a recent local construction project has had in your community by analyzing changes it has caused in three of the following:

■ Pedestrian or car traffic.

■ Noise or pollution levels.

■ Public transportation usage.

■ Available affordable housing.

■ Number or diversity of plants and animals.

■ Frequency of flooding.

■ Energy demands.

Make sure you record your observations over a period of two to four weeks. How would you improve the design of the project? Share your findings with your troop, group, friends, or family.

2 Identify a home repair or renovation that your family or a neighbor needs. Draw the existing conditions, then design a solution in a series of architectural drawings or sketches.

3 Take a group of younger girls on an exploration of some public spaces, such as parks and playgrounds, in their neighborhood. Help them translate their ideas for redesigning one of these sites with a crayon or pencil sketch.

4 Architects take many things into consideration when they plan their designs, including accessibility for people with disabilities. Since the passage of the Americans with Disabilities Act (ADA) in 1990, all new construction must meet certain accessibility requirements. Find out if you can do an accessibility study for a campsite or program area in your council. Or study the accessibility of your school or a public place. Chapter 2 of the Girl Scout publication *Focus on Ability: Serving Girls with Special Needs* will give you guidelines on how to conduct an accessibility study. Share your results and recommendations for better accessibility with site directors.

Career Exploration

1 Often, a portfolio is a requirement for admission to a school, for getting a job, or for entering a competition. Assemble a portfolio of your creative work thus far in your life. You may use photographs or other reproductions instead of the actual objects, which may be too large or fragile. You can include items such as a clay pot, a song, a drawing, a rug, or a piece of clothing that you made. Both the final result and the studies, sketches, and thoughts during the design process are worthy of documenting. Start your portfolio with your completed interest project products.

2 What is a typical day in the life of an architect, urban planner, or environmental designer? Arrange to visit the office of such a professional, or job-shadow her.

Make notes and drawings about the experience in a journal.

3 Select an architect to profile: for example, Frank Lloyd Wright, Louis Kahn, Le Corbusier, Eileen Gray, Alvar Aalto, or Mies Van der Rohe. Prepare a presentation for your troop or group on her or his work and life. Use photographs or other visuals to show the architect's work.

4 Interview an urban planner or environmental designer. If possible, arrange for one of them to visit a troop or group meeting. What advice might they offer to young people interested in these fields? What course of study would they recommend? Find out about their areas of specialization. For example, some planners work in waste management (garbage) and recycling. An environmental designer might work with a landscape architect or a parks department on improving or conserving a park or wildlife reserve. Ask them about specific tasks they do while on a project, as well as about the skills and training they bring to their jobs.

And Beyond

TO HELP WITH YOUR DRAWING, STUDY prints or postcards of favorite gardens, landscapes, and architectural specimens.

If architecture and environmental design intrigue you, build upon your skills with these related interest projects:

■ Build a Better Future

■ Visual Arts

■ Family Living

■ Folk Arts

■ Planet Power

■ Home Improvement

■ Photography

■ Travel

■ Math, Maps, and More

Artistic Crafts

Do you get satisfaction from working with your hands and being able to say, "I made it myself"? If so, you may also enjoy experimenting with different kinds of crafts. They can provide an outlet for your creativity. Whether you prefer to work alone or with others, you will find in this interest project many kinds of crafts to choose from to pique your interest!

Skill Builders

1 Choose your medium. You will probably want to experiment with several types of crafts before you find one that you really enjoy. Choose from among the following crafts: leather work, macramé, crocheting, quilting, decoupage, candle making, metalwork, stained glass design, pottery, ceramics, printmaking, woodcarving, woodworking, jewelry making, floral design, basket weaving, or clothing design. When you have made a choice, do the following steps:

■ Become familiar with the craft. Be able to explain the process and describe the tools needed and where you would find them.

■ Make a scrapbook with pictures, articles, and samples of this craft.

■ Develop at least three different designs; complete one of them.

2 Clay is a medium that offers many possibilities for expression. From bead making to pottery, you will find a variety of possibilities for using clay creatively. Traditionally, clay work has involved firing (baking) in a kiln. Today, there are many types of clay that can be baked in a regular oven or air-dried. Learn about hand building, or learn to throw clay on a potter's wheel. Make one finished piece.

3 Make your own woodcarving. Or try your hand at building something with wood—for example, a birdhouse.

4 Find out some of the places available in your community for crafts instruction: for example, community centers or craft stores. Compare the cost of each course and find out if anyone would be willing to teach your troop or group.

Technology

1 Choose three of the following crafts and find out about three tools used in each:

■ Candle making.

■ Stained glass.

■ Woodcarving.

■ Leather working.

■ Pottery making.

Consult artisans, crafts catalogs, and salespersons to determine the benefits and drawbacks of working with these crafts. Some factors to consider are the cost and availability of materials, and the size of the work space and special equipment you would need. Prepare a demonstration of what you learn and share it with your troop or group.

2 The Internet has sites for crafts organizations, companies, and individuals from all over the world. It is also a place where

many crafters exchange ideas and offer suggestions. Develop your own site or join a group site to exchange information about crafts with others your age.

3 Stenciling is popular in many countries. In America, it was used in colonial times to decorate walls, floors, furniture, and every-day objects. Find out the ways in which modern technology has changed how stencils are made and used. Experiment with stenciling on paper or cloth and then try a more advanced project, such as stenciling the back of a chair.

4 Visit a woodworker's shop. Ask for a demonstration of such tools as a jigsaw, a plane, a router, and a finishing sander. Find out what safety precautions must be taken when using these tools.

Service Projects

1 Teach a simple craft to younger girls, making sure that the skills needed are appropri-ate to the age group.

2 Make several craft items that you can donate to a nursing home, children's center, or other organization.

3 Contact local craft stores, schools, and community cen-ters to find out about courses, workshops, or seminars. Put this information in a newsletter, flier, or brochure and distribute it to others.

4 Work with your Girl Scout troop or group to develop your own how-to craft manual. Give copies to your council, local library, or community center.

Career Exploration

1 Interview someone in your community who earns part or all of her living through her craft. Find out how she got started, what she has learned, some typical aspects of her work, and what advice she would offer to someone just starting out. Or visit a crafts show, exhibit, or sale, and do the following:

■ Find out how many different media are represented in the show or fair.

■ After looking at the objects on display, decide which ones you like best and why. Be able to explain the reasons for your pref-erence to your troop or group.

■ Talk to one of the artists to find out:

■ How she got started.

■ What kind of training was required.

■ Whether she has other work that she does in addition to her craft.

■ What are the pitfalls and satisfactions of the artist/craftsperson.

2 There are many career options related to crafts besides being an artisan. These include crafts shop owner, crafts wholesaler, crafts show manager, and designer of crafts displays. Choose a crafts-related career and find out how you would pursue it.

3 When planning to sell your crafts, it is important to know your market. Interview a crafts store owner or show manager to find out the trends in crafts and craft design in the past 10 years. What does she predict for the next decade? What are the consequences of not knowing the trends in the crafts market? How can a craftsper-son keep up with these trends?

4 Occupational therapists help people with illnesses or dis-abilities improve their coordination and fine-motor skills. They also design devices to help improve daily living skills. Ask an occupa-tional therapist to explain or demonstrate how crafts activities might be used in her job.

And Beyond

IF YOU'VE HAD FUN CREATING WITH ARTISTIC Crafts, try these related interest projects:

■ Visual Arts
■ Fashion Design
■ Home Improvement
■ Graphic Communications
■ Paper Works
■ Textile Arts
■ Photography
■ Why in the World?
■ Exploring the Net
■ Dollars and Sense
■ Public Relations
■ Your Own Business

Collecting

Mention collecting as a hobby and only images of coins and stamps may come to mind. But people collect all kinds of objects: baseball cards, comic books, stuffed animals, crystals—the list is endless. If you're intrigued by the idea of starting a collection of your own or building on an existing collection, carry on.

Skill Builders

1 Start a collection. Use your current interests as a starting point or, if you already have a collection going, add to it. Find at least five items that are of interest. If you love a particular sport, for example, you might collect the caps, posters, or pennants of your favorite teams.

2 Find a way to use or display your collection. Colored beads or shells, for example, could be laid out artistically or made into beautiful jewelry. Postcards can be arranged to make a colorful collage. You could photograph your collection. Describe your collection to a group of younger girls. Or display your project at your school or at a troop or group meeting.

3 Read catalogs, magazines, and books on collecting to expand your knowledge. Visit stores, garage sales, street fairs, and collectors' conventions in your area.

4 Search through closets at home or your attic for interesting objects. Decide on a theme and put together a display showcasing your wares.

5 What do you do if your collection has grown too large? Why not donate all or part of it to a museum, library, school, or community center? Photograph and list all the items. Write a brief description of each item.

6 Begin a collection of Girl Scout memorabilia: for example, pins, badges, guides, uniforms, and photographs. Did you know that the U.S. Postal Service has issued three Girl Scout commemorative stamps? See if you can find them. You may also want to write to GSUSA, and obtain information about the National Historic Preservation Center.

Technology

1 Some collections must be stored under special conditions. In order to preserve early Girl Scout documents, for example, the archivist at the Girl Scouts' National Historic Preservation Center must keep them in a specially designed, temperature-controlled room. Does your collection need special treatment? Develop a storage system to properly preserve your collection.

2 Some collections start by accident. You find a fascinating stone on a camping trip and later learn that it is a rare mineral. On your next outing you keep an eye out for other finds. Although many archaeologists have made major discoveries in much the same way, they now have new technology to assist them. Find out how computers, satellites, magnetic imaging, and sound waves are helping the modern "Indiana Joans."

3 Find out some ways objects are dated: for example, carbon-dating for fossil remains. Experts must sift through different types of clues—it's like trying to solve a mystery. What is needed to date your collectibles?

4 Find out the methods used to detect forgeries, fakes, or imitations of valuable items.

3 Offer to help your local council catalog and preserve Girl Scout artifacts.

4 Volunteer your services at a local museum, historical society, or other center that has a collection. Find out how the collections are built and maintained.

5 Start a collectors' club for younger girls. Show them your collection and take them to exhibits in museums or elsewhere, if possible. Help them as a group to begin a collection.

find out how she goes about acquiring artwork.

4 Libraries must continually add to their collections of books. Interview a librarian to find out how she decides on which books to add to a collection. How does she keep track of all the books in the collection? How are valuable books and manuscripts preserved?

Service Projects

1 Organize a flea market for your troop or group. This could be a money-earning project. You can sell items collected and donated by you and your fellow troop members.

2 Some of the things accumulated over the years may benefit someone else. Clothes that no longer fit could go to a homeless shelter, old magazines to a library, and outgrown games and toys to children in a hospital. Take an inventory of your possessions and arrange to give some of them away.

Career Exploration

1 With your friends, brainstorm a list of professions in which people collect things or care for collectibles. Select one profession to learn more about, or a professional to shadow.

2 Work with an antiques store owner or flea market dealer for several hours. Ask her what makes something an antique and how the value of antique furniture, jewelry, artwork, and other items is appraised. Find out about her educational background and area of expertise.

3 Curators arrange art exhibits for museums. Arrange to meet with or interview a curator to

And Beyond

ADD TO YOUR COLLECTION OF SKILLS by learning more about these related interest projects:

- Women Through Time
- It's About Time
- Digging Through the Past
- Folk Arts
- Museum Discovery
- Home Improvement
- Just Jewelry
- Fashion Design

Fashion Design

C *lothes play a number of roles, some more obvious than others. Of course, your clothes keep you warm and protect you from the elements, but did you know they also reveal aspects of your personality and your mood? Complete this interest project to gain an appreciation of how you can express yourself through clothes and how your design ideas can be brought into the "material" world.*

Skill Builders

1 Create a fashion design for a specific population such as pregnant women, fire or police professionals, or people with physical disabilities. Be creative in your designs and try to address the special needs of the people in these groups.

2 Learn to knit or crochet a garment. Ask experts for help choosing materials or interpreting patterns or instructions. Your home economics or art teacher might be a good resource.

3 Ask someone how to create a pattern for a specific wardrobe item, or adapt one that you purchase from a store. Create the garment from the pattern.

4 Color is one of the most important aspects of fashion design. Not everyone looks good in every color. The colors you wear need to be suited to your skin, hair, and eye coloring, and even personality. With friends, collect pieces of fabrics about 20" x 40" in some pure basic colors—red, yellow, blue, purple, green, orange—and in black, white, and brown. Try to get some lighter, subdued tones of these colors as well: for example, pink, blue-green, beige, and gray. Have the group vote on which piece looks best on each person. Afterward, discuss why you think certain colors look best on some people. How will this knowledge affect your choice of clothing? Keep your own color chart to refer to when designing for yourself.

5 Fashion is a personal choice, but most importantly, fashion should fit the wearer. Knowing your measurements will enable you to adapt or create flattering clothes designs. Find out about proportions by making a chart that includes the following measurements: length from neck to waist; neck circumference; arm circumference and length; and measurement of bust, waist, hips, thighs, legs. Use these measurements to analyze your figure type to purchase clothing and select patterns with the proper designation of Junior, Petite, Misses, Woman, or Half Size.

6 Follow fashion trends by reading fashion magazines and trade journals. (Your local library may have copies of these publications.) Evaluate which trends have become established and which are really "fads." Predict your own fashion trends for next season.

7 Design clothing for a special occasion, such as a bridesmaid's gown for a wedding. You might want to collaborate with a seamstress or dressmaker.

Technology

1 Choose three synthetic fibers. Find out how they are made and what their special properties are. With this information, decide what types of clothes or accessories you would make out of each fiber.

2 Go to a computer store and review the types of software available to professionals in the fashion design industry. Ask the salespeople to explain the merits of the various packages.

3 Find out how technology has made a difference in fashion design and manufacturing. If possible, use design software to create a pattern or a new fashion design for a shirt, dress, pair of pants, or other wardrobe component.

4 Manufacturing sometimes causes pollutants to be released into the environment. Create a list of at least five ways in which clothing manufacturers can operate with the lowest impact on the natural environment.

Service Projects

1 Rummage through your closets and drawers for items—gloves, hats, sweaters, scarves, etc.—that are in good condition, but that you don't use anymore. Use felt, beads, yarn, thread, sequins, or fabric paint to add decorative touches to each item. Then donate them to a community clothes drive.

2 Host a fashion show for and by youngsters. Use decorations and music to liven up the event.

3 Teach a group of younger children a skill such as knitting, crocheting, or sewing. Have the group create an entire garment using a chosen technique.

4 Volunteer at a local theater or school to assist with costume design. Learn what you can about technical aspects of design while expressing your creativity.

Career Exploration

1 Participate in an organized job-shadowing experience. Choose a job such as fashion designer, costume designer, fashion consultant, fashion editor, or marketing merchandising director.

2 Go to a retail store in your area. Develop a list of potential careers simply by browsing. Compare your list to a list of careers in retail sales in the *Dictionary of Occupational Titles*, available at the library.

3 Create the résumé of a fictitious person who works in the fashion industry. You might want to imagine what you will be doing in 10 years and base your

résumé on this projection. This activity has no right or wrong answers. See pages 101–103 in *A Resource Book for Senior Girl Scouts* for guidelines on preparing a résumé.

4 Find out how unions have changed the conditions of clothing manufacturing in the United States. Look at the child labor laws for the nation and for your state. Discuss with two others the effects of these laws and agreements.

5 Get a part-time job in a retail store.

And Beyond

ENHANCE YOUR ARTISTIC AND FASHION flair with these related interest projects:

- From Fitness to Fashion
- Home Improvement
- It's About Time
- Women Through Time
- Artistic Crafts
- Visual Arts
- Folk Arts
- Just Jewelry
- Paper Works
- Textile Arts

Folk Arts

Folk arts and folk tales have existed throughout time in all cultures. Folk tales are stories that illustrate natural phenomena. Folk arts reflect the stories, myths, and symbols of a culture and are expressed in objects such as cooking utensils, textiles, and toys. Folk songs and dances reveal the mysteries of nature and the complexities of culture. Exploring the many facets of folk arts helps us understand and appreciate cultures around the world.

Skill Builders

1 Read several folk tales from different countries. Determine how the climate and geography of the area play key roles in the story. Look for characters that personify elements of nature. What impact do these characters have on the lives of the other characters? Create a presentation of the folk tale for younger Girl Scouts, and lead a discussion about it afterward.

2 Learn how to hook a rug by reading books that offer instruction on the subject or by taking a course. Obtain the supplies and tools you will need. Look at pictures in books or visit a museum that displays rugs from different cultures, for example, Persian or Navajo rugs. Design a rug. Describe the fibers you would use or get actual samples.

3 Develop papier-mâché masks to represent mythological characters from different parts of the world. Use these masks in a performance for younger children, such as a play or puppet show, or display them in a folk history or folk arts show.

4 Write your own fairy tale based on a particular culture, or rewrite an old favorite. Put the heroes through tests of strength and character. What struggles do they overcome? What rewards do they reap? Read at least three or four famous fairy tales, such as those by the Brothers Grimm or Hans Christian Andersen, for inspiration.

5 Design beadwork or other ornamental jewelry. The tools and materials you use are key. For starters, you will have to select a suitable thread. A standard necklace is 18–20 inches, and a choker is 14–16 inches. Silk, cotton, or nylon threads will accommodate most beads. Experiment with making different kinds of knots on the ends of several threads. Try stringing beads of different weights and choosing beads of various styles and from different cultures. What other materials will you need? Put together a list and purchase what you can. Perhaps share the cost with friends. Once you've tested and mastered the materials, you can focus on design. Look at pictures of distinct styles, such as African or Venetian beads.

6 Make an object in the folk arts tradition that requires a painting technique. For example, work on a box, a certificate, or a piece of furniture.

Technology

1 Make a quilt from start to finish. It could be small enough for a baby carriage or large enough for your bed. Choose a design pattern from one of the many fine fashion design programs now available via computer.

2 Find at least two computer programs that can be used to design folk art. Use a design on fabrics or articles of clothing. What method do you use to transfer the design to the fabric?

3 Find out about the technology of music and sound recording. Interview two professional musicians, music archivists, or recording engineers. How are old records or tapes preserved? Solo or with partners, sing and record on tape your favorite folk music.

4 Interview one or more people who are attempting to preserve antique examples of folk art for museums, for profit, or for their own personal pleasure. Look over a collection and discuss with your troop or group members the appeal of each piece and the techniques necessary to care for and preserve such art.

Service Projects

1 Put on a folk arts festival in your community. Invite neighbors, friends, art students, and professional artists or crafts people to set up booths with crafts to view or do in a variety of areas: for example, macramé, hooked rugs, woven baskets, beadwork, batik, quilting, decorative wooden objects, painted furniture, pottery, tinware, and carved soapstone.

2 Hold a storytelling hour at a local library or school. Read a selection of folk tales. Be dramatic! Use props such as slides, puppets, or sound effects. Leave time for discussion.

3 Make a collection to show the varieties of design found in one type of folk art, such as baskets, religious symbols, woven cloth, or pottery. If you can obtain pieces made in other countries, you may even have an international collection. Use photographs or illustrations if you do not have examples of the actual objects.

4 Host a folk song session in your local park or other community area with your troop or group, a friend, or neighborhood center. Invite people to share and sing folk songs together. Distribute the song lyrics.

5 Teach or demonstrate folk dances at a senior citizens' center.

Career Exploration

1 Shadow a professional in the folk arts field for one day. It could be an artist, a writer, an oral historian, a teacher, a musician, or an archivist at a museum. Take notes on what she does and the skills needed in her field.

2 Read a biography or work of a famous anthropologist such as Ruth Benedict or Margaret Mead. Where and how did they work? Discuss the book in a book discussion group or troop meeting. Or read a work by a famous folklorist or writer of fairy tales.

3 Learning about the traditional customs, folk tales, dances, art forms, and legends of a culture is one of the tasks that cultural anthropologists engage in. Call a local college's department of anthropology for the name of a professor of anthropology to interview. Ask her about her fieldwork or academic research. What does she observe or look for?

4 Explore the art of collecting. There are many people who collect folk art objects. How do they store, preserve, and display their collectibles? Visit at least two museum exhibits of folklore and folk objects. Historical museums and universities, as well as art museums, house such collections.

5 Find out about careers in curating and art conservation from the education department of a major museum or the fine arts department of a college, through research online, or by talking to professional artists and craftspersons. If possible, observe a conservation project in progress.

And Beyond

FOR FUN, MAKE SOMETHING "FOLKSY" for your home, like a weather vane, stenciled wallpaper for your bedroom, or a decorative jewelry box.

Develop your interest in folk arts into an ongoing hobby. For additional information, read the section on hobbies in the *Cadette Girl Scout Handbook* or on the arts and music in *A Resource Book for Senior Girl Scouts*.

To further your appreciation of folk arts, try these related interest projects:

- Collecting
- Museum Discovery
- Visual Arts
- Artistic Crafts
- Women Through Time
- Reading
- Once Upon a Story

Heritage Hunt

Are you fascinated by other cultures or stories of your ancestors? Do you love history and research? Looking to the past can be like taking a journey to an ancestral land. It is a way of appreciating and honoring your roots.

Skill Builders

1 Imagine you are a historian. Your task is to create a family history chart—a family tree—for yourself or someone you know well. Start by recording the full name, maiden name (for women), and dates and places of birth, marriage, and death of each person listed on the chart. Go back as many generations as you can. Begin by interviewing family members and family friends, and recording what they tell you. Find information in birth, baptismal, marriage, or death certificates, the family Bible, etc. When you have finished, make copies of your work for interested family members and/or your local library, historical society, or genealogical society.

2 Develop an activity or project that brings families and friends together to celebrate their heritage and cultural diversity in a festive way. Encourage people to contribute and share something about themselves. People could bring prepared foods, music, artifacts, photos, etc.

3 Do two activities that young women of previous generations would have done as part of their everyday lives:

■ Bake bread and make butter.

■ Weave on a loom.

■ Gather natural fabric materials and dye them.

■ Forage wild edibles with a naturalist or other trained person, and then prepare and eat what you gather.

■ Plant an herb garden.

■ Chop and split wood, square or hew a beam, or refinish a piece of wooden furniture.

4 Make a collection of pictures of old buildings in your community or local area. Include single- and multiple-family dwellings, religious buildings, work sites, barns and silos, and outbuildings such as springhouses, milk houses, root cellars, or bake ovens. Choose one building and learn all you can about it—its architecture, its use, its former inhabitants.

5 Family traditions are often observed at special times in our lives such as birth, coming of age, marriage, or holidays. What family traditions do you observe? Find out which family traditions are no longer being observed. Are some of the family traditions observed differently now than in the past? Why? Select an upcoming family tradition that will be observed and see if you can coordinate or assist in the planning of the occasion. Or revive a tradition that was once observed but has since died out.

6 Search out information about your community's heritage.

Who were the first people to live in your community, town, city, or county? When did various waves of settlers arrive? When was the area incorporated? What have been the special events in its history (influential visitors, celebrations, buildings and memorials erected, highways completed, etc.)? Using the answers you have found, make a time chart or display to illustrate your community's lifeline.

Technology

1 Locate an old work site, such as a mill, factory, lumberyard, mining operation, blacksmith's shop, train depot, canal lock, wharf, fishery, farm, or ranch. Find out all you can about how the work was carried out at that particular site by looking through old newspaper accounts in your local library or, if possible, talking to former owners or employees or their descendants. Find out about safety factors and working conditions such as the hours worked or lighting and ventilation inside a factory.

2 Compare the way records such as passports, birth and wedding certificates, and driver's licenses are produced today with how they were produced 50 years ago.

3 Make comparisons between the way people live today and 100 years ago. List the appliances and other household items in your home today that did not exist 100 years ago. Beside each item write its historical counterpart: for example, refrigerator = ice box. Share with your group in a discussion or display.

4 How is computer technology useful in gathering historical and statistical information? What online services provide this? Put together a directory of resources and services available for historical research.

Service Projects

1 Ask your family or older members of the community to tell you stories of their lives or stories they have heard told in their families. Compile an oral (tape-recorded) history and/or a pictorial history of these stories and share it in some special way with family members and others, perhaps during an informal presentation at your local library.

2 Plan a project to increase community awareness and pride in your cultural heritage. Examples of such a project might be a neighborhood cookbook or song book, a block festival, or an exhibit at a fair or in a library or mall. Work with others in your community.

3 Volunteer a couple of hours a week for approximately one month in your local community at one of the following places: the historical preservation society, library, chamber of commerce, museum, archaeological society, bureau of vital statistics, city hall, archives, etc.

4 Identify several examples of literature that represent the cultural diversity in your community. Read selections to a group of younger Girl Scouts.

Career Exploration

1 Choose a woman of the past whom you admire or find especially interesting and learn all you can about her. She can be one of your ancestors. Find out about her family, friends, hobbies, and work. Using your research, write a biography or make a scrapbook that represents her life.

2 Create a collage that represents five or six careers that women in your community have. Highlight the careers that were not open to women 100 years ago, 50 years ago, and 25 years ago.

3 Identify the various careers that are a legacy in your family: for example, firefighters, police officers, doctors, lawyers, and teachers. Find out as much as you can about why family members chose their professions. Who had an impact on their decisions?

4 Contact your local historical society and ask about services provided to the community. What kinds of jobs are available? What education and training are required for these positions?

5 Find out about current adoption procedures in your state and how they have changed in the past three or four decades. Contact an adoption counselor, social worker, or other professionals in the field.

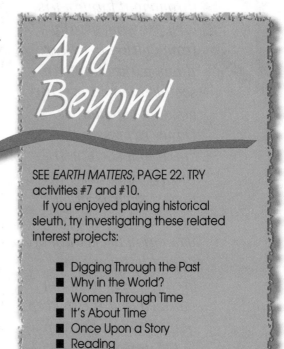

And Beyond

SEE *EARTH MATTERS*, PAGE 22. TRY activities #7 and #10.

If you enjoyed playing historical sleuth, try investigating these related interest projects:

■ Digging Through the Past
■ Why in the World?
■ Women Through Time
■ It's About Time
■ Once Upon a Story
■ Reading
■ Media Savvy
■ The Play's the Thing

Invitation to the Dance

Dance is a tradition throughout human history, varying greatly from culture to culture. It has played a role in social interaction, rituals, and ceremonies. Dance expresses the spirit of a society. It incorporates other art forms, such as music and art. Not only can you enjoy the beauty of dance, but you can greatly enjoy dancing yourself and it can keep you in shape. So, step up to the dance floor!

Skill Builders

1 Design or select a warm-up exercise or routine to prepare your body for participation in a dance activity. Include at least three exercises to stretch and strengthen the muscles and joints you will be using when dancing.

2 Learn five social dances, including three that were popular with your parents' or grandparents' generation. How are their dances similar to or different from those of your generation? Organize an intergenerational dance or a dance from another era: for example, a 1950's rock and roll dance.

3 Learn five folk dances. Such dances reflect how the cultural customs of many people who emigrated to the United States became part of the traditions of regions of this country. Find out about the cultural roots of at least two dances you have learned. Teach at least two of these dances to others and explain something about their history and background.

4 Learn three dances from three countries in different parts of the world. How do these dances express the life, customs, and values of the cultures they represent? Teach or demonstrate at least one of the dances to a group. If possible, wear the traditional costume for this dance: for example, the colorful dramatic costume of the flamenco dancer from Spain, a Chinese dragon costume, etc.

5 Explore dance concepts, such as movement and rhythm, that are involved in one of the following sports: ice skating, ice dancing, gymnastics, or rhythmic gymnastics. Learn and execute at least three moves in one of these sports that involve dance movements.

6 Choreograph your own dance routine. Select the music and style of dance you will use. Perform your dance for someone else.

Technology

1 Find out about the resources and materials that go into a dance performance. Find out more about dance shoes and dance surfaces and whether they have changed over the years.

2 Find out more about the role of modern medicine in helping dancers perform at their peak. What kinds of injuries are common to dancers and what precautions do they take to prevent them?

3 Find out from a fashion designer or a salesperson in a ballet store about the best and latest dance wear. Share her recommendations or knowledge with someone else.

4 Did you know that there's a language you can learn in which you can record your choreography? It's called Labanotation. Interview a dancer or choreographer who can show and explain Labanotation to you. Or research this system at a local or performing arts library.

5 Arrange a behind-the-scenes day with a dancer or dance troupe. Find out about the preparation required for a performance.

4 Working with experts in the field, create a *rhythmic cymetrics* program, which incorporates movements adapted for people with disabilities. You could supply bulbs with handgrips, adapt ribbon or rope movements for people in wheelchairs, and underinflate the balls so arthritic hands can use them.

5 Volunteer with an organization that brings dance classes and performances to disadvantaged youth. If no such organization exists in your area, start a class through your Girl Scout council, place of worship, or in an after-school program.

ask a professional in the world of dance for answers to any questions you might have. You may want to create an illustrated booklet on dance and dance-related careers.

4 All dancers work with music. Explore careers in composing, recording, and performing music expressly for dance.

5 Brainstorm six to eight careers or jobs related to dance, such as physical and dance therapists, teachers, chiropractors, and choreographers. Make a picture book, cartoon, play, video, or game that would expose young girls to these careers.

Service Projects

1 Share your love for dance with the young and "young at heart." Demonstrate a dance or dances you have learned and explain something about them in a presentation to younger children or senior citizens.

2 With your troop or group or others, put on a folk, square, or country dance. This could be a Girl Scout councilwide event. Invite the community to join in the fun. Learn the dances, select the music and the space, designate a caller if needed, and step lively!

3 Teach Daisy or Brownie Girl Scouts the elements of dance by having them choreograph movements and steps to a song or a series of sounds. For example, have Daisy Girl Scouts pretend to be jungle animals while playing original or taped music that incorporates jungle sounds!

Career Exploration

1 Are you serious about choreography? How do you develop all those steps to a dance? What sort of training do you need? Go to the library or, better yet, go to the source: a choreographer or dancer who can share with you directly. Or contact a college or conservatory to get information about dance courses.

2 Read or find out about three famous professional dancers, past or present. Learn about their background and their training. What special challenges did they have to overcome on their road to success? What other ways are they involved in the arts; for instance, do they appear on television or in the theater?

3 See a dance performance and read the program to find out the job titles of people involved in the production. Can you imagine for yourself a career as a choreographer? Artistic director? Are you unfamiliar with some of these titles? Do research at the library or

And Beyond

FOR MORE INFORMATION ON MEETING the demands of dance through physical fitness and exercise, review the booklet *Developing Health and Fitness: Be Your Best!*, especially chapter 2.

Go to the ballet and other dance performances whenever you can!

Whether you're a "twinkle toes" or "two left feet" type, dance your way to joy and express yourself through movement by doing these related interest projects:

- On a High Note
- Fashion Design
- From Fitness to Fashion
- The Performing Arts
- The Play's the Thing
- Once Upon a Story
- Sports for Life
- From Stress to Success
- Women's Health

Just Jewelry

tems of jewelry are some of the oldest artifacts that have been found among the ruins of ancient civilizations. In addition to being merely decorative, jewelry has, through the centuries, signified status and wealth, expressed religious beliefs, and held symbolic meaning. Try your hand at creative expression by designing and making jewelry for yourself or others. Be imaginative and innovative. For example, you can recycle old items into jewelry.

Skill Builders

1 **Activity #1 is required before doing other activities in this section.** Renderings or sketches of jewelry are usually the important first step in developing an item of jewelry. Look through magazines, browse through stores, and notice what others are wearing. Collect a sampling of photos, ads, or sketches of jewelry styles that appeal to you. Then draw an item of jewelry that you would like to have. Draw the piece of jewelry to size and indicate the materials that you will use. Use this rendering to execute a design in one of the other Skill Builders activities.

2 Put together a toolbox of equipment that you will need to make jewelry. Consult a craft book or talk with someone who works with jewelry to learn about some handy tools. Here are some items to consider: super glue, white glue, polymer clay, assorted wire, paper, pencil, polishing cloth, sandpaper, assorted threads and cording, paints, varnish, wire cutters, small needle-nose pliers, metal snips, and jewelry findings. (See activity #3.) Your kit will vary depending on the kind of designs you will do.

3 Learn about jewelry findings. These are jewelry elements such as the clasps that close a bracelet or necklace, the settings for stones, and the backs for pins or earrings. Investigate the different types of findings that you have on your own jewelry. Expand your search to include what friends may have or what you see on items sold in stores. Find at least five different types of clasps used on bracelets or necklaces. Investigate where you can buy simple, inexpensive findings or select a type (for example, a necklace catch) that you can make. If you do not have ready access to materials, think of at least two ways to improvise a finding with items in your home. Make an item of jewelry using findings.

4 Although jewelry is often crafted from precious metals and gems, it can also be made from inexpensive or easy-to-obtain materials. Use your imagination to craft a piece of jewelry from a commonly found item. Here is a list of common items that can be crafted into jewelry: buttons, safety pins, shells, nuts, paper clips, wood pieces, heavy foil, paper, stones, sea glass, pottery fragments, fabric pieces, bottle caps, bolts, or washers. You can decorate materials with paints, nail polish, pens and markers, glitter, or sequins. Mix and match materials.

5 Beads have been one of the most common jewelry elements from past to present. Assemble a collection of beads. Recycle beads from old necklaces and bracelets into new designs. Make your own beads using a variety of materials such as polymer clay that can be baked in a home oven, papier-mâché, self-hardening clay, or some other material that can be formed into beads (for example, coiled wire). Make a necklace or bracelet from your bead collection.

6 Make a pin or pendant using a combination of at least three different materials. For example, you can embroider a design and sew some small beads or buttons on a piece of heavy fabric, or paint and glue seashells on a piece of wood.

7 Do some research on the history of jewelry. Track a particular type of jewelry or find out more about jewelry of a particular culture or period. Display what you have learned in an attractive way.

Technology

1 Professional jewelers use many tools and techniques to complete their work. Work with a jeweler or knowledgeable person on a piece of jewelry using one or more of the following techniques: soldering; mold making; forming metal by twisting, hammering, pulling, and heating; casting metal; stone setting; metal engraving.

2 Learn about metals commonly used in jewelry making: copper, brass, silver, gold, and platinum. Compare the characteristics of each and determine why a particular metal might be used over another. Some terms to consider are: ore, malleability, tensile strength, melting point, oxidation, tarnish, and hardness. Select an item of jewelry that you own or would like to own and find out more about its metal composition.

3 The colorful stones and gems used in jewelry are minerals and crystals selected for their looks, color, luster, ability to reflect or refract light, hardness, and durability. Arrange a collection of 20 or more stones, minerals, gems, or crystals that are used in jewelry making. Select photographs, illustrations, or, when possible, actual samples of the minerals. Become familiar with the properties of the stones, minerals, etc. Don't just consider the gems that may be familiar. Chalcedony, jade, hematite, lapis lazuli, opal, car-

nelian, onyx, jasper, agate, chrysoprase, turquoise, malachite, and beryl are all used in jewelry.

4 Find out about technological advances that have occurred in jewelry composition and manufacture. Synthetic stones, new metal alloys, and electroforming have resulted in items of jewelry not possible years ago. Find examples of jewelry created through these new techniques and compare them with pieces done years ago.

Service Projects

1 Contribute an item of jewelry you have made for a troop money-earning project or some similar worthy cause.

2 Help a group of younger girls with a jewelry craft project. Design your own activity or consult with a leader on the type of project that would work with the group.

3 Help a group of younger Girl Scouts earn the Jeweler badge or the Art to Wear Try-It.

4 Many jewelers belong to craft guilds or art leagues. Find out if there is an association for artists or jewelers in your area. Contact it to find out more about how members help each other. Volunteer to help.

Career Exploration

1 Jewelry making can be as simple as one artisan crafting and selling her own work, or a huge business that involves industrial mining, or large retail operations.

Identify 10 or more careers related to jewelry making. Learn about a career that interests you.

2 Start a business selling jewelry you have made. Create a display and determine what your pieces should cost. Do not forget to factor in the time it takes to make each piece, as well as the cost of materials.

3 Find out about schools that offer courses in jewelry crafting and related fields. Write and get a course catalog that outlines the different classes available. Keep this for future reference.

4 Interview a professional jeweler. Develop a short profile of the training and experience that led to her current job. Find out what are the most rewarding aspects of the work as well as the negative aspects, if any.

And Beyond

VISIT JEWELRY STORES AND MUSEUMS TO view gem collections and craft exhibits.

If you love designing and making things with your hands, try these related interest projects:

- Fashion Design
- Visual Arts
- Textile Arts
- Paper Works
- Artistic Crafts
- Folk Arts

Also try Collecting and Women Through Time. For career moves, Your Own Business, Public Relations, and Dollars and Sense are valuable!

Museum Discovery

Museums offer visitors unparalleled opportunities to become absorbed in the past, to ponder the present, and to envision the future. Whether you are walking through a model of a human heart in a science museum or watching a re-enactment of a scene from colonial America at a historical site, museums can be magical and intriguing places. Discover something new about an old favorite, or explore online a new museum anywhere in the world.

Skill Builders

1 Visit a museum of your choice. Take in the exhibits on your own. Then, if possible, arrange for a "behind-the-scenes" tour. Determine how the museum is meeting its mission or objectives by asking your guide questions and by observing how others use the museum. Discuss with others what you like most about this museum, and how you might change it to appeal to or meet the needs of different age groups, cultures, or people with disabilities.

2 Develop a mini-exhibit for your Girl Scout council on Girl Scout history. You will need to research, organize, catalog, exhibit, and learn how to care for the display items.

3 Design your own museum! Choose a theme, determine your objectives, plan exhibits and activities, and diagram one or more of the exhibit spaces. Select a theme from the list below or come up with one of your own:

- Children.

- Film and broadcasting.

- History.

- Natural history.

- Science and technology.

- Automobiles.

- Fashion.

- Art.

- Women's history.

- Living museums such as zoos, aquariums, or botanical gardens.

4 Visit or learn about the exhibits at Juliette Gordon Low Girl Scout National Center in Savannah, Georgia, or GSUSA's National Historic Preservation Center. If possible, visit a historical exhibit at your council.

5 Build a model or draw a blueprint of a site, such as a medieval castle, a modern skyscraper, a sports arena, or a neighborhood. Describe your model in writing on an exhibit card.

Technology

1 Visit at least three American (including the Smithsonian) and three foreign museums online. Visit at least three virtual museums online, keep a log of what you see, and compare your experience to an actual trip. Develop an online tour for a family member or friend based on her interests.

2 Museums house priceless and irreplaceable collections of all kinds—from dinosaur bones to manuscripts from ancient times. Discover the high-tech security methods museums use to protect their collections from vandalism or theft.

3 If moon rocks were exposed to the air, they would rust. If medieval tapestries were placed in direct sunlight, they would fade. Find out about the special lighting, temperature, and humidity systems that museums use to exhibit rare and delicate objects.

4 Visit a local museum and check if it is accessible to people with disabilities. What technologies are used to aid people with disabilities to visit museums? After your visit, make a list of recommendations on how you would improve the facilities.

5 Find out how audiovisual materials such as videotapes, music cassettes, films, slides, and photographs are preserved.

Service Projects

1 Develop or facilitate an activity for younger Girl Scouts at a local museum. For example, you might arrange a sleepover at a historical site or a science museum.

2 Create a small exhibit on something you feel strongly about. Arrange to show or share this exhibit in your local Girl Scout council, house of worship, or school. Topics might include women in the arts, women's inventions, the history of your favorite music or dance, fashion, a conservation issue, or civil liberties.

3 Form a museum association for people your own age and explore ways to provide service to a local museum, library, historical society, nature museum, zoo, or botanical garden as aides, docents, or museum interpreters. Or participate in an existing volunteer program. Evaluate your training and experience.

4 Develop a directory of local and regional resources for your council or service unit, including museums, historical societies, archaeological sites, botanical gardens, zoos, arboretums, libraries, or exhibits. Make sure to include features (elevators, audio tours, Braille guides, etc.) that make each site accessible to a broad audience. Suggest how these places could provide educational experiences for Girl Scouts.

Career Exploration

1 Find out about three careers that are museum-based, such as conservator, exhibit preparer, curator, educator, librarian, graphic artist, researcher, public relations or communications staff, fund-raiser, or editor of a museum publication. Find out what educational preparation and training are required for these positions.

2 Identify two museum studies programs at colleges or universities. Find out if these programs might enable you to work in a specific kind of museum: for example, a museum devoted to art history, science education, American history, or zoology.

3 For one day, shadow a person with a museum-related career. If there is no museum in your area, check to see if there is a museum outreach program that comes to your community, a nature center, zoo, botanical garden, or other facility. Or shadow someone who contracts with a museum, such as an exhibit maker, storyteller, or artisan. What kinds of skills does the person practice on her job?

4 Learn about maintaining exhibits at living museums such as zoos, aquariums, and botanical gardens. Request a behind-the-scenes tour and ask questions about training and experience in this field.

5 Work as an intern or aide in a museum.

And Beyond

MAKE THE MARVELS THAT MUSEUMS display come alive with your own artistic efforts in these related interest projects:

- Artistic Crafts
- Visual Arts
- Folk Arts
- Home Improvement
- Architecture and Environmental Design

Explore other connections to museum life with these as well:

- Graphic Communications
- Public Relations
- Women Through Time
- It's About Time
- Collecting
- Heritage Hunt
- Digging Through the Past
- Inventions and Inquiry

On a High Note

Music is a universal language. Joyous or sad, lighthearted or somber, it often evokes a strong mood or feeling. Around the world and throughout the ages, music has played a key role in people's lives. In this interest project, enhance your singing, listening, composing, performing, and appreciation skills. You may even take the first steps toward a career in music.

Skill Builders

1 Take a poll in your class or Girl Scout troop or group of the most popular types of music. Plan a musical program that includes music from the top three or four musical categories. Present the program at a special assembly, to commemorate an event in your community, or as part of a Girl Scout program activity.

2 Karaoke singing has become very popular in many communities around the world. Karaoke machines make it possible for people to sing along with the instrumental music of popular songs. Many places offer this activity as entertainment. Arrange for a karaoke party for your Girl Scout troop or group. With enough practice, your group could put on a show.

3 Investigate the roles of music in your own and another culture. Is it a part of celebrations? What instruments are used? Compare the two cultures and create a visual and/or audio presentation. Share it with others.

4 Music has long been a part of religions around the world. Listen carefully to the music in your place of worship. Then visit other places of worship or discuss with friends from other faiths how their religious music is similar to or different from your own.

5 Opera has a very long and rich history. From your school or local library, borrow and listen to tapes of operas in three languages different from your own. Share one of your selections with your family, friends, or other Girl Scouts.

6 Attend at least three different types of musical performances or concerts. Keep a journal. Note, for example, the selection and quality of music played and its high points. Include sketches of the musicians and their instruments. Using your journal notes, put on your critic's cap, and write an article about one of the performances for a school or Girl Scout publication.

Technology

1 Computers are now a part of the world of music. Visit a music store to find out what instruments rely on computer technology to make sounds. If you can, use software for composing music electronically.

2 Visit a museum that displays musical instruments. What changes have taken place in the equipment? Create a scrapbook of pictures of old and new products in the musical field.

3 Go online and explore the various "music" rooms and information available on the World Wide Web. Chat on the Internet with other teens about your own musical interests and favorite artists.

4 Learn about advances in music-recording technology. Compare the same song recorded several decades ago with one recorded recently.

Service Projects

1 Put on a singing show at a local nursing home. You can invite the audience to sing along.

2 Most of you are probably familiar with the instruments in school bands and orchestras, but do you know about other instruments, including handmade ones, used around the world? Work with a group of younger girls to create their own world band, using both handmade and school-band instruments.

3 Background music is an integral part of films and other entertainment involving visual images. Listen to a few musical scores from movies or television shows. Then create your own original background music score. Tape the music or play it "live" to enhance a slide presentation, puppet show, story-telling, or poetry reading.

4 Learn song-leading techniques. Or help to create a Girl Scout chorus or band with a group of younger girls. Select

musical pieces appropriate to the age of the girls. Practice over the course of several weeks and put on a concert for the parents and friends of the girls.

Career Exploration

1 There are many careers in music that you can explore: for example, composer, lyricist, promoter, recording or performing artist, sound technician, and musicologist. Visit a music school or a music department at a college or university, an opera house or a theater, a music store or a recording studio. Talk to the people you meet and find out how they got started in the field of music.

2 Music can involve setting poetry to a tune. Get together with a partner and put your words to her music or vice versa. Or set to music one of the poems from either the *Cadette Girl Scout Handbook* or *A Resource Book for Senior Girl Scouts*.

3 Practice being a radio or live disc jockey and create a half-hour musical program. Select the music and write or record your introductions to the songs. Include commercials or public service announcements in your programming. You might want to put on your show for a local children's hospital or community center.

4 Learn some basic conducting techniques from your music teacher or another music professional, or by watching instructional videos. For practice, you can conduct while playing some of your favorite music. Shadow your school's band or orchestra leader to improve your conducting techniques.

5 It is said that music can have a healing effect on someone who is ill. What does a music therapist do? Arrange to shadow or interview someone in such a career. Ask her about the challenges and rewards of her profession.

6 Play the role of a music critic and review a performance for a school or local newspaper or for a class.

And Beyond

HOLD A MOVIE NIGHT WITH FRIENDS AND watch videos about famous musicians or hit musicals such as *The Sound of Music*. Related interest projects that can fan the musical flame include:

- The Performing Arts
- Invitation to the Dance
- Folk Arts
- Games for Life

Once Upon a Story and Media Savvy bring music to your other activities.

Paper Works

From crafts to computers, paper is an integral material in everyday life. Let your imagination run wild and envision all the uses for a blank piece of paper. Fold it up and it becomes a paper airplane floating through the air or a beautiful piece of origami adorning a bureau. Write on it and it becomes a vehicle for communication. Cut it up and it becomes confetti for celebrations. Try this interest project and you'll discover piles of activities for the paper in your life.

Skill Builders

1 Papermaking was developed in China centuries ago, as an alternative to writing on silk. You can make your own paper by following these directions. Get permission from a parent or guardian before starting this activity.

MATERIALS

Newsprint or other uncoated paper (to start, you will need two or three times as many sheets as you wish to make); large bowl; blender; water; flat rectangular pan, or vat; framed screen smaller than the dimensions of the pan; iron; gelatin (optional); cloth or towels.

PROCEDURE

■ Cut or tear paper into 1" square pieces.

■ Fill the blender about two-thirds full with water. Add about a cup of paper squares, and let soak at least 20 minutes. Blend on high for about 10 seconds, then pour into the vat. Repeat this process three or four times.

■ Take the screen, mesh side up, and in one continuous motion, lower it into the vat, until it is horizontal along the bottom. Then lift the screen slowly, just until it breaks the surface of the water. Gently shake it from side to side to even out the pulp. Continue to slowly lift it out of the water to drain.

■ Slowly peel the sheet of paper off the screen and set it aside to dry, on a towel, in a bathtub, or in a shower stall. Layer cloths between the sheets of paper. Press down lightly to force out as much water as possible (a board or pan may do this more evenly).

■ Set the iron to a low setting, and iron one sheet at a time until dry. You can also air-dry sheets by hanging them with clothespins on a drying rack overnight.

■ Seal the paper so that ink or watercolors will not bleed on it. Follow the directions for mixing the gelatin with water. While the gelatin is still watery, brush it on each sheet. Let dry.

2 Papier-mâché is popular because it is easy to learn and involves easy-to-find materials. All you need are strips of old newspaper and a bowl of starch or paste. Because the process is messy, cover your work surface and wear an apron. Make a mold for your project from a bowl, an inflated balloon, or a wire frame. Saturate your strips in the paste or starch. Then layer them until the surface is covered, and there is a thickness of 1/4" or more. Let your project dry, and determine if any areas need more layers for strength. When your project is completely dry, sand the rough edges, paint it, and then add a finish with a shellac or varnish.

3 Paper cutting is an art form practiced in many cultures. The finished products often resemble fine lace. Find out about the tools and expertise needed for this craft, and participate in a class or try a kit on your own.

4. Decoupage is a craft in which sections of paper are cut out and glued on to a surface, which is then decorated. Once the design is completed, the entire surface is coated with a protective layer of varnish or similar protectant. Create your own design with paper pieces glued onto a smooth, flat surface. Once the design has dried, use a small brush to "paint" a mixture of 1 part water to 2 parts white glue onto it.

5. Origami is the art of paper folding to create three-dimensional pieces. Refer to a book on the topic or work with someone who knows the art and complete at least three different designs.

Technology

1. Visit a paper plant or processing facility. Find out the types of equipment needed to make various products. How has technology improved the development of paper products? How does the process differ from your own paper-making process?

2. Archivists as well as artists, craftspersons, and photographers rely on different types of paper for storing and preserving their work. Find out how the following affect the longevity of paper products: acid-free stock, rag content, dyes, and finishes.

3. Use a computer program to design your own stationery, posters, greeting cards, or some other product. Compare the results from color printers with the results from black-and-white printers.

4. With the aid of a computer or hand-held design tools, develop a catalog of craft projects that you and your friends have made. Include illustrations, if possible. Develop a price list. Print and distribute your catalog to others.

Service Projects

1. Organize a paper drive to collect a supply of paper that can be used in craft projects by troops or groups or a local recreation program. Try to collect a variety of paper goods, including old newspapers, pieces of construction paper, wallpaper scraps, or wrapping paper.

2. Using a variety of paper products, learn the technique of bookmaking. Make a scrapbook or journal, and give it to a girl in your area who may be attending a wider opportunity. Ask her to record her trip and share it with others when she returns.

3. Help a group of Brownie or Junior Girl Scouts complete an art project that involves the use of paper.

4. Design and make a selection of greeting cards for a holiday or event. Donate these cards to a group that could use them: for example, Thinking Day cards that your council can send to those who have helped the council.

Career Exploration

1. Many people are involved in processing paper from its raw pulp state to the finished product in available stores. Find out about at least two of the following careers: chemist, wallpaper designer, paper wholesaler, gift shop owner, greeting card buyer, and printer.

2. Develop a money-making project for yourself or a group by designing invitations, greeting cards, gift tags, or gift wrap. Use a computer in the design and production of your

product, or try calligraphy, stenciling, or fabric bonding.

3. Visit a local paint store, home improvement center, or home furnishings department in a store to find out what types of wallpapers are available and how they might be used for different decorating purposes. Ask what decorating services the professionals in each place provide to their customers.

4. Develop a list of arts-related careers that use paper in some way. Find out the skill level and training needed for each, and rank them accordingly. Make a list of schools in your area that provide such training, and share this information with friends who may be considering such careers.

And Beyond

IF YOU'VE ENJOYED PLAYING WITH paper, try interest projects in other media, including:

- Visual Arts
- Photography
- Once Upon a Story
- Writing for Real
- The Play's the Thing
- Media Savvy
- From A to V: Audiovisual Production
- Just Jewelry
- Folk Arts
- Artistic Crafts
- Textile Arts

Put your ideas to constructive use on paper with:

- Architecture and Environmental Design
- Graphic Communications
- Desktop Publishing

The Performing Arts

*D*o you like to get up in front of people and act, sing, dance, or play an instrument? Do you like being in the limelight? Or are you shy about performing but wish that you could? Participating in the performing arts can help you sharpen your communication and team-building skills, handle stress better, be creative, or just add joy to your life!

Skill Builders

1 All performers need to warm up before they perform. Look through relevant magazines and books or talk with a music, dance, or theater teacher and ask her or him to show you three different warm-up exercises. One should be for large muscles (legs, arms, etc.), one for vocalization or breathing control (lungs, vocal cords), and a third should focus on small muscles (like the fingers, toes, or lips.). Practice each of these warm-up exercises at least five times over a two-week period.

2 Before there was television, millions of people listened to the radio. Actors read stories that were enhanced by sound effects and music. Practice reading a story aloud to a small group of your friends or to younger kids. Talk with a librarian, teacher, or coach, attend a reading given by an author, listen to a book on tape, or listen to a short story reading on a local radio station, to learn storytelling techniques. Then tell the story to your group.

3 Most performers experience stage fright at some point. Many learn how to transform that nervous energy into creative energy! Interview or read about two or three performers, and identify and write about three techniques they use to overcome stage fright. Try one out as a public speaker or performer.

4 Join your local choir, chorus, band, dance, or theater group. Rehearse and perform for others as a part of this group.

5 Give a solo performance! Sing, dance, act, or play a solo on an instrument in front of a group of people. Practice your solo for at least two weeks before your debut. Keep a journal. Ask yourself questions. For example, "Do you prefer performing solo or with a group? Why?" "Is the preparation for a solo different? In what way?"

Technology

1 More and more performers are incorporating technology into their presentations. Observe a production and list all the technology used in it. Include the obvious workings of technology (lights, sound, fog, etc.) and the less obvious (acoustical materials, turntables, etc.).

2 Visit a concert hall, auditorium, or theater with a friend or a group, and practice speaking without a microphone. Find out if there are audience sections where the sound carries better, and why.

3 Floors used for professional dance are specially constructed to protect dancers from injury and allow them to perform at their best. Talk with a dance instructor in your area (or via the Internet), or do library research and learn how the floors are built. What sorts of injuries do they or don't they prevent?

4 Find out about different ways of recording performances (for example, audiotapes and video-tapes). Watch two or three recorded performances and observe what techniques were used. What are the advantages/disadvantages of a recorded performance rather than one that is live? What is lost or gained?

5 Find out how technology has shaped music over the last 20 years. Talk with performers or knowledgeable people at music stores or through Web sites. Or read about audio and media technology in trade magazines. Or do library research on the history of the music industry.

Service Projects

1 Participate in a read-a-thon at your local library. Choose your selection carefully. Look for something interesting, entertaining, and age-appropriate.

2 Introduce younger Girl Scouts to the performing arts. They can either perform or be observers, but plan on taking at least two or three trips to concert halls, theaters, or arts centers.

3 Work with a troop or group to create a performance

based upon a "message," such as how to resolve conflicts or how to contribute to a community. Perform your play for an audience.

4 Sing, dance, play, or act at a local senior citizens' center. Your audience may have vision and/or hearing impairments that need to be considered in your presentation.

5 Participate in a performance that helps the community: a dedication of a park or new school, a summer parks program, a multicultural awareness day, as a clown for the children's ward of a hospital, etc.

Career Exploration

1 Read, watch, or listen to a biography/autobiography of a famous performer. How did she or he succeed? Could you succeed in the same manner now? Why or why not? What obstacles did she or he overcome?

2 How much do teachers and performers have in common? Talk with teachers at three different grade levels and find out if and how they use performance techniques throughout their day. For instance, do they use dramatic role-playing in history class?

3 What qualities does a good speaker need to be in command of an audience? Make a chart or poster that illustrates three to five skills, such as having a good ear or animated speech. Are these qualities you possess or would like to develop?

4 Interview two or three professional, amateur, or "behind the scenes" performers or workers, such as a production assistant, a stage manager, a lighting or costume designer, or a musician who plays in a stage orchestra. Ask about their training, the challenges they have encountered, the availability of work, and any advice they can give to a young person starting out.

And Beyond

IF YOU ENJOY PERFORMING IN THE spotlight, or if backstage is the place you'd rather be, try these related interest projects:

- Invitation to Dance
- On a High Note
- Media Savvy
- The Play's the Thing

Photography

t's been said that a picture is worth a thousand words. Taking photographs is like drawing with light. Photographs are pictures that stir memories, evoke feelings, inform, tell stories, and record history.

So get ready to create your lasting impressions. Who knows, the image of a fleeting moment that you capture on film may be your claim to fame.

Skill Builders

1   Visit a camera store or talk to an experienced photographer about the different kinds of cameras on the market. Ask about point and shoot cameras, 35 mm cameras, and cameras for underwater photography. Also, inquire about different types of lenses, like telephoto, wide angle, and zoom lenses, that are used to create special effects. With your own or a borrowed camera, take pictures of a favorite subject. Experiment with different lenses and angles.

2   Learn the basics of using a 35 mm camera from an amateur photographer or from a book. Be sure to find out how to load and unload the camera, when to change the shutter speed and f-stop, and how to focus. Experiment by shooting a couple of rolls of film and recording the settings of each picture for reference.

3   There is a wide range of accessories to use with all kinds of cameras, including tripods, lamps, and filters. Make a list of the ones you will need for two of the following: close-up photography, portraits, nature shots. Next, go to two or three stores to compare prices on all the cameras and equipment on your list.

4   Talk to an amateur photographer about the basics of composition, including background, distance, depth of field, and lighting.

5   Take a series of pictures based on an interesting theme or idea, such as circles and squares, children at play, or reflections. Put them together in a scrapbook or framed display.

Technology

1   Try your hand at black and white or color developing and printing by taking a photography course. Your school may have a darkroom you can use. Work with an experienced photographer or mentor.

2   Photographers use different film speeds for various types of lighting (indoor, bright light, clouds). Over a period of time, shoot the same subject under different conditions. Which lighting achieves the most dramatic or artistic effect? Use the best pictures for a display or to create note cards for your troop or group.

3   The treasured photograph of a beloved relative, friend, or pet has cracked and is missing a piece. Is all hope lost? Don't despair; it can be fixed! Find out how computer technology can be used to restore damaged photographs.

4   Digital photography is gaining in popularity because of the speed with which you can obtain an image and even manipulate it.

Regular cameras use film that has been coated with silver halide crystals that are physically transformed by light. This film then has to be developed. Digital cameras capture images by electronically recording the light that enters into it—no chemicals, no darkroom, no waiting! Discover how your local newspaper or advertising firm is using this technology to create images and give them a special look. Large photocopy centers and photo labs are beginning to use this technology, too, so they may be a good source of information. You also can speak to a photographer or go to the library to find out more about digital photography.

5 Can you take a photograph of heat? Not with conventional film that reacts to light. You can take a picture of the heat that comes off of an object, though, if you use infrared film. Infrared film is used extensively for aerial photography because it can penetrate haze. Find out how ecologists, botanists, and people concerned with energy efficiency use infrared photography in their line of work. Practice taking your own pictures with infrared film during the day and at night—you'll be surprised by how striking they'll look!

6 Find out how digital cameras record and manipulate images. Speak with one or more of the following: a photographer, a librarian, someone at a local newspaper or advertising firm, or an employee at a large photocopy center or photo lab.

Service Projects

1 Create an album of troop or group events for your council's archives.

2 Offer to photograph a holiday or special event for younger children or senior citizens.

3 Compile a list of community resources in the field of photography for your council. Include professional photographers, stores, labs, courses, photography galleries, etc.

4 Photograph a community event and send it to the chamber of commerce. Suggest its inclusion in a brochure.

5 Organize a troop or council-wide one-day photo shoot on a particular theme: unusual architecture, train depots, recreation, bodies of water, or maybe even "a day in the life of our town." Collaborate with other organizations in publicizing the event. Ask professional photographers for help.

Career Exploration

1 Shadow a news photographer for several assignments. Does she "pose" her subjects, take candid shots, or use artificial lighting? Does she interview her subjects or just observe their actions?

2 Photography is used in a number of fields—advertising, public relations, journalism, travel, police work, law, medicine, etc. Read the "Photographer" Career Focus on page 113 in the *Cadette Girl Scout Handbook*. Help organize a career fair and invite professionals to show and discuss their work, their training requirements, and job benefits.

3 Get a part-time or summer job in a camera store or take a basic or advanced photography course to learn new skills.

4 Study the careers of some famous female photographers, such as Berenice Abbott, Dorothea Lange, Margaret Bourke-White, and Diane Arbus. What obstacles did they have to overcome to achieve success? What was their training?

5 Join the school newspaper or take photographs of troop or council events to become adept at fast action shooting.

6 Offer to take "head shots" (portraits from the neck up) for a friend.

7 Become an intern at a photographic lab, portrait studio, or other business that deals with photography. Or job-shadow someone working in one of these places. Keep a photo diary and written diary of your experience.

And Beyond

FRAME YOUR FAVORITE PHOTOGRAPHS and give them as gifts for special occasions. Expand your artistic sights and observation skills with these related interest projects:

- Visual Arts
- Museum Discovery
- Fashion Design
- From A to V: Audiovisual Production
- Women Through Time
- It's About Time
- Architecture and Environmental Design

Bring your camera to record whatever you like. For instance, focus on the natural worlds of All About Birds, From Shore to Sea, Plant Life, and Wildlife.

The Play's the Thing

Have you ever wondered just how the "magic" of theater really works? How does a play go from an author's concept to a fully costumed, stage-designed, and well-lighted production? Or have you ever pondered just what a director or producer does? This interest project goes beyond the play as a book of words to give you an overview of stage-craft—scenery, costumes, and lighting—as well as a chance to make your directorial debut.

Skill Builders

1 Be an offstage star! Work as a stagehand or technician for a school or community production. Plays, concerts, dance performances, and even school assemblies all need technical help. Receive training in woodworking, scenery painting, set construction, lighting design and operation, sound, costume design and creation, or making props for at least five days. Work the show, performance, or assemblies for another five days (this includes rehearsal). Keep a journal of your experiences, with names in it of people from whom you can learn more in the future.

2 Actors bring a play to life. Select a monologue from a favorite play and perform it for an audience of friends. Try to convey feelings through your voice, stance, and movement. Have your friends critique your performance. Then recite your lines again.

Or try this improvisational activity: Act out a situation from either the *Cadette Girl Scout Handbook* or *A Resource Book for Senior Girl Scouts* with some of your friends. Topics like "Communication," "Life Success Skills," "Peer Pressure," and "Job Hunting" are perfect for such a role-play. Each girl should create a character for herself, including age, family background, and motivation. Change roles with the other girls and see what happens.

3 Write a short play to help other girls deal with a contemporary issue, such as peer pressure. Have your friends read the first draft aloud. Note what flows and seems natural, and what doesn't. Listen to their suggestions as actors/readers and make changes where appropriate. Then revise your play.

4 Direct or produce a play. Directors cast the show and work with the actors on their blocking (where they move on the stage) and the way they deliver their lines. Directors also decide what the set and lighting should look like, the time period in which the play takes place, and the types of costumes characters will wear. Producers locate and "book" a theater, hire a director, obtain the rights to a play, and arrange for the finances needed to put on the production. Keep a journal of your experiences as a director or producer. You might want to use it as the basis for your next show!

5 Become a seasoned theater critic. Attend at least three different types of plays, and write a review of each. If there isn't that much theater being performed in your community, check the listings for any PBS productions or check your local video store for video-taped play performances. Try to get your reviews published in your school or local paper. Or publish them yourself on your own World Wide Web home page!

Technology

1 Learn about different types of stages: for example, a

proscenium arch and round, three-quarter, and thrust stages. What are four strengths and challenges of working with each stage? Which would be better for a small cast? For a big musical comedy? For a slapstick comedy? For a drama? Why? Explain your reasons to at least two other members of your troop or group, club, etc.

2 Learn about stage lights by reading industry magazines and catalogs, or through library research. Consult a theater designer, if possible. Identify different types of stage lights. How does each work? Which lights are used for what type of effect? How does the crew operate them? What is the purpose of lighting "gels"?

3 Create a set design or lighting design for a particular play. Consult a theater designer, or use theater books and magazines to learn how to sketch the outline of the stage, as well as the types of symbols used to identify set pieces and/or lighting areas. Create a set or lighting design for two different scenes, including any special effects that you want to have. Get feedback from your players or director.

4 Fog suddenly rolling in! Snow falling! Bombs bursting! Lightning flashing! Grotesque aliens firing laser guns from landing spacecraft! Superhuman heroes flying through the air! No, this is not a story line from a comic book, but special effects that stage designers may use to make a play come alive. Pick three of these effects, or others you might prefer, and find out how each is done by speaking with the stage designer at your neighborhood playhouse, talking with a drama teacher, or reading a library book.

Service Projects

1 Volunteer as a gofer, ticket person, usher, or program writer for your local community theater. Make a commitment of at least two weeks.

2 Volunteer to work with children in a day-care center or hospital. Introduce them to theatrical play: bring "dress-up" clothes (costumes), face-painting kits (makeup), and assorted props. Encourage them to create characters, interact as those characters, and change their characters through dress-up and makeup. Make at least a five-session commitment to these children.

3 Help your council with its theater camp by assisting with the administrative and/or creative end of things for at least one week.

4 Volunteer at your local Lighthouse or Guild for the Blind. Tape-record plays and books, or organize others to do the recordings. Or, if you're technically inclined, you might want to help the organization maintain its sound equipment.

Career Exploration

1 Read about or watch a televised biography about two famous actors, playwrights, lyricists, designers, or directors. Identify five things that they did in order to succeed in theater. Decide if those are things that you would want to do or be able to do.

2 Look through college catalogs and identify five schools with good drama programs. Compare the cost of each institution, as well as the entrance and graduation requirements. Create a resource for students in your school who might be interested in this field.

3 Talk with the teachers who design and direct the shows at your school. Find out about the training and experience needed. Then talk with community theater directors and/or designers. Ask about their training and experience. Decide if, and plan how, you can go about making a living while aiming for the stars.

4 Create a story or a coloring or a picture book to teach younger girls about one of the following careers: actor, playwright, director, designer, or producer. Have three or four girls review your work, and make changes based on their comments. Be sure that the material is interesting and appropriate for their age. Share the book with a troop or group.

And Beyond

DEPENDING ON YOUR TALENT AND theatrical inclination, try any of these related interest projects:

- The Performing Arts
- Visual Arts
- Fashion Design
- Textile Arts
- Do You Get the Message?
- Once Upon a Story
- On a High Note
- Invitation to the Dance

If you'd like to produce, try It's About Time and Dollars and Sense. Public Relations, Writing for Real, Reading, and The Lure of Language will round out your onstage and offstage talents. Take time to "sit back and enjoy the show"—your own as well as new and old favorites.

Textile Arts

*D*o you see the colors and textures of different fabrics and think of a million things you could do with them? If you are interested in trying your creativity in areas such as weaving, handwork, or quilting, you may find just the activities you're looking for here. Whether you want to try something large or small, this interest project offers ideas to try from fiber to finish, and everything in between!

Skill Builders

1 Collect samples of wools, cottons, linens, and silks, as well as several synthetic fibers, such as polyester, nylon, and microfibre. Find a variety of textures and thicknesses. (The type of craft you choose may determine the kinds of materials you use.) Make a folder or notebook of your samples and note their special qualities, instructions for care, and the types of clothing or decorative items that each would be used for. Refer to this folder when completing a design.

2 Until synthetic dyes were developed in the nineteenth century, people used natural materials for putting colors in their fabrics. Indigo dye from plants was used to make denim and other fabrics blue, while yellow could be made from such natural sources as onion skins, marigolds, and goldenrods. Experiment with some of these natural dyes or others of your choosing. Be sure to wear protective clothing while working. Make sure the utensils and containers that you choose won't be used later for food preparation or storage. Stainless steel, plastic, or shatterproof glass items work best. Test your dyes on cotton, linen, or other natural fabrics and complete a project with your dyes.

3 Different handwork techniques such as knitting, crocheting, lacemaking, embroidery, and stitching are used to adorn clothing, linens, and other household items. Learn one of the techniques and use it to decorate something for yourself or a friend.

4 Some forms of weaving, such as card weaving and finger weaving, do not require a special loom. Investigate three kinds of loomless weaving and prepare a simple project using a technique of your choice. Teach this technique to a group of younger Girl Scouts or children.

5 Quilting is a craft that has a long history and is enjoying a revival. One reason for this is that technology has made quilting so much easier. Just a few decades ago, it might have taken several women weeks or even months to make one quilt. Today, one woman can finish a quilt in a few days or a few weeks by using a rotary cutter and mat, a sewing machine, and a quilting pin gun. Find out how these tools are used. What advantages do they offer over the traditional hand methods? Make a quilt piece using either simple hand tools or the new sewing technology.

Technology

1 Weaving is one of the oldest and most enduring crafts, having spanned centuries and crossed many cultures. Simple weaving can be done on a loom you make yourself. Make a cardboard, wood-frame, inkle, backstrap, or other simple loom and carry out one of the projects listed below. Experiment with two of these techniques — plain weave, tapestry, or rya knots.

Remember, use of color can make a simple project more exciting.

■ On a cardboard or wood-frame loom, make a pillow or wall hanging.

■ On an inkle loom, make a belt, a guitar strap, or a bell pull.

■ On a backstrap loom, make a belt.

2 Computer programs offer a way to design a textile project before cutting, dyeing, sewing, or otherwise committing to a project. By trying out your ideas beforehand, you get a sense of what the finished product will be. Use one of these programs to coordinate colors, design a quilt, enlarge a design, or whatever you choose. Show someone else how this flexibility can help you plan your craft project.

3 Visit a local crafts dealer to find out ways technology has transformed craft making. For example, items such as glue guns, iron-on bond, and sergers can speed up the process in some crafts.

4 Select a craft or skill that involves textiles and find out more about production methods or tools.

Service Projects

1 Make sure your meeting room and home are stocked with durable crafts supplies. They don't have to be expensive. Sometimes merchants will donate or place on sale many crafts items, such as beads, buttons, yarn, and fabric.

2 With your troop or group, compile directions for making some of your favorite textile craft projects. Make activity cards or a booklet to share with other troops and groups in your council, or suggest that some of the activities be included in your council newsletter.

3 Invite members of a senior citizens' group to join your troop or group in sharing craft ideas. Find out what some of their favorite crafts are and how they compare with yours. Together, plan a crafts exhibit and teaching event for your council or community.

4 With your troop or group, organize an event surrounding demonstrations of textile-related crafts from the past and present. Invite adults of all ages to assist you in demonstrating these crafts, which may include quilting, darning, tatting, fabric painting, and stitchery, among others. Give participants an opportunity to make some of the crafts themselves.

Career Exploration

1 Plan your own small-scale, money-making project by yourself or with a friend. Here are some suggestions: gift baskets, toys for young children, decorated clothing, decorative containers (boxes, baskets, etc.), simple jewelry, decorative frames, or photo albums.

2 A number of occupations revolve around the design, care, and use of textiles. Find out about the requirements for at least two of the following careers and how these careers relate to the fiber and textile industries: weaver, pattern maker, seamstress, chemist, engineer, designer, historian, and preservationist.

3 Some interior designers specialize in textile-related design elements. Collect information from books and magazines, and try at least one of the following projects in home decoration:

■ Find out about two or three decorating techniques using fabric or sheets.

■ Try making a simple window treatment by draping fabric through holders or on rods, or cover a valance and install it.

■ Use scraps of fabric, lace, and old buttons to design pillows for various rooms in the house.

■ Try stenciling, weaving, or embroidery to make place mats, napkins, or table runners.

4 Visit at least three craftspersons in your area and find out how they went about learning their craft. How much training did they need? How did they begin selling their crafts? How do they sell their crafts—through a studio, craft shows, or some other way? Ask them for suggestions on developing a portfolio of crafts.

And Beyond

IF YOU ENJOYED TEXTILE ARTS, CONTINUE to weave a web of beauty with these related interest projects:

■ Visual Arts
■ Just Jewelry
■ Artistic Crafts
■ Paper Works
■ Folk Arts
■ Fashion Design
■ Photography

To help you to package and promote your crafts:

■ Graphic Communications
■ Public Relations
■ Desktop Publishing

Visual Arts

Even if you can't draw a straight line, you can enjoy the visual arts. Research reveals that a strong link exists between creating visual images and a good memory. Sketching pictures in a notebook can help some people to memorize facts and learn better!

This interest project focuses on developing your skills in the visual arts—drawing, painting, sculpture, pottery, and design—as well as enriching your world.

Skill Builders

1 Design a "home studio." It can be as simple as a table in the corner of your bedroom, the living room, or the family room. Stock it with construction paper, scissors, tape, glue, crayons, markers, colored pencils, and any other drawing medium.

2 Work with a local artist or craftsperson in her studio. Decide together what your responsibilities and time commitment will be.

3 Create a painting, drawing, or sculpture that expresses something you feel deeply. Show the artwork to others.

4 Visit a museum, gallery, or shop that sells postcards of paintings. Do an art activity based on paintings you especially liked. For example, arrange to sketch the inside of a diner or restaurant that reminds you of an Edward Hopper painting of an urban scene.

5 Take a walking tour with friends and stop at points where art objects may be seen. Look for sculptures or murals in public spaces, mosaic tile art on floors or walls of buildings, posters inside stores, and department store window displays.

6 What skills do you need to become a fine artist? Learn about and practice at least two of the following skills in a class at school, by attending a museum course, by reading a book, or from an art mentor:

■ Perspective.

■ Composition.

■ Color and design.

■ Light and shadow.

Technology

1 Create an original work of art in any two-dimensional medium. For example, work on a painting, a woodblock, a lithograph, a pen-and-ink drawing, or a silk-screen. Learn the procedures and try individual ways of handling your chosen medium. Learn about the chemicals, solvents, and tools used in your medium. Make sure that you choose nontoxic products and use a work space with adequate ventilation.

2 Find out about etching or another printing method by reading about it or visiting a museum or gallery. Create your own plate or block from which to print. To learn about the craft of printing, visit a professional printmaker's studio, speak with an art teacher, or attend a print-making class.

3 How are fabric designs created? How are fabrics designed for permanency (permitting the fabric to be washed or dry-cleaned)? Ask a textile designer or teacher for answers to these questions, then create a design for fabrics you would like to see in stores.

4 Make a sculpture of a human figure using an *armature*, a wire frame upon which you apply pieces of clay. Use self-drying clay that can dry indoors or in the sun.

Service Projects

1 Help to design and paint a mural depicting a scene that stresses cultural appreciation. Display your work in your meeting place, the lobby of a public library, at your school, or in your Girl Scout council office.

2 Use recyclable materials to create a sculpture that shows the need to reuse materials to protect the environment and the benefits of recycling.

3 With a group of younger girls, use popsicle sticks, clay, colored paper, and any other materials to create a 3-D model of an ideal playground structure that could be used in a park in your community.

4 Become an expert in one visual art technique and volunteer to help a group of seniors use this skill in a project. For example, you might teach them about

drawing cartoons, sketching portraits, or painting with watercolors.

Career Exploration

1 Interview or shadow for a day an artist in your community to determine her special qualities and skills.

2 Art therapists help people analyze their behaviors and feelings through the use of drawing and painting. Visit or call a hospital, rehabilitation center, or college that has an art therapy program. Ask a therapist about the rewards and challenges of her job. Find out from her about the employment prospects in her profession.

3 Arrange to interview two art teachers working at different age levels (perhaps one at a middle school and another at the college level). Ask them how they arrange their schedules so that they can both teach and create their art. What are the challenges of their lifestyles? Ask them for any advice they can offer a young artist starting out.

4 Meet with or read about an artist who works in a craft such as pottery, photography, weaving, silk-screening, jewelry making, or quilting. What steps did she take to develop her career? What does she think is the most interesting aspect of her career?

5 Become a docent, or tour guide, at an art museum.

6 Visit an art museum to view the work of a favorite artist. Read about the life and work of this artist. Find out:

■ What kind of childhood the artist had. (For instance, the well-known children's author/illustrator Beatrix Potter drew from nature as a young girl.)

■ What the artist's early career was like.

■ What challenges were overcome.

■ How her style changed over time.

And Beyond

CONTINUE TO APPRECIATE ART BY VISITING art galleries and museums. Make your own art at home, at school, or with your troop or group.

Visual art takes many forms. Try any of these related interest projects:

■ Just Jewelry
■ Paper Works
■ Textile Arts
■ Home Improvement
■ Fashion Design
■ Artistic Crafts
■ Photography
■ Graphic Communications
■ Desktop Publishing
■ Media Savvy

Use your artistic vision when trying Plant Life, Wildlife, and Build a Better Future.

Women Through Time

Throughout time, women—pioneers, writers, homemakers, adventurers—have made vast and varied contributions to society. Often, the accomplishments of women have not been highlighted. Do this interest project as a way to take a look back in history and to discover the power and presence of women in all walks of life.

Skill Builders

1 Explore your personal history by finding out about the women in your family. Look back at least two generations by reading family records or by talking to relatives to find out about rites of passage, educational or work experiences, travels, illnesses, or major family events. How did those events reflect what was happening in the world at the time? Record interesting details about the women's lives, personalities, and traditions in a scrapbook, on audiotape, or on videotape.

2 Conduct an oral history interview with an older woman. Ask her what it was like growing up. What were the educational and work opportunities? What are the major changes from her childhood to now? Ask about changes in technology, communication, travel, entertainment, social roles, and responsibilities.

3 Go to a library or a museum and look through magazines or newspapers from 20 or more years ago. How were women written about? If possible, go back even further in time. Can you see changes in the roles of women from one period to the next? What are the differences and similarities between images then and now? Be creative and make a historical or artistic collage to illustrate your findings.

4 Explore the life of Juliette Gordon Low. Visit her birthplace in Savannah or read about her in historical materials. What events in her life gave her the strength and vision to inspire the Girl Scout movement? Write an essay or discuss your findings with your troop or group.

5 Read a diary, journal, or autobiography of a woman who lived at least 25 years ago. Keep your own journal for at least a month.

6 Select an era in American history that interests you: for example, colonial America, the American frontier in the 1850s, the Roaring Twenties, or World War II. Find out what it was like to be a woman during that time period. Read a book, view a documentary, or visit a museum. Share your discoveries in a troop or group discussion, in an essay, or through illustrations.

Technology

1 After searching the Web for information on female leaders throughout history, develop an interactive game, videotape, or audiotape describing their accomplishments.

2 Find a way to share information and to celebrate the role

of women in science and technology for National Women's History Week (March), National Science and Technology Week (April), or other appropriate celebration.

3 Put together a multimedia program that honors the contributions of women in a particular field: for example, the visual and performing arts or the sciences.

4 Learn a skill, domestic art, or craft practiced by women in earlier times but replaced by technology and busy lifestyles, such as home canning, quilting, knitting, soap making, weaving, or basket making. Make something as a gift for someone.

Service Projects

1 Develop a display about women's history or a women's issue for your local library or school: for example, women aviators or the suffragettes, who fought for the right of women to vote. Present the information to younger girls in a lively way.

2 Create a walking tour that addresses the historical contributions of women in your community. Include streets and buildings named after women, historic residences, places of business, and historic events.

3 Help develop a brochure or hands-on activity for a historical museum that interprets the daily lives and times of girls and women. Or assist as a guide.

4 Become well-informed about an issue affecting women, such as breast cancer, domestic violence, elder care, or child care. Volunteer to help an organization that deals with the issue.

5 Organize or participate in an event to honor the contributions of women: for example, a women's history fair, a women's film festival, an awards program to honor the contributions of women in your community, or an event honoring Girl Scouts.

Career Exploration

1 Interview someone who works in a field that deals with women's history: for example, a research librarian, an archivist, a costume maker, an author or journalist, or a women's studies teacher. Find out what she likes about her job and how she sees it as connecting the past with the present and future.

2 Research the changes in women's career opportunities in professional sports over the past 30 years. Find out about the lives of three or four women who have contributed to changes in this area. In a troop or group meeting, discuss the changes and what these women have envisioned as the future of women's professional sports.

3 Explore women's roles and opportunities in the U.S. military service or in politics. Trace women's historical impact and present-day service. Interview a woman who has served in the military or in politics.

4 Read about a woman who was a "pioneer" in a nontraditional career. Or interview a woman who works in a career such as engineering or aviation, in which there

are relatively few women. What obstacles did she face, if any? Did anyone serve as her mentor?

5 Investigate at least three different women's history or women's studies courses in schools of higher education. What areas are encompassed in women's studies, and to which possible career options do they lead? If possible, interview someone who is a student or adviser in one of these programs.

And Beyond

LOOK AT TOYS IN A MUSEUM (OR READ about the toys girls played with historically) and compare them with what is being offered for girls today. Have toys changed? Compile a list of toys for girls that avoid sex-role stereotyping, or design your own.

Consider reading historical novels or biographies about outstanding women.

Can you think of more ways—from sewing to science—in which women through time have influenced and shaped history? No field is without a woman's contribution. To find out more, try these related interest projects:

- Games for Life
- Reading
- Leadership
- From Fitness to Fashion
- Family Living
- Artistic Crafts
- Heritage Hunt
- It's About Time
- Child Care
- Women's Health

Sports
and
Recreation

Backpacking ■ Camping ■
Emergency Preparedness ■
Games for Life ■ High Adventure
■ Horse Sense ■ On the Court ■
On the Playing Field
Orienteering ■ Outdoor Survival ■
Paddle, Pole, and Roll ■ Rolling
Along ■ Smooth Sailing ■ Sports
for Life ■ Water Sports

Backpacking

Become familiar with these minimal impact camping principles:

- *Plan and prepare.*
- *Camp and travel on durable surfaces.*
- *Pack it in; pack it out.*
- *Properly dispose of what you can't pack out.*
- *Leave what you find.*
- *Minimize the use and impact of fires.*

Outdoor Education in Girl Scouting *is an excellent resource and some camping experience will prove beneficial. Get out your pack and hit the trail softly!*

Skill Builders

The two starred Skill Builders activities are required.

1 Make a list of equipment and clothing needed for a backpacking trip. Add specialized items to this list for the following environments: desert, mountain, and beach. Learn ways to take care of yourself by the use of appropriate clothing, food, and water. To learn ways to reduce the size and weight of the items you carry, talk with an experienced backpacker or read a book about lightweight backpacking. Pages 163–164 in *Outdoor Education in Girl Scouting* will be helpful.

* 2 Get into shape from the ground up. Choose and break in hiking shoes or boots appropriate to terrain you will be hiking on. Learn proper foot care, including what socks to wear. Develop a plan for conditioning your legs and increasing cardiovascular strength to meet the demands of the terrain and altitude. Take a practice hike with your backpack loaded and make any needed adjustments. Learn to spot signs of fatigue and dehydration and what you can do to avoid them. See pages 34, 39, and 159–160 in *Outdoor Education in Girl Scouting*.

3 Learn the first-aid treatment for burns, cuts, blisters, sunburn, heat exhaustion, heatstroke, hypothermia, shock, insect stings, ticks, contact with poisonous plants, and a bite by any poisonous animal common to the areas where you plan to travel. Assemble a light-weight first-aid kit. Review how you can put a first-aid plan into action. See pages 83–94 in *Outdoor Education in Girl Scouting*, and complete the activities in each section.

4 Learn to use a compass and read a topographical map. Read pages 103–111 in *Outdoor Education in Girl Scouting* or pages 123–124 in the *Cadette Girl Scout Handbook*. Then trace out a hiking route on a topographical map. Describe what you would see along the way by visualizing the terrain from the map symbols.

* 5 Put your minimal impact skills to the test by planning and carrying out a backpacking trip of at least two days. Follow *Safety-Wise* guidelines, obtaining permission for each trip and the area where you plan to camp. Submit a written plan that describes the route, emergency procedures, group safety rules, equipment, menus, and names of participants. Develop a plan for building teamwork and sharing leadership among the individuals going on each trip. Before taking the first trip:

- Be able to explain why a group of four to ten people is most appropriate in a backcountry setting.

- Know ways to avoid and prevent encounters with wildlife when on the trail or when storing food overnight.

- Know how to avoid insect and tick bites.

Upon your return, evaluate the trip. Make appropriate changes in procedures, teamwork strategies, and gear before your next outing.

Technology

1 Visit an outdoor store to find out about the variety of backpacks and frames available. Learn about the materials and design components of internal and external frame backpacks. Try on a pack that adjusts to fit you. Make sure that it includes padded shoulder straps and a hip belt. Compare the kinds of sleeping bags and tents on the market, and ask for recommendations for ones most appropriate for the type of backpacking that you plan to do.

2 Learn about the most common water pollutants in the area where you will be hiking. Find out about methods of purifying water on trips to the backcountry, including at least one "high-tech" way. Practice purifying water by using one method.

3 Compare backpacking stoves operated by butane, propane, blended fuel (propane and butane), and gasoline. Compare ease of use, weight of stoves, cooking times, suitability for different altitudes, and recommended temperature range. Arrange to try out at least two different kinds of stoves. Which stove(s) would be best for general use? Which would work best when backpacking at high altitude or in cold weather? See pages 49–58 in *Outdoor Education in Girl Scouting*.

4 Plan the food for at least one backpacking trip. Learn about lightweight foods as well as those that pack best and last without refrigeration. What's the difference between freeze-dried and dehydrated foods? With your group, consider the cost and size per serving, the efficiency of the packaging, and which foods will provide the maximum energy. If needed, repackage food to eliminate excess weight.

5 On the Internet, search for information on backpacking, hiking, or outdoor adventures. Look for Web sites with backcountry weather reports, maps, or information on wilderness areas. If possible, use the Web to help plan a trip.

6 Draw your own design for a piece of equipment or clothing that would be useful on a backpacking trip or improve on a current model. If possible, construct and use it on a trip.

Service Projects

1 Teach younger girls skills such as campsite selection, safe use of a backpacking stove, equipment selection, proper backcountry hygiene, food selection and repackaging.

2 Join a trail maintenance or campsite cleanup effort.

3 Contact a search and rescue group. Train to become a member of a search and rescue team.

4 Work with an environmental organization to complete such tasks as replacing natural resources, collecting and planting native seeds, and protecting wilderness and park areas.

Career Exploration

1 Visit a store that sells camping and backpacking equipment. Learn about job opportunities in this retail business. Ask someone what kinds of skills and experience are necessary for different levels of jobs.

2 Shadow a wildlife biologist, geologist, botanist, or other natural resource professionals for a day. Or interview at least two people who work in outdoor recreation. Find out what they do in their jobs, what challenges they enjoy

and don't enjoy. Ask them to trace their career paths for you.

3 Contact by phone or in writing two manufacturers of camping and backpacking equipment for information about careers in designing and manufacturing outdoor equipment.

4 Talk with two trip leaders or outfitters of various high adventure programs such as backpacking, white-water rafting, or horse packing. Ask questions about what they must do to plan trips, provide meals, and offer a safe but challenging program. What kinds of training, permits, and insurance are necessary to run an adventure-based business?

5 Investigate career opportunities related to backpacking such as working with recreational, outdoor, or environmental clubs and organizations.

And Beyond

TO GET THE MOST OUT OF YOUR BACKpacking adventures, you will need to master many skills and build stamina. Try these related interest projects:

- Camping
- Orienteering
- Emergency Preparedness
- Eco-Action
- All About Birds
- Wildlife
- Outdoor Survival
- High Adventure
- Paddle, Pole, and Roll
- Travel
- Sports for Life

Camping

*S*leeping under the stars, listening to the whistle of the wind, or hiking in the early morning are part of the camping experience. Completing the Camping interest project will enable you to refine your skills while enjoying the pleasures of the great outdoors. For more information on many of the topics included here, read Outdoor Education in Girl Scouting. Challenge yourself to be your best on an outdoor adventure.

Skill Builders

1 Learn how to select a site and a route for a camping trip appropriate to the skills of your troop or group. Determine how your group can minimize its impact on a site by considering the following:

- Time of year and the size of the group.

- Clothing and equipment.

- Food preparation and use of portable cooking stoves.

- Camping and traveling on durable surfaces.

- Proper disposal methods and plans to pack out waste and trash.

- Leaving the site in a natural condition.

2 Collect 10 recipes for outdoor meals that will minimize food preparation time and the use of cooking fuel. Be careful to select foods that will not spoil. For a three-day camping trip, plan a well-balanced menu. Learn the proper procedures for setting up, fueling, and cooking on the stove you will be using. Show how to keep food and cooking supplies safely away from animals.

3 Develop emergency procedures for a camping trip. Know what to do in case of fire, flood, and injured or lost campers. Learn the procedures to follow if you become separated from your group. Show that you can set up and recognize international distress signals. Demonstrate how to be prepared for weather emergencies and find out about methods for obtaining water and shelter. Assemble a first-aid kit. Know how to treat for shock, bleeding, sprains, burns, bites, hypothermia, frostbite, sunburn, heat exhaustion, and heatstroke.

4 Demonstrate two ways to build group readiness and spirit for a camping trip. Keep in touch with the feelings that come from living and working together in the outdoors by writing a song or poem, recording your thoughts in a journal, or sharing them with a friend or at a Girl Scouts' Own ceremony.

5 Plan a trip to challenge your skills. Create maps, plans, and checklists. Backpack, bicycle, ride horseback, canoe, sail, ski cross-country, or find some new, exciting way to get to your campsite (perhaps an extended scavenger hunt or mystery ride).

Technology

1 Learn to use a baseplate compass and to read a topographical map. Sketch a map of your neighborhood or camp area from field notes you have taken. Measure the length of your pace and show that you can judge distance. Demonstrate your navigational ability by planning and, with an adult, co-leading a hike for a group.

2 Be prepared for changing weather conditions. Show that you understand the significance of a barometer reading, wind direction and speed, and patterns of weather movements typical of your region. Before leaving, check the current forecast to make sure you have the proper clothing and equipment. Record weather observations for two days before your trip and make your own weather prediction. Record the conditions during the trip and compare them with your prediction.

3 Find out about new types of materials and fibers used to create camping equipment. What makes something waterproof? Or lightweight? Heat or cold resistant? Visit a local outdoor store and examine the latest products. Read through catalogs and comparison shop for several items. Find out about the types of insulation in sleeping bags and which is best for your area and the type of trip you are planning.

4 Surf the Internet and find out which camping organizations and clubs are represented in cyberspace. Do a Web search and find sites on camping gear, travel destinations, and safe outdoor practices and minimal impact (for the last topic, see the National Outdoor Leadership School's Web site).

Service Projects

1 Look into how to make a camping experience more accessible to people with disabilities. Together with your troop

leader, you may wish to consult *Focus on Ability: Serving Girls with Special Needs*. Then, using the assessment tools from the book, determine which of your campsites are most suitable for people with disabilities, and how you can improve any existing conditions at them.

2 Offer your services to maintain a hiking or nature trail. Or, create a new trail at a local Girl Scout camp or park. Learn the proper ways to cut unwanted growth, control erosion, and divert water off the trail.

3 Teach camping skills such as selecting proper equipment, meal planning, or pitching a tent, to a group of younger Girl Scouts. Visit their troop meeting, demonstrate the skills, and help them practice.

4 Volunteer to plan and conduct a weekend camporee, a habitat improvement project, or an outdoor skills day. Or collaborate on a camping-related service project with another group.

Career Exploration

1 Learn about jobs in the outdoors such as lifeguard, camp counselor, camp director, camp administrator, program specialist, site manager, or food services manager in the recreation industry. Interview someone who has one of these jobs and report back to your troop or group on your findings.

2 Look through several magazines about camping and outdoor activities. Use the ideas to make a list of outdoor careers. Find out about the skills, education, and experience needed for three of the careers you listed.

3 Interview someone with a career related to safeguarding the environment. What does it take to be an educator, a lawyer, an engineer, a lobbyist, or a scientist devoted to environmental issues?

4 Come up with an idea to start your own business in the area of outdoor recreation. For example, some people have started up outdoor clothes and equipment catalog businesses or ecotourism companies. What product or service could you sell? What would you do to make sure your company is environmentally aware? Think about how your business could contribute to preserving the environment and still make money for you.

And Beyond

CAMPING OPENS UP NEW VISTAS AND taps many abilities. Whether you are a weekend camper or planning a longer trek, consult any of these related interest projects:

■ Wildlife
■ Outdoor Survival
■ Backpacking
■ Orienteering
■ Eco-Action
■ Digging Through the Past
■ Plant Life

Emergency Preparedness

The Girl Scout motto, "Be Prepared," applies to many life situations, including readiness to deal with emergencies and disasters. Knowing the kinds of emergencies and disasters that might happen in a given area is the first step to being prepared. Making a plan to ensure your own and your family's safety is next. This interest project will enable you to prepare yourself through practice and knowledge so that you can take care of yourself and others in an emergency situation.

Skill Builders

* Activities with an asterisk must be completed.

***1** Complete a basic first-aid course offered by the Red Cross, a local hospital, fire station, or school. Know how to stop bleeding, give artificial resuscitation, do the Heimlich maneuver, and treat for shock.

***2** Complete a certified cardiopulmonary resuscitation (CPR) course offered by the Red Cross, American Heart Association, a local hospital, fire department, or other certifying agency. Know how to administer CPR to an adult as well as a child whose breathing and pulse have stopped. Keep your certification up to date.

3 Read "Life Success Skill #4: Staying Safe" in the *Cadette Girl Scout Handbook* or pages 56–57 in *A Resource Book for Senior Girl Scouts*. Complete a personal safety course offered by a women's group or your local police. Learn basic principles of self-defense and how to avoid situations that might put yourself in danger.

4 Evaluate your home or apartment for fire hazards and help to remove any that you find. Prepare evacuation plans for all areas of your house to be adopted and practiced by your family. Know how to test doors prior to opening them. Establish meeting areas outside of the home in case of a fire. Make sure that your home has sufficient and charged smoke detectors, as well as recommended fire extinguishers for the kitchen and other areas. Know when, how, and where to use a fire extinguisher.

5 Make up first-aid and emergency preparedness kit(s) for your home and family car. Include items that are recommended by your local emergency managers or the Red Cross for disasters. Discuss with your family what to do in case of a crisis: if you are all at home and if you are separated. Choose and make plans for three different disasters that might happen in your community, such as a forest fire, tornado, hurricane, lightning storm, toxic spill, power failure, flooding, water contamination or drought, tsunami (tidal wave), earthquake, snowstorm, or ice storm. Practice disaster plans at home. Include one disaster that would require evacuation from your house.

Technology

1 Visit a local or state command center (police station, hospital, fire station, U.S. Forest Service, emergency manager, military) to learn about different technologies used for communication and handling emergencies in your community. Find out what back-up technologies are available for use in case of a disaster.

2 Learn about ham or CB radio operation through a club meeting, special training, or by spending time with an active member. Learn basic radio procedures and take part in a conversation, drill, or actual emergency communication operation for your community, state, or another part of the world.

3 Know how to turn off the utilities where you live. Ask your parents or the building superintendent to show you how to locate the electrical control panel or fuse box and the water and gas turnoff valves. Learn how to reset a circuit breaker or change a fuse. Know what to do if there is a gas leak. Learn how to test and change smoke alarm batteries. Know what to do in case of a downed electrical wire. See that you have easy access to candles, matches, and flashlights in an emergency.

4 Make an emergency plan for how you, your family, and your community would deal with a severe oil shortage. Which services and products do you use that are oil dependent? For example, electricity from power companies is often generated by using oil. Does your community have an emergency plan? If not, discuss ways that your family and neighbors can cut back on oil use and how your community can still provide basic services.

5 What if your home was without electricity for between three and five days? How would you and your family keep warm or cool, cook food and keep it fresh, and keep water pipes from freezing? How would you do your homework? Think about ways to work cooperatively with neighbors. How could neighborhood cooperation improve the situation for everyone?

6 Learn how to operate an electric generator, propane or gaslight, and propane or gas stove for use in an emergency. Know how to store and handle fuel and where to place equipment safely. Know fire-safety procedures to use with each piece of equipment.

Service Projects

1 Become a trained emergency volunteer for your community. For example, work in developing a community disaster plan, on a search and rescue team, for a crisis "hot line," at a community or women's shelter, as a lifeguard, or as a member of a ski patrol.

2 Learn about the mission of disaster relief agencies such as the Federal Emergency Management Agency (FEMA) and the Red Cross. Help collect or pack items for a disaster relief effort in your community, state, country, or abroad or distribute disaster relief information in your community.

3 Organize or facilitate an event for young children that focuses on home safety, first aid, fire prevention, personal safety, and emergency response. Consider using the Federal Emergency Management Agency's *Disaster Dudes* video as a part of your program.

4 Help develop a plan for assisting wildlife or domestic animals affected by an environmental disaster, such as a wildfire, flood, oil spill, severe storm, or drought, or assist in the aftermath of a disaster with wildlife or domestic animals.

Career Exploration

1 Interview and, if possible, job-shadow someone responsible for community safety, such as a police officer, firefighter, safety manager, emergency medical technician (EMT), state or local emergency manager, or health department official. Find out what kind of education, training, and/or experience is needed for her position.

2 Interview or invite a health department worker or public health nurse to speak on control of health emergencies in your community. Find out what you can do to assist in preventing or controlling a health emergency such as food poisoning, contaminated water supplies, outbreak of a communicable disease, or severe air pollution.

3 Interview four parents of school-age children. What are some of the emergency situations that they have had to handle with young children? Based on the information you have collected, prepare a "Tips for Baby-Sitters" sheet and distribute it to your friends.

4 Develop and/or disseminate information on common household emergencies for parents of small children. This could be a collection of fliers, a news column, awareness posters, or a video.

5 Read a book about someone surviving a natural disaster. Determine what knowledge, preparation, and attitude are needed to survive a natural disaster, based on the survivor's experience.

And Beyond

IF YOU WANT TO DEVELOP YOUR SURVIVAL skills, try these related interest projects:

- Outdoor Survival
- Camping
- High Adventure

To safeguard your home or if you are around young children, look at Family Living and Child Care.

Games for Life

Games are found in all cultures and are enjoyed at all age levels. Games provide a way to share time with others as well as offer lessons in teamwork, fair play, competition, skill development, and self-confidence. Games can be a great leisure-time pursuit for one, two, or more people, so whether on your own, with friends, or with family, team up and have fun! And remember, practice makes perfect.

Skill Builders

1 Read the chapter "Getting Started" in *Games for Girl Scouts*. Learn games from three different countries (one of which can be the U.S.A.) and teach them to a group of younger girls.

2 Learn about games that can be used as "ice-breakers" for groups of people coming together for the first time. Facilitate an appropriate ice-breaker in a group you are a part of, other than your own troop.

3 Develop a file of games for different age groups that can be used for child care, travel, or group activities. Include indoor and outdoor games, and small-group and large-group games. Include games that can be adapted for differing abilities.

4 Find out about games that do each of the following: increase physical strength, develop mental capabilities, and build character. Teach at least two of these games to others.

5 What are the elements of a competitive or educational board game? Brainstorm a list with a friend. Use the list as a springboard for developing a board game for use with peers. Create the game yourself or with a "team."

6 Learn how to play a game of strategy, such as bridge or chess.

7 Learn at least five singing games or five jump-rope games and be able to teach them to others.

Technology

1 Learn to play a variety of educational, interactive computer or electronic games and share them with younger girls.

2 Compare a game that is played in a non-tech version and in a tech version, such as chess and computer chess. Play both versions. What are the pros and cons of each version? Has technology changed the way games are played?

3 Read two magazines that evaluate computer games and on-line games from the Internet. Note the criteria used, and compare the published evaluation with those made by friends who have played these games.

4 Make a list of computer games you would recommend based upon criteria such as degree of difficulty, educational value, fun, and artwork. Share your list with others.

5 Create a computer game that can be played by one or more people. Field-test it with at least four people, evaluate the feedback, and make changes.

Service Projects

1 Develop and host a "games day" for families, younger girls, or senior citizens that introduces a variety of games in different formats.

2 Help Brownie Girl Scout troop members earn their Play Try-Its.

3 Create a box in which you can store board games, like a large treasure chest, that can be used in a homeless shelter, women's shelter, retirement center, nursing home, or day-care setting. Include games appropriate to the setting and age levels you are serving.

4 Develop at least two instructional games for a community center or troop house that can be used by adults or leaders when working with younger girls or by the younger girls themselves when exploring a contemporary issue. Be sure to work with your council program director, service unit director, or older girl adviser before trying out the games with girls.

5 Interview several children or adults with different kinds of disabilities. Find out what their favorite games are, or what games they would really like to play. Work with them to develop new strategies or techniques, or to adapt a piece of equipment to play a specific game. Share this information or adaptation in your community.

6 Volunteer to help at a cultural event, such as one held in honor of a national holiday, or at a living history reenactment that features games played in the past by a specific cultural group.

Career Exploration

1 Examine some careers that involve games directly or indirectly: youth leader, referee, computer programmer, toy manufacturer, game developer, sporting goods and games retailer. Arrange to interview or job-shadow an individual whose career you are interested in. Find out what training and experience are necessary for the job.

2 Explore some professional or interest-based organizations that are in existence because of games, such as a local chess club or on the computer. Find them through research in the library. Look for special publications, magazines, or computer bulletin boards having to do with games. Choose one organization to explore in depth or develop a list or resource file for your library, resource center, or school.

3 As a parent or simply as an adult you will undoubtedly have to make some decisions about games on the market for children.

Develop criteria for evaluating children's games that include safety, educational value, ease of playing, and fun. Make recommendations to parents or kids through a display or special program.

And Beyond

CONSIDER BECOMING A CADETTE OR Senior Girl Scout Program Aide with a concentration in games. Consult the resource books *Outdoor Education in Girl Scouting* and *Games for Girl Scouting*.

If you like to play games, on boards or outdoors, try these related interest projects:

- Leadership
- On the Playing Field
- On the Court
- Computers in Everyday Life
- A World of Understanding
- Dollars and Sense
- Math, Maps, and More

Explore ways to play games with all ages, in Child Care, Generations Hand in Hand, Family Living, and Understanding Yourself and Others.

High Adventure

Whether you are canoeing the rapids, helping your group cross a river filled with alligators, or hiking to a mountaintop, you'll need to learn about taking safety precautions and working with others to achieve a common goal. High adventure challenge courses, which are offered through Girl Scout camps, schools, outdoor store networks, and private instructors, can equip you and your friends with these skills.

Note: All activities must be done under the guidance of someone with the required training. For high ropes or climbing, see the relevant activity checkpoints in *Safety-Wise* or *Safety and Risk Management in Girl Scouting*. Before engaging in these activities, you should obtain your council's approval of equipment, instructors, and the site.

Skill Builders

1 With your group, play "get acquainted" games that help people get to know each other and develop teamwork. Look for these in *Games for Girl Scouts* and other books that describe team-building activities. You might want to use these three resources from Project Adventure, Inc. (listed in the resource section of this book): Silver Bullets, Cowtails and Cobras I, and Cowtails and Cobras II. Develop a selection of games to use with different ages.

2 Learn from a challenge course instructor, a physical education teacher, an instructor at a youth or recreation facility, or another expert some simple warm-up and stretching activities to get the circulation going, increase coordination, and develop limberness and flexibility. Be able to lead at least three activities with a group.

Note: These activities should always be done prior to any climbing or physical challenge activities.

3 Successfully complete at least three parts in a "low elements" course, such as "The Triangle," "Cross the River," "Fidget Ladder," or "The Bridge Is Out." How do these activities contribute to the skills of listening, problem solving, teamwork, and confidence building?

4 Successfully complete at least three elements in a "high elements" course, such as "The Catwalk," "The Perch," "The Giant's Ladder," "The Burma Bridge," or the "Zip Line." Discuss what you have learned about yourself, including challenges you met and teamwork developed with your group.

5 Learn from an expert basic rock-climbing techniques to employ on a rock surface or specially constructed wall, and how to rappel from the top of a rock face or a climbing wall. This includes checking out the equipment, putting on and adjusting the safety harness, tying knots used in climbing, and wearing safety gear and proper clothing. Practice using foot holds and hand holds as well as how to hold yourself and the rope, as you move right or left along the face of the rock. Learn how to use commands such as "on-belay" and "belay" and how to act as a spotter for others while they are climbing.

6 Find out about the safety equipment used in challenge courses or rock climbing. Know about the two kinds of carabiners (regular clip-on and L-lock) and determine in what situations you would specifically need a locking or nonlocking carabiner. Find out what kinds of braking systems are employed in belaying. Learn to "flake" a rope (string it out so it is free of coiling and twisting). Find out from an expert how to recognize signs of wear in equipment and courses themselves (for example, wear due to weathering).

Technology

1 Search the Internet, including the World Wide Web, for information and resources on activities, equipment, and places to go if you are interested in high adventure. Some key words to use in your search might be *camp, ropes course, climbing, recreation,* and *outdoor magazines.*

2 Build some simple pieces of initiative game equipment, such as "centipede walkers," a "walking A-frame," stilts, or a spider web (that can be strung between trees) and use them with a group.

3 Design your own dream "low element" and "high element" course to scale, with at least six elements in each area, using such tools as toothpicks, dental floss, clay, Styrofoam, ruler, and a topographical map.

4 Visit an American Camping Association conference or a similar meeting where you can talk with exhibitors who build challenge courses. Make a list of techniques and materials that interest you.

5 Study, evaluate, and discuss the environmental impact of an adventure course that has been constructed by utilizing existing resources (such as trees and rocks), as opposed to one that has been built using materials brought into a site (treated poles and structures).

Service Projects

1 Develop a collection of cooperative or initiative games that can be taught to younger girls and plan a program for a meeting or camping activity.

2 Help with the grounds maintenance or assist in the setup and breakdown of a challenge course for a period of time.

3 Investigate the availability of challenge-course instruction for people with disabilities. Assist an organization in making its challenge course available to people with disabilities, or link people with disabilities to organizations that can accommodate their needs.

4 Be trained as a challenge-course assistant. Learn how to assist in equipment care and storage, ensure the safety of participants, do basic emergency procedures, instruct in the successful completion of activities, and evaluate the experience with participants.

5 Develop a brochure, a bulletin board of inspirational quotes and pictures, a Web site, or a photo record for a challenge course site or facility.

Career Exploration

1 Find out about at least one of the following industry-standard high-adventure groups: Association for Experiential Learning, Project Adventure, Outward Bound, or National Outdoor Leadership School (NOLS). What kinds of careers and training are represented in the organization? Does the organization offer advanced training for trainers? Certification?

2 Make a list of local people who might be involved in a high-adventure business, such as outdoor store personnel, equipment manufacturers, designers, trip leaders, instructors. Interview two of them. What are the special skills and challenges of such a career?

3 Find out about people who are consultants or trainers for businesses that use challenge courses and initiatives to develop corporate or business teamwork.

4 Investigate the use of high-adventure activities (a certified course) in the juvenile justice system in your state as an alternative or complement to lockup for juvenile offenders. Find out how successful the program has been in redirecting the way young people think about themselves and their actions. What kind of training, in addition to high-adventure training, would one need to work with this kind of program?

And Beyond

JOIN A LOCAL CLIMBING CLUB TO PURSUE your new hobby or explore other outdoor recreational opportunities.

Kindle your adventurous spirit with these related interest projects:

- Camping
- Orienteering
- Outdoor Survival
- Backpacking
- Paddle, Pole, and Roll
- Water Sports
- Games for Life
- Leadership

Horse Sense

Horses have been a major part of human history. Whether you live in the country or in a city, have your own horse or ride at a nearby stable, this interest project will help you better understand horses, increase your riding skills, explore careers and hobbies that involve horses, and share your love of horses and horsemanship with others.

Skill Builders

1 At a riding academy, stable, or riding program, learn how to do the following activities safely: groom, lead, tie, bridle, saddle, and mount a horse. Learn how to post, to go from walk to canter, to gallop, and to turn left and right on a horse. Find out how to hold a horse for a farrier (blacksmith) or veterinarian. See page 91 in *Safety-Wise*.

2 Identify six safety rules to use on and off the horse and in the stable, ring, or on the trail. Create posters, signs, etc., listing these rules. Offer to post them to help others.

3 Help plan and/or take part in a group overnight trail ride. Properly pack gear that will be carried by the horses. Take part in the care and maintenance of the horses and their tack while on the trail. Or demonstrate your skills as a rider during at least three group trail rides of one hour or longer. Perhaps pack and carry a trail meal with you.

4 Learn about horse breeding. Talk to a horse breeder or visit the library and read a book about horse breeding. Select one breed of horse that interests you and research its history. Identify essential characteristics of the breed. Make a drawing of the ideal horse in this breed.

5 Visit a library or museum to learn about two topics from this list, or a topic of your own:

■ Mythology and horses.

■ Horse images in art.

■ How horses were introduced to North America, and their effect on the American Indian culture.

■ The domestication of horses.

■ Horses in the lives of royalty or gentry.
  Create a photo essay or visual and text display of your findings.

6 Learn to assess a horse physically and temperamentally. Consider personality traits, physical attributes, age, training, and learning ability. Find out what faults a horse might have and how to correct them. Using this information, create on paper a "perfect horse," listing the qualities suitable for you and your riding style. Or visit a ranch or stable and select a horse to ride based on these qualities.

Technology

1 Find out how modern science has contributed to the health, breeding, training, and care of horses. What technology was involved?

2 Learn about *tack* (bridle and saddle) and how to care for it. Name two or three different saddles, bits, girths, and pads. Which would you choose for your riding style? Explain to a group why some equipment is better-suited to particular riding styles. Explain and/or demonstrate the different types of tack and equipment and how to care for it to a group of beginning riders. Be able to recognize worn and unsafe tack. Or enter a horse show or rodeo. Identify five pieces of the equipment that you will need. List five criteria that the judges will be looking for in the particular event in which you will be competing.

3 With permission, visit two or three stables and interview the owners about as many of the following as you can:

■ Boarding prices.

■ Stall accommodations.

■ Storage of hay and feed.

■ Number of horses.

■ Feeding schedules.

■ Types of riding rings and trail systems.

■ Amount of pasture.

■ Types of bedding.

■ Method of manure disposal.

■ Quality and amount of water easily available to horses.

Keep a record of your findings, and list the technology that is used in the care, feeding, and hygiene of horses.

4 For a minimum of two months, track the financial responsibilities involved in owning a horse. Include the cost of rent or purchase, tack, farrier's bills, veterinarian's bills, training, supplies, food, etc. You may also need to include other expenses, such as show fees, riding instruction, and transportation, if they apply.

5 If you have access to the Internet at home, at school, or at the public library, track information about horses. Print it out, and share the reading material with friends or fellow riders.

Service Projects

1 Volunteer to assist in the care of horses at a local animal shelter or elsewhere. Or find out about programs that protect wild horses. Find a way to support the effort, and volunteer your services for at least one day.

2 Find out how horses are used in therapeutic programs for people with disabilities, what the programs entail, and how horses can help. Locate a nearby stable where there is such a program (or any horse-related program that helps people with disabilities), and find out about volunteer opportunities.

3 Make a bibliography of storybooks about horses. Include illustrated and multicultural books. Select your favorites and read them to a group of younger girls. Share your own experiences with them.

4 If you have your own horse, think of ways in which you and your horse can benefit someone else. Advertise your services by word-of-mouth or by posting fliers.

Career Exploration

1 Find out about three careers related to horses and explore three of them. Find out about the training required, salaries, job market, etc. To what professional organizations do members of each field belong? Give a presentation of your findings to a troop or group.

2 Follow a veterinarian on her horse calls to observe what she looks for when treating a horse. Ask her about the advantages and disadvantages of her career, and what she likes best about it.

3 Shadow a horse trainer. Learn about her daily responsibilities. How do they differ from the responsibilities of a veterinarian?

4 Attend a rodeo or visit a library and get information about rodeos. List three different rodeo careers that involve horses. Select one that interests you and interview or read about a woman working in that career. Find out about her skills, and about the benefits and challenges, even dangers, of her work.

5 Find out about the skills involved in the production or restoration of carousel horses, such as carpentry, woodcarving, designing, and painting. Visit your local carousel for information. Some cities have carousel organizations that restore old carousels in city parks. See your local historical society or chamber of commerce. Make a collage of carousel horses using original photographs, drawings, or magazine illustrations. At a carousel near you, treat yourself and a young child to a ride.

6 Interview a mounted police officer. Learn about the role of horses in police work and how they are trained.

And Beyond

READ THE POEM "THE JUMP" ON PAGE 117 in the *Cadette Girl Scout Handbook*. Animal lovers will enjoy these related interest projects:

■ Wildlife
■ Pets
■ All About Birds

On the Court

From recreational athletes "shooting hoops" in the backyard to pros smashing serves at world-class tennis events, a variety of sports are played on different courts all around the world. Learning to play a new sport, or becoming more adept at one that you already love, can enable you to meet people with similar interests and become physically fit in the process! So get out on the courts and try this interest project!

Skill Builders

* This skill-builder is required before doing any of the other activities.

*1 Before you start playing any sport, you should warm up and stretch the muscles you will be using. Although your physical education teacher, coach, or athletic trainer will be able to show you the best warm-ups for specific muscle groups, generally start by slowly stretching the muscles you'll be using for a minimum of 15 seconds. Repeat the stretch and hold for another 15 seconds. In addition, several minutes of a low-intensity aerobic activity (running, skipping, jogging, biking, etc.) will also warm the muscles.

2 With the help of a knowledgeable person, learn the basic rules for basketball. What is a foul? What is a foul shot? What does a "double dribble" mean? What are the three basic positions? Then learn three basic skills: dribbling, passing, and shooting. Be able to travel half the court while "holding" your dribble; complete a pass to another player; and make a basket from the foul line.

3 Get on the tennis court with a friend or coach. Learn how to serve the ball and how to hit forehand and backhand strokes. See if you can maintain a rally for five exchanges. Learn the rules of the game, how to score, and the meaning of such calls as "net," "out," and "fault."

4 Working with someone who is knowledgeable about volleyball, learn about the different positions, such as "hitter" and "setter." Understand how player rotation works. Learn how the game is scored, the difference between a "point" and a "side-out" as well as the basic strategy of "bump, set, spike." Be able to serve the ball (either underhand or overhand), set a ball, and hit a ball over the net, either by bumping or spiking it.

5 Become better at one particular sport. Keep a record of your progress over a three-week period. With the help of a coach, teacher, or knowledgeable adult, develop a program that concentrates on basketball, volleyball, or tennis skills while increasing your overall fitness level.

6 Learn more about the skills needed to be the official or referee who enforces the rules. Watch two or three games in a sport of your choice. Make a list of the major rules the officials must monitor during a game, like "traveling" or "foot faults." If possible, record part of the game and review the official rulings in two or three cases. Do you agree or disagree with each ruling? Why?

Technology

1 How has sports equipment changed over the years? Choose one piece of equipment and chart its evolution, focusing on both the design and materials used. What do you predict will happen to sports equipment in the future?

2 Sports medicine and rehabilitative therapy training equipment have improved the ability of athletes to perform at their maximum levels. Follow the treatment of one athlete through the news (television, newspaper, radio) as she recovers during a season. Keep notes on the medical terminology and processes she undergoes, as well as the rehabilitative treatments she receives.

3 Choose one sport and determine how equipment has been adapted for athletes with disabilities, depending on their specific needs. Were changes made in the rules of the sport? Why?

4 Do a survey to determine which court sports, at which level, get the most media coverage. Keep track of both women's and men's teams, on both the college and professional levels. Also include in your survey the types of media coverage. How have the media affected the playing of a particular sport, players' rights, and salaries?

3 Volunteer at a sports clinic for girls in your community or work with a group of younger Girl Scouts to help them develop sport skills.

4 Work with either a teacher or organization leader to develop a sporting event for girls. For more details in setting up a tournament, read pages 119–121 in the *Cadette Girl Scout Handbook*.

5 Volunteer in a sports program that helps children with disabilities. While developing the activities, find out about the challenges that these children face. Follow through with your work to help the children complete an event.

6 Compile information about Title IX. Research how it has affected the sport of basketball, volleyball, or tennis for women. Interview at least three women of different ages about their opinions and experiences with Title IX and sports. Make the information available to others.

sports photographer. Find out pertinent information from this photographer and then spend some time with her. Take notes on her work and experiences.

5 Observe a sports announcer. What does she do? How does her sportscasting affect your understanding and enjoyment of the game? Investigate the field of sportscasting by finding out about the experience and education of three different announcers.

6 Write an article for your school or community paper focusing on girls' or women's teams. Observe both the game (or series of games) and the spectators. Interview the players, coaches, and family members to obtain quotes to use in your article. Don't forget to include statistics as well as human interest.

Service Projects

1 Develop a resource list of sports programs for girls or women in your community. Contact schools, parents or guardians, youth-serving organizations (such as Girl Scouts), or a community recreation agency. You might also check the sports section from the local newspaper for information.

2 Find out which colleges and universities offer sports scholarships for women. Investigate four colleges that would be of interest to you and find out if they offer athletic scholarships and in what sports. Or select a sport in which you excel and find at least six colleges and universities that offer that sport and have scholarships available.

Career Exploration

1 Invite a professional female athlete to give a talk or demonstration at your school or to your team. Publicize the event in a variety of ways—fliers, radio spots, etc.

2 With a group of friends, watch a movie about the life of an athlete or coach. Discuss what was inspiring about this individual.

3 Shadow a coach at either the high school or college level. Spend at least one day with the coach and have her describe her profession, participation in the sport, and future plans.

4 Learn about sports photography as a career. Contact a community newspaper to locate a

And Beyond

LOOK BEYOND THE COURTS TO OTHER sports and fitness-related interest projects:

- Rolling Along
- Sports for Life
- On the Playing Field
- Water Sports
- Paddle, Pole, and Roll
- Backpacking
- High Adventure
- Outdoor Survival

The well-rounded athlete will also benefit from:

- Leadership
- Invitation to the Dance
- Women's Health
- The Food Connection
- From Fitness to Fashion
- From Stress to Success
- Camping
- Orienteering

On the Playing Field

*P*laying on an athletic team thrills many people because it is physically, mentally, and emotionally challenging. Through competition in sports, people learn the value of cooperation, teamwork, and dedication to a goal. Of course, involvement in sports is not all about winning and losing. Going out on the playing field means being with friends, getting fit, and having fun!

Skill Builders

1 Read pages 127–129 of *A Resource Book for Senior Girl Scouts* and take note of the sports safety tips, or get some background information on different sports by referring to pages 117–124 of the *Cadette Girl Scout Handbook.* Set up a one-month schedule to reach a sports-related goal and follow it.

2 Enroll in a sports clinic offered in your community or school.

3 Become an expert. Learn the rules, basic skills, and strategies of a specific sport.

4 Create a scrapbook or poster devoted to the accomplishments of female athletes all over the world. Scan the sports section of newspapers, sports magazines, and other journals for articles and pictures to use in your project.

5 With the help of a coach, physical education teacher, or medical professional, develop a conditioning program designed to improve your level of fitness or to prepare you for participation in a specific sport. Understand the reasons for including each activity in the conditioning program. Decide on a period of time to carry out your program. Compare your level of fitness before, during, and after participation in this conditioning program.

6 Teach a friend a sports skill at which you are particularly proficient. You might show someone how to throw a softball correctly, or spend some time reviewing the rules or strategies of volleyball or field hockey with someone who is unfamiliar with the details of the game.

Technology

1 There are a huge number of sports-oriented computer and video games. Most of these products, however, concentrate on men's sports and male athletes. Being as creative as you can be, develop on paper or on a computer, if possible, an idea for a game that features female athletes. Think about the objectives and rules of your game.

2 From batting cages to rowing machines, all sports have highly technical equipment to help athletes hone their skills. Choose one sport and brainstorm a list of the various kinds of equipment that athletes might use. Try to test out at least one piece of equipment.

3 Technology helps physical therapists and athletic trainers reduce injuries among athletes or recover from injuries. Arrange to interview a physical therapist or athletic trainer. Have her show what new advances have improved the type of medical care that can be given, and for what types of injuries they are used.

4 Get online to help girls who are interested in sports to learn about opportunities that exist in your community. You can create a directory of sports programs and teams open to young women. Try to include school sports, including intramural teams, community recreation programs, and Girl Scout sports programs.

5 Sports photography is a field that requires professionals to have in-depth knowledge of specialized equipment. Go to a camera store and ask the employees what types of film, lenses, cameras, filters, tripods, etc., are used by the experts. If possible, take a series of pictures using some of the special equipment and techniques you learn about. You may be able to borrow a camera and other equipment from your high school newspaper, your council, or maybe from your religious or community center.

Service Projects

1 Volunteer to take photographs of a Girl Scout sports event to help publicize the project in the community.

2 Together with other Girl Scouts and members of the community, clean up a park or a vacant lot and establish a field where sports like soccer, softball, field hockey, or ultimate frisbee might be played.

3 Be a referee in a league for younger children who play a sport you know about or for which you can receive training as a referee or coach. Make sure you know all of the rules and be fair in calling the game.

4 Volunteer to coach a team of younger children. Help them to develop the skills and attitudes necessary to be successful athletes. Read about the benefits of playing team sports on pages 118–119 of *Cadette Girl Scout Handbook* and find out more about how sports can affect your outlook on life on pages 128–129 of *A Resource Book for Senior Girl Scouts*.

5 Collect sports equipment to distribute to individuals who are unable to purchase their own. You may want to establish a loan system or you may want to give the donated equipment away permanently.

Career Exploration

1 Watch a professional sporting event on television and make a list of at least five careers associated with that game other than "professional athlete." Share this list with other members of your troop or group.

2 Create a sports networking list. Start by brainstorming all the people you know who are involved in sports-related careers and to whom you feel you could talk. Call at least two of these people and conduct an "informational interview." Ask them questions about their profession, their educational background, what a routine day is like, etc. At the conclusion of each interview, ask if the person knows someone else to whom you might speak. You might want to speak to these people when you are seeking a summer job or an internship.

3 Most organized sports have professional associations that monitor the manner in which the games are played. Using the *Encyclopedia of Associations*, find the name and address of an association for the sport that most interests you. Either by writing or calling, find out what prospects women have for careers in that sport. Ask the association what other careers might be related to that sport.

4 Read the biography or autobiography of two female athletes on professional teams. Try to determine if their fields interest you. Are professional sports as glamorous as they might appear in the media? Do women receive a fair amount of recognition for their accomplishments? After reading, host a discussion in your troop or group on these topics.

And Beyond

BECOME A SPORTSWRITER FOR YOUR HIGH school newspaper.

Read sports magazines and watch for special clinics and events that offer opportunities to participate in sports that you have not tried before.

To improve your skills, on and off the playing field, try these related interest projects:

- On the Court
- Sports for Life
- Rolling Along
- Water Sports
- Backpacking
- Orienteering
- From Fitness to Fashion
- From Stress to Success
- High Adventure
- Your Best Defense

Women's Health focuses on mental and emotional, as well as physical, benefits of sports.

Orienteering

Would you enjoy increasing your physical fitness while competing in a sport that draws participants from around the globe? Or would you like to use map and compass skills to find your way while hiking, horseback riding, or wilderness camping? The map and compass skills you learn in this interest project could be useful all of your life. You will find Outdoor Education in Girl Scouting *a valuable resource for completing this project; see pages 103–116.*

Skill Builders

1 Obtain a U.S. Geological Survey (USGS) topographical map or an orienteering map. Show that you can identify and explain the map symbols for water, vegetation, human-constructed features, and contour features. Be able to explain what is meant by a *contour interval* and why it is important. Learn how to use the map scale and practice determining the actual distance between points on a map. Draw a map of your neighborhood, schoolyard, community park, or Girl Scout camp. Be sure to include the scale and legend.

2 Be able to identify each of the basic parts of a protractor compass. Learn to take a compass bearing from a map using a baseplate protractor compass. Be able to demonstrate your skill at taking a bearing from a map and then walking to your destination.

3 Using a U.S. Geological Survey (USGS) topographical map of your community, learn how to orient the map to magnetic north. Fold the map so you can focus on the area where you are located. Practice the orienteering skill of "thumbing the map" by marking your place on the map with your thumb as you go for a walk around your neighborhood.

Maintain contact with the map with your thumb at all times while keeping the map oriented.

4 Learn to select the proper clothing and footwear to participate in an orienteering meet. Consider the time of year, the terrain, and the distance of the course. Learn to dress appropriately to protect yourself from ticks, poisonous plants, and snakes. Know what to do if you become lost. Be able to explain the meaning and importance of a *safety bearing.* Show that you can follow a safety bearing to a road or major trail.

5 Apply your knowledge. Take part in a local orienteering meet. Complete a white (beginner) or yellow (advanced beginner) level course. After the meet, compare your route choices with others. Discuss what you did well and what you might have done differently.

Technology

1 Use a computer graphics program or a CAD (computer-aided design) program to create a map of your neighborhood, schoolyard, or local park. Be sure to include the scale and legend.

2 Explore the Internet for topics related to maps, compasses, and orienteering. Subject areas you might investigate include orienteering, backcountry, hiking, maps, weather, U.S. Geological Survey, and geography. Find several bulletin boards that post messages about orienteering. Talk to others interested in orienteering through online chat sessions.

3 Find out how a compass is constructed and the different features to consider when purchasing a compass. Learn how designers of compasses use computer technology to create their products.

4 Learn about the U.S. Geological Survey National Mapping Program. What resources are available and what tools are used? Information is available online or through the U.S. Geological Survey and the Department of the Interior.

5 Find out how a Global Positioning System (GPS) works. What types of recreational activities and professions might utilize a GPS device and in what ways?

Service Projects

1 Prepare an orienteering map of one acre or more for a Girl Scout camp, local park, or schoolyard. Field-check features for accuracy; include a legend, a scale, and contour intervals.

2 Work with an orienteering club to organize an orienteering meet in your community. You can also organize a meet on your own by consulting printed resources. Find out the duties of the meet director, registrar, course setter, and persons in charge of the start and finish. Practice being a course setter. Use an orienteering map and set out 5–10 controls for a white (beginner) course.

3 Contact your local orienteering club or the U.S. Orienteering Federation to find out about string orienteering, a program for young children. Set up a string orienteering course for Daisy or Brownie Girl Scouts.

4 Organize an orienteering meet or workshop for Girl Scouts in your neighborhood or council. If possible, ask volunteers from an orienteering club to help you. Provide instruction for the participants in the use of a map and compass. Make an orienteering map available, recruit assistants, design a course, set the controls, and plan an awards ceremony.

Career Exploration

1 Learn about people who use maps or orienteering skills in their jobs. Make a list of careers that involve the significant use of a map and compass. Interview two people with such careers in person, by telephone, by fax, or by e-mail. Find out about educational requirements and employment opportunities.

2 The ability to use a map and compass accurately is an important skill for someone who leads sea kayaking, backpacking, or other high adventure trips. Discuss career possibilities with outfitters or trip leaders. What other skills and educational requirements are required to do these jobs?

3 Orienteering is a lifetime recreational skill. Join an orienteering club and participate in at least three club activities.

4 Be the route finder on a wilderness trip with your troop or group.

And Beyond

APPLY YOUR SKILLS IN ORIENTEERING. Compete in an orienteering meet by completing a course at the yellow (advanced beginner) level or above.

If you'd like to use your new orienteering skills, try them out with these related interest projects:

- Travel
- Paddle, Pole, and Roll
- Smooth Sailing
- Camping
- Backpacking

Outdoor Survival

Whether you are taking a trip, going on a weekend camping expedition, or traveling in a wilderness area, there is always the potential of a life-threatening situation arising. Your most important survival tool is your head. Being prepared, avoiding panic, and learning to work with others are keys to survival. This interest project will provide you with the skills and confidence needed to meet the challenges of outdoor survival.

Skill Builders

1 Read books or view videos about survival experiences and adventures involving physical and mental endurance. Talk about ways to deal with hunger, thirst, pain, and panic in crisis situations. Discuss the importance of the determination to survive. Agree on ways to make decisions, such as when to turn back, to stay put, or to change plans.

2 When traveling outdoors, know how and where to report an accident and how to get help. Have a local search-and-rescue group (for example, county sheriff's office, Civil Air Patrol, ski patrol, Coast Guard, or park security force) provide you with information on signaling methods and symbols, using flares and other devices, and locating help in an emergency. Create a "lost plan" for a group going on an outing. Include emergency numbers and contacts and what each person's role should be in an emergency. Review appropriate activity checkpoints and "Planning Trips with Girl Scouts," pages 126–140 in *Safety-Wise*, if applicable.

3 Take a course with special emphasis on outdoor survival techniques. Put together your own essentials to meet the need for shelter, water, warmth, energy, and signaling to carry in your daypack, backpack, or vehicle.

4 Evaluate what shelter sites and materials can be used most effectively to protect you from wind, cold, heat, lightning, or falling objects. If it is environmentally sound and permission is given, construct a shelter using fallen branches, other found materials, or the natural features of a site; for example, construct a snow cave for winter survival or storm-lash a backpacking tent. Or create an exhibit of small-scale models of improvised shelters.

5 Water is a priority for survival along with air and shelter. Learn two methods of water purification—for example, boiling water, using special chemicals or filters that eliminate *Giardia lamblia* (water-borne parasites). Learn how to construct and use a simple solar still in the ground to extract water, and above-ground to turn sea water into fresh water. Practice ways to avoid hypothermia. Refer to *Outdoor Education in Girl Scouting*, pages 36–37.

Technology

1 How do you find out about weather conditions prior to departing on a trip? Use two different technologies to access information about weather.

2 Compare the properties of cotton, wool, and synthetic fabrics for protection from wet, cold, and heat. Interview someone at a store specializing in outdoor equipment for recommendations and, if possible, test different fabrics yourself for warmth and *wicking* (water traveling by capillary action in fabric) when wet. How does "down" compare with other materials? How does a "space blanket" work? When might it be needed in a survival situation?

3 Become confident with a compass. Use a compass to orient a map, to navigate accurately around obstacles, and to backsight to return to your original location. Go on an orienteering course or travel from one point to another cross-country to test your compass skills. Demonstrate two methods to find direction without a compass. Discuss how conditions, such as fog, a sandstorm, or a snow white-out, would complicate direction-finding and what you should do in case of each of those conditions.

4 Know when, where, and how to start a campfire for warming, drying, lighting, cooking, and signaling. Know when and where fires should not be used. Specifically, learn how to: light a fire (find two methods) without using a match; light and maintain a fire under difficult conditions such as on a wet day or in a deep snow; produce a fire without wood fuel; make a fire starter for your survival kit; extinguish fires safely, leaving no trace; and use a backpacking stove to heat water.

5 Consider the safety of staying in a car in a snowstorm, severe lightning storm, or desert survival situation. Assume that you and another person are stranded in a car. Describe how different parts of the car might be used to ensure survival. Investigate safety precautions (for instance, with a car's heating system).

Service Projects

1 At a school, campground, or camp, plan and present a "what to do if you become lost" program or skit for younger children. Include discussions on how to handle panic; simple equipment to carry (such as a whistle) on outings; dressing for any weather; encountering animals; and what to do if separated from a group. Discuss occurrences common to your area, such as flash floods, extreme weather conditions, or city safety.

2 Plan and facilitate an outdoor skills game that promotes learning about survival skills for peers or a Junior Girl Scout troop or group.

3 Using the first-aid skills and survival training you already have, plus any special training needed, volunteer your services. Work with a search-and-rescue group, ski patrol, or other emergency rescue group in your community. Participate in an actual search or disaster drill.

4 Develop a survival board game, poster, video, or outdoor game that highlights outdoor safety and survival tips for your council's resident campsite, program center, or library, or for use in a local elementary school.

Career Exploration

1 Interview someone professionally involved in outdoor survival or search and rescue. This person could be a wilderness guide or instructor, member of a sheriff's patrol or search-and-rescue team leader, U.S. Coast Guard member, ski patrol coordinator, wilderness ranger, search-and-rescue dog trainer, or mountain rescue paramedic. Find out what training and certification they have for their jobs, and what career paths they would recommend.

2 Tour an outdoor goods store or company that manufactures outdoor gear. Find out about jobs in retail, equipment/clothing design, or manufacturing that relate to outdoor gear. Learn how equipment is designed and tested to enhance safety.

3 Relate how you might incorporate your interests in survival with a different career path (such as teaching, research, writing, business, medicine, or law) and talk with someone with this experience.

4 Host a panel discussion on a survival topic, such as disaster preparedness, hypothermia, or a local concern.

And Beyond

YOU MIGHT WANT TO VOLUNTEER OR continue to volunteer for a search-and-rescue group and apply it to a Community Service Bar with additional training; or become certified as an instructor for a challenge course.

Outdoor survival skills can be valuable in other settings. Put them to the test with these related interest projects:

- Camping
- Backpacking
- Emergency Preparedness
- Orienteering
- Paddle, Pole, and Roll
- Smooth Sailing
- Water Sports
- Wildlife

Paddle, Pole, and Roll

f you are a water baby with an adventurous edge, Paddle, Pole, and Roll is an interest project with many appealing canoeing and kayaking activities for you. **Note**: *Always wear a personal floatation device (PFD) when participating in canoeing or kayaking activities on the water. Read the requirements for canoeing and kayaking in Safety-Wise.*

Skill Builders

* Activities #1 and #2 are required before doing the other activities in this section.

* *1* In the presence of a certified lifeguard or instructor, demonstrate your ability to go under and back up to the surface of the water confidently and your comfort level in the water while wearing a PFD. Or pass an American Red Cross swim test.

* *2* Show an instructor that you can handle a canoe or kayak. Demonstrate that you can:

- Balance your craft and get in it safely.

- Start, stop, dock, and beach your craft.

- Go straight for 50 yards.

- Go backward for 50 yards.

- Go sideways for 50 yards.

- Make a left turn, a right turn, and a 360° turn.

- Swamp your canoe and paddle back to shore.

- Lift your craft over your head safely for portaging.

3 Demonstrate with proficiency for your instructor the following strokes:

- Stroke

- Sweep stroke

- Feather stroke

- Reach and pull

- Rudder

- Forward paddle

- Double-blade paddle

- Single-person paddling

- Double-person paddling

4 Write the maintenance and storage checklist for your craft and equipment. Include basic care for transportation and long-term storage, and repair instructions for trouble such as leaks, punctures, broken ribs, and bends in the gunwale. Check the accuracy of this information with your instructor. Submit this list to your local Girl Scout camp for posting in its waterfront boathouse, if such a list is not already available.

5 Know basic first aid for water safety, including hypothermia, drowning, shock, cardiopulmonary resuscitation (CPR), breaks, sprains, heatstroke, dehydration, and bleeding. Enroll in a standard first-aid course and CPR course. Create a list of the contents for a first-aid kit, including an emergency management plan with contact persons included.

6 With your instructor's or leader's assistance, role-play the following situations and demonstrate how you would handle them.

■ A medical emergency happens while you are canoeing: for example, the friend who is accompanying you suffers sunstroke.

■ A person is thrown into fast-moving water. The other person is alone in the boat.

■ A canoe overturns, leaving one person with a broken arm and the other with a PFD in the water.

■ Your paddle falls into fast-moving water.

■ A severe storm, with lighting and thunder, rolls in while you are out boating in the middle of a large lake.

7 Help plan and take part in at least a one-day canoe/kayak trip. Learn to "read" the water conditions and know the international scale of difficulty. Understand the importance of planning a safe trip; include in your plan time for reading the river, checking the weather, and assessing whether or not you will portage your craft at any point on the river.

Technology

1 Assemble a waterproof fanny pack of river supplies and tools and submit it for your instructor's approval. Include river-reading tools, compass, repair kit, map, first-aid kit, rescue tube, flare, food, and written emergency procedures.

2 Use the Internet to locate information on four rivers in different regions of the country. Research a nearby campground for each river, including cost per night, the facilities available, and area activities. Write down the uniform resource locator (URL) for each Web site you discover on an index card for your troop or group planning box.

3 Interview a salesperson at an outdoor supplies store about the materials used to construct today's canoes, kayaks, water clothing, and supplies. Find out why these materials continue to change and where this technology is going in the future. Report back to your troop or group.

4 Know the major parts of a canoe or kayak. Construct a small-scale model out of cardboard, clay, bark, or synthetic materials. Explain the function of each part. For an added challenge, construct a model canoe or kayak from your own design and explain its advantages.

Service Projects

1 Create a file of articles and brochures about river trips as well as a list of outfitters who guide such trips. Share this information with others in your council or community.

2 Volunteer at your local Girl Scout camp during its pre-camp training session. Help bring canoes out of storage; scrub them down in preparation for summer camp use.

3 Help develop a detailed canoe/kayak trail guide of a single navigable river or waterway. Include some interesting facts about the area, such as its geology, animal and plant life, and ecology.

4 Demonstrate how to choose a proper-fitting personal flotation device (PFD). Share information about the role of clothing in preventing hypothermia with a group planning a water adventure.

Career Exploration

1 Find out the necessary skills and age and certification requirements for a job as a river guide by contacting a local trip outfitter.

2 Conduct a canoe/kayak skill and safety demonstration for other Girl Scouts in a swimming pool.

3 Consider the career of owning your own canoe/kayak tripping business. Make a flier advertising your business that states why people should choose your company as its recreational water outfitter. (Consider safety, fun, cost, etc.) Show your flier to your troop or group and ask for feedback.

4 Prepare for a job at a Girl Scout camp. Check *Safety-Wise* for requirements and ask your Girl Scout council for a waterfront boating staff job description. Write a résumé for this job.

And Beyond

ENROLL IN A BASIC CANOE OR KAYAK course with the American Canoe Association.

If water adventure whets your appetite further, try these related interest projects:

■ From Shore to Sea
■ Smooth Sailing
■ High Adventure
■ Camping
■ Water Sports
■ Outdoor Survival

Rolling Along

In-line skating, skateboarding, and cycling are three great ways to get around. Sports that are incorporated into your daily life have far-reaching benefits. Not only are your bones, heart, and lungs strengthened by exercise, but your stress level is reduced and your mood improves, too. And who knows, such a combination of good physical and mental health might be reflected in improved schoolwork and more energy for other fun stuff!

Skill Builders

* The first Skill Builder activity is required before completing any of the other activities in this interest project.

* **1** Before you start any sport in Rolling Along, do at least five different stretches to prepare the muscles you will be using. Hold each stretch for at least 15 seconds, and keep breathing throughout the stretch. The idea is to slowly and gently expand your range within the stretch, not to force it and pull a muscle.

2 Create your own bicycling workout plan and bike at least three times a week for a couple of months. Make a personalized list of rules to follow based on the climate and terrain you will encounter. Start with these: *Always* wear a helmet, make sure that your brakes are aligned and in good repair, and check the tire pressure on both wheels. *Always* ride with the traffic on the far right-hand side of the street, unless you are preparing to make a left-handed turn. *Always* signal your stopping and turns, so that drivers can anticipate your actions. Teach these safety rules to others, including any partners who may wish to bike with you.

3 Demonstrate your ability to do the following:

■ Know, understand, and comply with the vehicle codes for the state in which you will cycle.

■ Know and demonstrate hand signals. Contact the police department or local bicycle clubs to help you with these.

■ Know how to execute basic bike maneuvers such as braking and turns to avoid an obstacle.

4 Plan a bike trip with others. Map out a route that avoids heavily trafficked areas or pavements unsuitable to biking. Have someone use a car odometer to track your route. Or you can use a pedometer to measure your distance. Start with 20–25 minutes and then work up to one or two hours (with breaks as needed).

5 Learn safety rules for in-line skating and teach them to two others. For instance: *Always* wear a helmet and protective gear (wrist guards, elbowpads, and kneepads). Wearing long sleeves and pants will also help protect you if you fall. Learn to brake properly by having someone knowledgeable demonstrate the technique or by following directions given at a sports center, skating supply store, or skating class. Find out about the best type of braking system, front stoppers, back stoppers, etc. Create and follow an in-line skating plan for a one-month period.

6 Master the sport of skateboarding. Learn and follow safety rules; create and follow a workout plan for one month.

7 Become an expert! If you already know how to skate, skate-board, or bike, advance your skills and learn something new. For instance, learn how to skate backward or do jumps and stunts on your in-line skates and skateboard.

Or take a two-day bike trip, or try mountain biking.

Technology

1 Skating, biking, and skateboarding require protective gear: for example, helmets, kneepads, and padded gloves. Visit a sports store, or look through catalogs and magazines to learn about the varieties of protective gear available. Learn about the maintenance and replacement schedule you should observe. Research and identify the next item of protective gear you will need.

2 Not so long ago, bicycles had only one gear, tennis shoes were used for cycling, and in-line skates didn't even exist! Compare the older and newer versions of three to five types of sports gear, and list three improvements in the new ones. Discuss your findings in your troop or group or club.

3 Learn how to maintain, repair, and upgrade your skates or board. Talk with a sports pro in your area or online and find out how to repair or replace parts. Once you've mastered the repairs, teach or help someone else do the same. Or demonstrate a thorough knowledge of bicycle repair, including repairs to the following: tires, braking system, wheels, spokes, hubs, derailleur, headset, stem, handlebars, seat, and power train. Or attend a clinic on cycle maintenance and repair. Demonstrate your ability to set up a maintenance schedule for your bicycle and stick to it. Demonstrate your ability to change a flat tire.

Service Projects

1 Offer help to a service organization that is running an event such as a bike-a-thon or skate-a-thon. Assist with route planning, first aid (if you're certified), registration, or to set up, clean up, pack up, and assist participants.

2 Run a clinic to teach bike or skate repairs and maintenance.

3 Run a basic skills workshop to teach younger girls skills on wheels, from bikes to skates.

4 Work with a bike or sports store to organize or run a "bikes/skates for kids" program. Older equipment is donated by the community, repaired by children and adults, and given to children in need. Remember that certain adaptations might be needed for children with disabilities.

5 Volunteer to be one of the guides or counselors for a bike trip lasting two or three days.

Career Exploration

1 List four careers other than professional athlete that relate to the design or use of sports-on-wheels equipment: a textile designer or product representative, for example. Find out and then discuss in your club or troop or group what the job requirements are.

2 Do you know a talented skater or cyclist? Ask her how she sees the sport affecting her life. Is she more productive at work? Less? What advice could she give an aspiring athlete about competition, conditioning, or the value of attaining a goal?

3 You are a sports gear or footwear designer called into the Olympics to design new in-line skates, footwear, etc., for the athletes. Draw your design, providing descriptions and rationales for the materials you choose. Also, specify how and on whom you will pilot-test your new product.

4 How could excellence in skateboarding, cycling, or in-line skating be put to use in working with children, including those with disabilities? Design a program specifying age, exercises, and goals. Find a local youth-serving organization or school where you can "try out" your program for at least two sessions. Or offer to assist in an existing program.

5 Interview a physical therapist about her work with people in wheelchairs, and also about how she uses skates/skating for people with certain kinds of disabilities. What was her training? What advice can she offer for a young person considering a career in physical therapy and sports?

And Beyond

FIND OUT ABOUT SPORTING EVENTS FOR persons in wheelchairs. Attend, assist at, or publicize such an event in your community.

If motion is your thing, look at these related interest projects:

- Car Sense
- Sports for Life
- Women's Health
- Travel
- Invitation to the Dance

Design a better car or rollerblades with Build a Better Future and Rolling Along.

Smooth Sailing

*S*ailing brings you into harmony with the wind and the water, the craft and the crew. Whether you are skipper or crew in a boat small or tall, you make a difference when you pull together with others under sail.

You must follow Safety-Wise *guidelines*, work with a qualified, experienced adult sailor and wear a life jacket (PFD.) Under supervision of a lifeguard, perform the water-safety exercise in the activity checkpoints for boating in Safety-Wise.

Skill Builders

* Activities #1 and #4 are required before doing any other activities in this section.

*1 Show you know how to be safe on the water including:

■ What to do to prevent and treat hypothermia, near-drowning, heatstroke and sunburn.

■ How to prevent and respond to emergencies including falling overboard, capsizing, swamping and collisions.

■ How to determine weather patterns and wind direction and follow safe weather rules.

■ How to choose, check and care for life jackets and other safety gear.

■ How to use a checkboard system and/or file a float plan.

2 Learn the communication signals and language used by sailors. Show that you know the meaning of nautical terms including: port and starboard, bow and stern, fore and aft, mast and boom, sheet and halyard, cast off and make fast, jibe and tack, lift and luff, heel and trim, head up and fall off; leeward and windward.

3 Show you "know the ropes."

■ Tie and show the use of a figure-eight knot, bowline, cleat hitch, round turn and two half hitches, and reef (square) knot.

■ Practice handling line: making a coil, getting kinks out of a line, tying to a post, ring or rail; making fast to a cleat, throwing a line for docking or towing.

*4 Show you can get underway and handle a boat:

■ Show how to step aboard, sit and move around.

■ Rig or ready the boat and raise and lower sails.

■ Start, stop and use the safety position.

■ Go through an overboard recovery.

■ Pick up a mooring, come alongside, make a landing and/or anchor the boat.

5 Master maneuvering. Show that you know how to trim sail; steer a steady course; tack and jibe; and "get out of irons." Identify the points of sail on upwind, downwind and crosswind courses.

Technology

1 Get the general forecast from the newspaper, weather channel, radio, or World Wide Web. Using a barometer, radar, storm signals, and/or National Weather Service radio, predict local conditions:

- Use a tide table to figure the time of sunrise, sunset, tides, or currents that affect your sailing.

- Tell wind direction and estimate wind speed from telltales, flags, the wind's effect on the boat, wave heights, and other water conditions.

- Predict weather changes by clouds and wind shifts.

2 Know how to tell where you are and how to get where you want to go. Do two of the following:

- Be able to tell direction by the sun and the stars.

- Practice dead reckoning, taking bearings, fixing your position, and estimating time of arrival.

- Figure the latitude and longitude of your home port.

- Read chart symbols for aids to navigation and hazards on and under the water.

- Plot courses for a day's run. Figure the true, magnetic, and compass courses.

3 Fine-tune your boat for racing under sail. As crew or skipper, show how to get the most speed out of the boat, figuring when and how much to adjust your weight, sails, lines, centerboard, and rig. Or compare and contrast three sail rigs and their suitability for day sailing, cruising, or racing on different waters.

4 Get good at electronic communication and navigation aids: Using proper protocol, monitor and communicate on marine radio. Work with the GPS, depth sounder, radar, and other devices.

Service Projects

1 Help organize or volunteer at a sailing event, such as a sailing clinic, a race, a regatta, or a parade of tall ships.

2 Help maintain sailboats for active use or winter storage.

3 Teach someone how to choose and put on a PFD and other basics of safe sailing. (Contact the U.S. Coast Guard Auxiliary or the boating law enforcement agency for your area.)

4 Volunteer at a maritime museum, lighthouse, Coast Guard station, or naval site, or on an historic sailing ship.

5 Teach younger girls to tie knots, bends, and hitches used by sailors, and how to whip and splice a line. Make something useful like a ditty bag or heaving line.

Career Exploration

1 Interview someone whose job is sailing-related: a sailing instructor; a trip leader for an eco-adventure company; a boat builder; a sail maker; a yacht broker; a deckhand; a ship's cook; a licensed captain. Find out what kind of training and experience are needed.

2 Identify a college or training program for two of the following: nautical archaeologist, marine architect, admiralty lawyer, marina resort manager, marine biologist, member of the Navy or Coast Guard, or maritime museum curator or historian.

3 Bring maritime heritage to life. Learn and enjoy a tradition related to sailing, such as scrimshaw, macramé, ship modeling, or chantey singing.

4 Find out about programs and membership in local sailing groups that are part of national organizations, such as U.S. Sailing, U.S. Coast Guard Auxiliary, or the American Sail Training Association.

And Beyond

READ A SHIP'S LOG OR ABOUT "CRUISING" voyagers for whom sailing is a way of life. Sail on with these related interest projects:

- Paddle, Pole, and Roll
- Water Sports
- High Adventure
- From Shore to Sea

Sports for Life

nvolvement with sports can benefit you mentally as well as physically. Sports activity not only can strengthen muscles and improve your cardiovascular system, but can also reduce stress and improve your mood! So it's up to you to make time for sports in your busy life!

Skill Builders

*You must complete activity #1 as a prerequisite for the other Skill Builders activities.

*1 Before you start any sport you should gently stretch and strengthen the muscles you will be using. Talk to your gym teacher, coach, athletic trainer, dance teacher, or other professional for guidance to find out what stretches and exercises are appropriate for your sport.

2 A good pair of running shoes, a nice day, and a route are all you need to start walking, jogging, or running. Your physical education teacher or coach, an athlete, or a family member can help you to learn the proper techniques. Start out covering an easy distance. As your stamina improves, increase the distance. Keep safety in mind when planning your course. Avoid areas near heavy traffic or across rough or uneven surfaces. At the end of your run you don't want to find yourself far from home as well as tired, out of breath, and thirsty, so end your course right where you started. Remember to stretch your muscles before you've begun and after you're finished. Begin your regimen with a three-day-a-week frequency. Rest on the other days to allow muscles to recuperate and adjust to their new workout. If you are running or jogging and you feel stress in your knees, shins, or back, slow down to a walk!

3 Cold weather offers a great opportunity for downhill or cross-country skiing, ice-skating, and snow boarding. Learn how to get started, stop, make turns, and get up from a fall. Practice with a friend for safety and security reasons. Falling in any of these sports can cause injury, so take a lesson from a certified trainer before you go out on your own!

4 Weight lifting and body conditioning can strengthen muscles and improve performance. You need loose, comfortable clothing, a pair of supportive sneakers, and a set of weights. Identify four or five muscle groups you want to tone and develop. Learn how to stretch and strengthen each muscle group, and how to do two exercises for each muscle. Increase your difficulty level through repetitions before increasing the weights. To ensure that you get the most from your workout, ask a knowledgeable friend to watch your form.

5 Investigate at least two types of martial arts: for example, tae kwon do, karate, yoga, judo, tai chi. Learn some basic moves or take a class in the sport you have chosen. Observe how mental attitude influences your physical performance. Demonstrate some of the exercises you've learned to the girls in your troop or group, or to others.

Technology

1 Clothing for outdoor sports is designed to keep you dry and comfortable. If your body is

too cold, the potential for injury or hypothermia increases. The thermometer doesn't have to dip below freezing for these to be a threat. Too much heat can also be a problem. It can cause heat exhaustion and dehydration. Read a sports catalog or magazine or visit a sports shop and make a list of the different types of clothing items and fabrics that protect athletes in the outdoors. Make a list of what you need to consider for the sport of your choice.

2 Sportswear now features reflective fabrics, so that an oncoming driver or athlete can more easily see you. Look at a variety of reflective sportswear. Evaluate the effectiveness of reflective wear. Are the reflective portions placed in easily visible areas? Improve upon or design your own reflective sportswear and equipment.

3 Many sports have protective gear. Learn about the materials and design used in the protective gear for your sport. How have they changed over the years? How might they change in the future?

4 As technology improves, more and more people who were once excluded from sports because of a disability or an injury can now play. Find out about two different adaptive/therapeutic devices, such as knee braces, orthotics, inhalers, and prosthetics. How do they compensate for a disability? Talk with a sports physician, a physical therapist, a sports association member, a supplier/manufacturer of the devices, or a salesperson for information.

5 While some sports have been played for many years, in some cases the quality of the equipment has improved. Runners used to wear plain tennis shoes, not the sophisticated footwear you see today. Learn about the equipment for the sport(s) you are most interested in. Learn how to maintain and repair your sports equipment.

Service Projects

1 Create a listing of local sports facilities accessible to people with disabilities, both as participants and spectators. Provide copies to your local chamber of commerce and to the facilities mentioned in the listing.

2 Volunteer to assist an athletic trainer or recreational therapist.

3 Volunteer to help children in your community become involved in sports. You could host a sports event that enables youngsters to learn new skills. Ask sports stores or organizations to donate the use of their equipment, or arrange with the school to use their facilities. Or assist in an event such as a Special Olympics.

4 Volunteer to work with professionals in your community to adapt an existing sports facility so that it is accessible to people with disabilities, both as spectators and participants.

5 Become an assistant coach for a season on a local girls' track and field team.

Career Exploration

1 Sports medicine involves a wide variety of professionals: for example, orthopedic surgeons, chiropractors, physical therapists, licensed massage therapists, psychologists, athletic trainers, medical supply manufacturers, and medical technicians. Investigate one of these careers. Interview a professional in the field of sports medicine. If possible, observe her at work. Make a record of your experience or write an article for your school paper.

2 Contact your local sports facilities and schools to find athletic trainers whom you can observe at work. Ask them about their qualifications and special areas of interest, such as aerobics or weight training.

3 Find out what colleges offer sports programs in areas of interest to you. See if they offer scholarships for athletes in those sports. Compile a listing of these colleges for future reference.

4 Offer younger girls information about a sports career. For example, put together a photo essay or create a video.

5 Recreational therapists provide services to children and adults who have suffered some sort of trauma. They work at nursing homes, hospitals, and residential institutions. Ask if you can observe or interview a recreational therapist in order to learn about her work.

And Beyond

REGISTER FOR A 5K RUN OR WALK, A MINI-marathon, or a biathlon or triathlon. Make sure you are ready, physically, to compete.
Keep in shape with these related interest projects:

- On the Playing Field
- On the Court
- Water Sports
- Smooth Sailing
- Paddle, Pole, and Roll
- High Adventure
- Outdoor Survival
- Women's Health

Water Sports

To do this interest project, you must pass a swimming test in front of a lifeguard. Jump into the water fully clothed (including shoes), right yourself, and stay afloat for five minutes.

Read Safety-Wise before doing any water-related activity. Always have a buddy, make sure there is a lifeguard, and wear a personal flotation device (PFD) for any water activity other than just swimming or splashing around. If you plan to work with others, read Safety Management at Girl Scout Sites and Facilities.

Skill Builders

1 Demonstrate basic self-rescue in the water with and without a PFD. Complete a swimming, emergency water safety, lifeguarding, or boating safety course to advance your skills in water safety.

2 Identify how exposure to the sun, wind, and water can be harmful, and which strategies will avoid these harmful effects. Learn how to recognize and administer basic first aid for sunburn, heatstroke, heat cramps, heat exhaustion, hypothermia, frostbite, and seasickness. Know when to seek a doctor's help.

3 Demonstrate proper technique in at least three basic swimming strokes. Measure your endurance and set a goal to improve it. Or participate in one of the following ways: competitive, synchronized, therapeutic, or lap swimming.

4 Attend a water aerobics class for at least six sessions. Learn proper warm-up and stretching exercises, aerobic exercises, body sculpting exercises, and cool-down exercises.

5 This activity is for very accomplished swimmers only. Learn to use a snorkel, mask, and swim fins in a pool, lake, or ocean, under the guidance of an experienced person. Know what to look for in a mask, snorkel, and fins, and how they should fit you. Practice defogging the mask and clearing the snorkel, as well as how to avoid ear problems with increased water pressure. Practice entering and leaving the water, surface swimming, and dives. Discuss basic safety and what you should know about the water environment before entering. Take care to leave underwater life and habitats undisturbed.

6 If you are an accomplished ocean swimmer, learn to surf. With an experienced instructor or advanced surfer, discuss your knowledge of ocean conditions such as the bottom, tides, currents, and wave action. In surf that matches your ability, demonstrate ways to avoid falling off your board, and ways of falling or diving from the board safely. Discuss and demonstrate ways of controlling the board. Be sure to do warm-up exercises and cool-down stretches for legs, arms, and back.

Technology

1 Visit a university or water sports training center. Learn what kinds of equipment and technology are employed to analyze and improve swim strokes or other water sports techniques. If possible, use some of this sports equipment under the guidance of a qualified expert.

2 Visit a sporting goods store, review water sports magazines, view a video, or speak to someone who uses the equipment to find out about the latest advances in equipment for a water sport of your choice. Consider snorkeling, scuba diving, windsurfing, water skiing, or surfing.

3 Use the Internet or World Wide Web to find out what is happening around the world in water sports. Do a key word search and keep a log of the resources you find. Are there any organizations, magazines, or chat groups of interest? Find out if your state or community has an online directory of water sports areas.

4 Learn how to monitor the water quality of a swimming area. Find out which tests are needed for the water in which you will swim. What is done when the conditions are not within safety guidelines? What tests are performed to test for water quality in public areas? What happens if water quality in a lake or public beach does not meet these standards? Find out about specific laws governing water testing in public swimming areas, and who monitors the testing.

5 Learn how to use a shortwave radio, CB radio, or other communications systems on a watercraft. Learn how to navigate by radio signals, landmarks, or the stars.

Service Projects

1 Take part in or organize a waterfront or shoreline cleanup. Use proper safety gear (such as gloves, goggles, flotation devices). Or help address the root of the problem by assisting with a public education program aimed at stopping shoreline littering and pollution.

2 Volunteer to work with an organization sponsoring a swimming meet, regatta, or sailing event. Help in both the planning and implementation stages.

3 Assist in or lead a water aerobics class. Use exercise routines that work all parts of the body. Consult with someone with expertise in this area.

4 Help promote a backyard pool safety program or water safety program in your community. Learn local laws and water safety tips and find a way to help users become more aware of water safety.

5 Attend a hearing or do a project concerned with use or preservation of waterfront property. Are there landfills or ecological hazards affecting bodies of water in your area? Research and prepare a report of your findings. Include drawings or photos, if you wish.

6 Create a swimming relay game or water game for young swimmers. Use several different strokes and plan activities with balls, inner tubes, rafts, and ropes. See the chapter "Wide Games and Special Events" in the Girl Scout resource *Games for Girl Scouts*.

Career Exploration

1 Visit or shadow an aquatics director at a Girl Scout camp, community center, or other recreation facility. Find out what part-time or full-time opportunities are available in aquatic sports facilities as an instructor, coach, manager, massage therapist, or dietitian. Explore education, training, and certification requirements for three of these positions.

2 Volunteer or work as a lifeguard for several Girl Scout events or an ongoing program. Or assist in a swimming instruction program for younger girls. In order to do this activity, you must meet all the necessary requirements outlined in *Safety-Wise*.

3 Hydrotherapy, or water therapy, is useful to both people and animals. Investigate the medical, educational, or engineering fields that provide the therapies and/or design the equipment for hydrotherapy by interviewing two professionals in the field. Learn how hydrotherapy helps people or animals.

4 Combine a curiosity for science and a love of water to find out about jobs in oceanography, marine biology, fish and wildlife, aquarium management, or research. Visit or talk to someone by phone or online at a university marine biology or fisheries program, a fish hatchery, an aquarium or sea park, or a water wildlife preserve to find out how her job combines fieldwork, management, and research.

5 Observe a YMCA or Red Cross baby or toddler swim class. Learn what safety methods are recommended for small children around pools. Discover ways to introduce small children to water so that they enjoy and respect it.

And Beyond

WORK WITH A COMMUNITY CENTER OR your local YWCA/YMCA to earn your Community Service Bar. To offer instruction or serve as a lifeguard in a water sports program, you must meet *Safety-Wise* age standards. Consult your Girl Scout council for opportunities to specialize in waterfront activities for CIT II.

Continue to make a splash with these related interest projects:

■ Paddle, Pole, and Roll
■ Smooth Sailing
■ Photography

Help build skills you can face from shore to sea with Backpacking, Orienteering, Outdoor Survival, and Camping.

Interest Projects:
Charting Your Progress

DIRECTIONS: Next to each interest project that you do, fill in the five columns below. Write in the numbers of the activities you completed. For example, if you completed Skill Builders #2 and #4 in Car Sense, then write those numbers in that box.

INTEREST PROJECTS

LIFE SKILLS

	SKILL BUILDERS	TECHNOLOGY	SERVICE PROJECTS	CAREER EXPLORATION	DATE/ SIGNATURE
Car Sense					
Child Care					
Conflict Resolution					
Cookies and Dough					
Dollars and Sense					
Family Living					
From Fitness to Fashion					
From Stress to Success					
Generations Hand in Hand					
Home Improvement					
Law and Order					
Leadership					
Travel					
Understanding Yourself and Others					
Your Best Defense					
Your Own Business					

INTEREST PROJECTS

NATURE, SCIENCE, and HEALTH

	SKILL BUILDERS	TECHNOLOGY	SERVICE PROJECTS	CAREER EXPLORATION	DATE/ SIGNATURE
All About Birds					
Build a Better Future					
Creative Cooking					
Digging Through the Past					
Eco-Action					
The Food Connection					
From Shore to Sea					
Inventions and Inquiry					
It's About Time					
Math, Maps, and More					
Pets					
Planet Power					
Plant Life					
Space Exploration					
Why in the World?					
Wildlife					
Women's Health					

INTEREST PROJECTS

COMMUNICATIONS

	SKILL BUILDERS	TECHNOLOGY	SERVICE PROJECTS	CAREER EXPLORATION	DATE/ SIGNATURE
Computers in Everyday Life					
Desktop Publishing					
Do You Get the Message?					
Exploring the Net					
From A to V: Audiovisual Production					
Graphic Communications					
The Lure of Language					
Media Savvy					
Once Upon a Story					
Public Relations					
Reading					
A World of Understanding					
Writing for Real					

INTEREST PROJECTS

THE ARTS and HISTORY

	SKILL BUILDERS	TECHNOLOGY	SERVICE PROJECTS	CAREER EXPLORATION	DATE/ SIGNATURE
Architecture and Environmental Design					
Artistic Crafts					
Collecting					
Fashion Design					
Folk Arts					
Heritage Hunt					
Invitation to the Dance					
Just Jewelry					
Museum Discovery					
On a High Note					
Paper Works					
The Performing Arts					
Photography					
The Play's the Thing					
Textile Arts					
Visual Arts					
Women Through Time					

INTEREST PROJECTS

SPORTS and RECREATION

	SKILL BUILDERS	TECHNOLOGY	SERVICE PROJECTS	CAREER EXPLORATION	DATE/ SIGNATURE
Backpacking					
Camping					
Emergency Preparedness					
Games for Life					
High Adventure					
Horse Sense					
On the Court					
On the Playing Field					
Orienteering					
Outdoor Survival					
Paddle, Pole, and Roll					
Rolling Along					
Smooth Sailing					
Sports for Life					
Water Sports					

Resources and Organizations

Below is a list of organizations to get in touch with for more information. When you call, ask for printed material on the subject you are interested in, for example, careers in engineering or summer sailing programs for teens. Be prepared to send a stamped, self-addressed envelope, and allow several weeks for return delivery.

If printed materials are not available, ask if and when you can speak briefly with a staff member. In some cases, you can tell from the name of an organization what service or subject is addressed, for instance, the American Camping Association. In cases where the title does not reflect a specific subject, a phrase word is listed—for instance, self-defense, for the Empower Program. Web sites and e-mail addresses were valid at the time of the writing of this book, but they do change frequently.

Because of space considerations, this list is not complete. For more listings, search the Internet, look at reference books at your library, and consult the Yellow Pages of your telephone book. You'll be surprised at all that's available at your fingertips!

The Adopt-a-Stream Foundation
600 128th Street, SE
Everett, Wash. 98208
(206) 316-8592

American Alliance for Health, Physical Education, Recreation and Dance
1900 Association Drive
Reston, Va. 22091
(703) 476-3400

American Association of University Women
1111 16th Street, NW
Washington, D.C. 20036
(202) 785-7700

American Astronomical Society
Executive Office
2000 Florida Avenue, NW
Suite 300
Washington, D.C. 20009
(202) 328-2010
http://www.aas.org

American Camping Association, Inc.
5000 State Road 67 North
Martinsville, Ind. 46151
(317) 342-8456

American Center for Design
233 East Ontario, Suite 500
Chicago, Ill. 60611
(312) 787-2018

American Chemical Society
1155 16th Street, NW
Washington, D.C. 20036
(202) 452-2113
education@acs.org
http://www.ChemCenter.org

American Council for the Arts
One East 53rd Street
New York, N.Y. 10022-4201
(212) 223-2787

American Counseling Association
5999 Stevenson Avenue
Alexandria, Va. 22304-3300
(703) 823-9800

American Craft Council
72 Spring Street
New York, N.Y. 10012
(212) 274-0630

American Film Institute
John F. Kennedy Center
for the Performing Arts
Washington, D.C. 20566
(202) 828-4000

American Folklore Society
4350 North Fairfax Drive, Suite 640
Arlington, Va. 22203
(703) 528-1902

American Historical Association
400 A Street, SE
Washington, D.C. 20003
(202) 544-2422

American Institute of Architects (AIA)
1735 New York Avenue, NW
Washington, D.C. 20006
(202) 626-7527
http://www.aia.org

American Library Association
50 East Huron Street
Chicago, Ill. 60611
(312) 944-6780

American Marketing Association
250 South Wacker Drive, Suite 200
Chicago, Ill. 60606

American Medical Association
1101 Vermont Avenue, NW
Washington, D.C. 20005
(202) 789-7400

American Meteorological Society
45 Beacon Street
Boston, Mass. 02108-3693
(617) 227-2425
http://atm.geo.nsf.gov/AMS/

American Nurses Association
600 Maryland Avenue, SW, Suite 100W
Washington, D.C. 20004-2751
1-800-274-4262

American Psychological Association
750 First Street, NE
Washington, D.C. 20002-4242
(202) 336-5500

American Sail Training Association
Box 1459
Newport, R.I. 02840
(401) 846-1775
Fax (401) 849-5400

American Society of Artists
P.O. Box 1326
Palatine, Ill. 60078
(312) 751-2500

American Society of Mechanical Engineers
(Call your Girl Scout council for the
address of the local ASME chapter.)

American Society of Travel Agents
1101 King Street
Alexandria, Va. 22314
(703) 739-2782

American Society on Aging
P. O. Box 41
Fayetteville, N.C. 28302
(919) 323-3641

American Translators Association
1800 Diagonal Road, Suite 220
Alexandria, Va. 22314
(703) 683-6100

American Veterinary Medical Association
1931 North Meecham Avenue, Suite 100
Schaumberg, Ill. 60173-4360
(847) 925-8070

American Women's Self-Defense Association
713 North Wellwood Avenue
Lindenhurst, N.Y. 11757
1-800-43-AWSDA

American Yoga Association
513 South Orange Avenue
Sarasota, Fla. 34236
(813) 953-5859

**American Society for the Prevention of Cruelty
to Animals (ASPCA)**
424 East 92nd Street
New York, N.Y. 10128
(212) 876-7700

Associated Press
50 Rockefeller Plaza
New York, N.Y. 10020
(212) 621-1500

Association of American Geographers (AAG)
1710 16th Street, NW
Washington, D.C. 20009-3198
(202) 234-1450
http://www.aag.org

**Association of Science-Technology Centers
(ASTC)**
1025 Vermont Avenue, NW, Suite 500
Washington, D.C. 20005
(202) 783-7200
http://www.astc.org

Ballet Theatre Foundation
890 Broadway
New York, N.Y. 10003-1278
(212) 477-3030

Books and Beyond
309 North Rios Street
Solana Beach, Calif. 92075
(619) 755-3823

The Center for the Book
Library of Congress
Washington, D.C. 20540-4920
(202) 707-5221

Center for Creative Leadership
P.O. Box 25300
Greensboro, N.C. 27436-6300
(910) 288-7210

Center for Marine Conservation, Inc.
1725 DeSales Street, NW, Suite 500
Washington, D.C. 20036
(202) 872-0619

Chamber Music America
545 Eighth Avenue
New York, N.Y. 10018
(212) 244-2772

Children's Book Council
568 Broadway
New York, N.Y. 10012
(212) 966-1990

Children's Defense Fund
25 East Street, NW
Washington, D.C. 20001
(202) 628-8787
Child advocates, laws, etc.

Dramatists Guild
234 West 44th Street, 11th Floor
New York, N.Y. 10036-9366
(212) 398-9366

Educational Broadcasting Corporation
356 West 58th Street
New York, N.Y. 10019
(212) 560-2000

Educators for Social Responsibility
23 Garden Street
Cambridge, Mass. 02138
1-800-370-2515 or (617) 492-1764

The Empower Program
7300 Pearl Street, Suite 220
Bethesda, Md. 20814
(301) 469-3938
Self-defense

Everybody Wins! Foundation, Inc.
13605 Sir Thomas Way, # 44
Silver Spring, Md. 20904
(301) 890-0646
Literacy, mentorship

Family Service America
11700 West Lake Park Drive
Milwaukee, Wis. 53224
(414) 359-1040

Gemological Institute of America
1660 Stewart Street
Santa Monica, Calif. 90404
(310) 829-2991

Geological Society of America
3300 Penrose Place
Boulder, Colo. 80301

**Hostelling International—United States
of America**
American Youth Hostels
733 15th Street, NW, Suite 840
Washington, D.C. 20005
(202) 783-6161

International Association for Financial Planning
Two Concourse Parkway, Suite 800
Atlanta, Ga. 30328
(404) 395-1605

International Food Information Council
1100 Connecticut Avenue, NW, Suite 43
Washington, D.C. 20036
(202) 296-6540

**International Graphic Arts
Education Association, Inc.**
4615 Forbes Avenue
Pittsburgh, Pa. 15213
(412) 682-5170

International Reading Association
800 Barksdale Road
P.O. Box 8139
Newark, Del. 19714-8139
(302) 731-1600

International Youth Hostel Federation
9 Guessens Road
Welwyn Garden City
Hartfordshire AL8 6QW, England

Junior Engineering Technical Society (JETS)
1420 King Street, Suite 405
Alexandria, Va. 22314-2715
(703) 548-5387

Learning Disabilities Association of America
4156 Library Road
Pittsburgh, Pa. 15234
(412) 341-1515

Merrie Way Community for Arts and Humanities
13601 Ventura Boulevard, Suite 371
Sherman Oaks, Calif. 91423
Fax (818) 501-3933
Arts, humanities, film, and media education

Museum Store Association
501 South Cherry Street, # 460
Denver, Colo. 80222-1325
(303) 329-6968

Music Teachers National Association
441 Vine Street, Suite 505
Cincinnati, Ohio 45202-2814
(513) 421-1420

**National Aeronautics and
Space Administration (NASA)**
To write to astronauts:
Astronaut Office/CB
NASA Johnson Space Center
Houston, Tex. 77058
To request materials:
NASA Educational Division
Code FEO, NASA Headquarters
Washington, D.C. 20546
http://www.nasa.gov/NASA_homepage.html

**National Alliance of Breast Cancer
Organizations (NABCO)**
9 East 37th Street, 10th Floor
New York, N.Y. 10016
(212) 719-0154
http://www.nabco.org

**National Association for Girls and
Women in Sport**
1900 Association Drive
Reston, Va. 22091
(703) 476-3450

National Association for Search and Rescue
4500 Southgate Place, Suite 100
Chantilly, Va. 20151
(703) 222-6277

**National Association for the Education
of Young Children**
1134 Connecticut Avenue, NW
Washington, D.C. 20009
(202) 232-8777

National Association of Underwater Instructors
P. O. Box 14650
Montclair, Calif. 91763
(909) 621-5801

National Association of Women Artists
41 Union Square West
New York, N.Y. 10003
(212) 675-1616

National Audubon Society
700 Broadway
New York, N.Y. 10003-9501
(212) 979-3120

National Bar Association
1225 11th Street, NW
Washington, D.C. 20001
(202) 842-3900

National Center for Learning Disabilities
381 Park Avenue, Suite 1420
New York, N.Y. 10016
(212) 545-7510

**National Coalition for Parent Involvement
in Education**
Box 39
1201 16th Street, NW
Washington, D.C. 20036

National Council for the Social Studies
3501 Newark Street, NW
Washington, D.C. 20016-3167

National Council on Family Relations
3989 Central Avenue, NE, Suite 550
Minneapolis, Minn. 55421
(612) 781-9331

National Dance Association
1900 Association Drive
Reston, Va. 22091
(703) 476-3436

National Endowment for Financial Education
4695 South Monaco Street
Denver, Colo. 80237-3403
(303) 220-1200

National Federation of Music Clubs
1336 North Delaware Street
Indianapolis, Ind. 46202
(317) 638-4003

National Federation of Press Women
Box 99
Blue Springs, Mo. 64013
(816) 229-1666

National Home Furnishings Association
P. O. Box 2396
High Point, N.C. 27261
(919) 883-1650

National Indian Youth Council
318 Elm Street, SE
Albuquerque, N.Mex. 87102
(505) 247-2251

National Institute for Dispute Resolution
1726 M Street, Suite 500
Washington, D.C. 20036
(202) 466-4764

National Maritime Historical Society
5 John Walsh Boulevard
P. O. Box 68
Peekskill, N.Y. 10566

The National Museum of Women in the Arts
1250 New York Avenue, NW
Washington, D.C. 20005
(202) 783-5000

National Newspaper Association
1525 Wilson Boulevard, Suite 550
Arlington, Va. 22209
(703) 907-7900

National Press Club
National Press Building
529 14th Street, NW
Washington, D.C. 20045
(202) 662-7500

National Press Photographers Association
3200 Croasdaile Drive, Suite 306
Durham, N.C. 27705
(919) 383-7246

National PTA–National Congress of Parents and Teachers
330 North Wabash Street, Suite 2100
Chicago, Ill. 60611-3604
(312) 670-6782

National Safety Council
1121 Springlake Drive
Itasca, Ill. 60143-3201
(603) 285-1121

National Ski Patrol
Ski Patrol Building, Suite 100
133 South Van Gordon Street
Lakewood, Colo. 80228
(303) 988-1111

National Theatre of the Deaf
P. O. Box 659
Chester, Conn. 06412-0659
(203) 526-4971

National Tree Trust
1120 G Street, NW, Suite 770
Washington, D.C. 20005
(202) 628-TREE

National Trust for Historic Preservation
1785 Massachusetts Avenue, NW
Washington, D.C. 20036
(202) 588-6000

National Women's History Project
7738 Bell Road
Windsor, Calif. 95492
(707) 838-6000

Overseas Press Club of America
320 East 42nd Street, Mezzanine
New York, N.Y. 10017
(212) 983-4655

Professional Photographers of America
57 Forsyth Street, NW, Suite 1600
Atlanta, Ga. 30303
(404) 522-8600

Reading Is Fundamental
600 Maryland Avenue, SW, Suite 500
Washington, D.C. 20024
(202) 287-3220

Save the Children Federation
54 Wilton Road
Westport, Conn. 06880
(203) 221-4000

Sierra Club
85 Second Street, Second Floor
San Francisco, Calif. 94105
(415) 977-5500

Society for American Archaeology (SAA)
900 Second Street, NE, Suite 12
Washington, D.C. 20002-3557
(202) 789-8200
http://www.saa.org

Society for Asian Arts
Asian Art Museum
Golden Gate Park
San Francisco, Calif. 94118
(415) 387-5675

Society for Historical Archaeology
P.O. Box 30446
Tucson, Ariz. 85751
(520) 886-8006
sha@azstarnet.com
www.azstarnet.com/~sha

Society of American Archivists
600 South Federal Street, Suite 504
Chicago, Ill. 60605
(312) 922-0140

Society of American Travel Writers
4101 Lake Boone Trail, Suite 201
Raleigh, N.C. 27607
(919) 787-5181

Society of Illustrators
128 East 63rd Street
New York, N.Y. 10021
(212) 838-2560

Society of Vertebrate Paleontology
University of Nebraska
W. 436 Nebraska Hall
Lincoln, Nebr. 68588

Society of Women Engineers
120 Wall Street, 11th Floor
New York, N.Y. 10005-3902
(212) 509-9577
http://swe.org

Solar Cookers International
1919 21st Street, #101
Sacramento, Calif. 95814
(916) 455-4499
sbci@igc.apc.org

Tele-Communications Association
701 North Haven Avenue, Suite 200
Ontario, Calif. 91764-4925
(909) 945-1122

Tread Lightly, Inc.
298 24th Street, Suite 325
Ogden, Utah 84401
(801) 627-0077
Minimum impact recreation

U.S. Department of Education
Office of Educational Research and
Improvement
OERI Education Information
555 New Jersey Avenue, NW
Washington, D.C. 20208-5641

U.S. Department of Education
Partnership for Family Involvement in
Education
600 Independence Avenue, SW
Washington, D.C. 20202-8241
Literacy and other initiatives

U.S. Sailing
P.O. Box 1260 or 15 Maritime Drive
Portsmouth, R.I. 02871
(401) 683-0800
Fax (401) 683-0840

UNICEF
633 Third Avenue, 23rd Floor
New York, N.Y. 10017
(212) 824-6275
Peace, international relations,
conflict resolution

United Press International
1400 I Street, NW
Washington, D.C. 20005
(202) 898-8000

U.S. Geological Survey Map Sales
Box 2528
Denver Federal Center
Denver, Colo. 80225
(303) 236-7477

Volunteers—The National Center
1111 North 19th Street, Suite 500
Arlington, Va. 22209
(703) 276-0542

The Wilderness Society
900 17th Street, NW
Washington, D.C. 20006-2596
(202) 833-2300

Women's Council of Realtors
430 North Michigan Avenue
Chicago, Ill. 60611
(312) 329-8483

Women's National Book Association
160 Fifth Avenue, Room 604
New York, N.Y. 10010
(212) 675-7805

Women's Sports Foundation
Eisenhower Park
East Meadow, N.Y. 11554
(516) 542-4700

Women in Communications, Inc.
10605 Judicial Drive, Suite A4
Fairfax, Va. 22030
(703) 359-9000

Women in the Arts Foundation
1175 York Avenue, Apt. 2G
New York, N.Y. 10021
(212) 751-1915

More About Resources

Anyone or anything can be a resource, from your great-aunt to your next door neighbor—who may be a paramedic or an actor—to your local automobile club or travel agency.

In addition to the organizations and associations listed, you can get help and information from agencies right in your own backyard. These might include your local arts and cultural centers, theater groups, museums, libraries, historical societies, schools and colleges, service organizations (like the Kiwanis or the Rotary Club), places of worship, sports organizations, town recreation departments, chambers of commerce, animal shelters, health organizations (such as your community's board of health, hospitals, clinics, or counseling services), youth boards and bureaus, police and fire departments, radio and TV stations, newspaper education programs, and state departments of environmental conservation, education, or labor. Consult the *Encyclopedia of Associations*, an annual directory that lists national organizations, at your library.

You get the picture. Once you start digging through the telephone book, exploring the Net, or talking to people in your community, these interest projects will bring a world of understanding and a wealth of skills to your doorstep.

Index

Membership and Program
5/97